BUSH'S BRAIN

BUSH'S BRAIN

HOW
KARL ROVE
MADE
GEORGE W. BUSH
PRESIDENTIAL

JAMES MOORE AND **WAYNE SLATER**

WILEY

John Wiley & Sons, Inc.

For general information on our other products and services, or technical support,
please contact our Customer Care Department within the United States at
800-762-2974, outside the United States at 317-572-3993 or fax 317-572-4002.

Wiley also publishes its books in a variety of electronic formats. Some content that
appears in print may not be available in electronic books. For more information about
Wiley products, visit our Web site at www.wiley.com.

ISBN 0-471-42327-0

Printed in the United States of America.

10 9 8 7 6 5 4 3 2

For Mary Lou and Amanda
Whose faith in all things good and true has never faltered
—J.M.

For Dianne and Todd
Two fixed stars guiding with love
—W.S.

An Unfallen Soldier

A patriot must always be ready to defend his country from his government.

Edward Abbey

No one who knows Karl Rove has been surprised to hear his name as a prime suspect in the scandal involving the leak of a CIA agent's name. That is how Karl Rove has operated in the political arena for his entire career. If he had an Achilles' heel as an operative, it was his temper. When crossed, Rove's anger was legendary, and was always manifest in the tactics he deployed to exact retribution against those he felt had wronged him. The greater shock for Washington, and journalists who have reported on Karl Rove's career, would be if he were not involved in outing undercover agent Valerie Plame.

Back in Texas, one of Rove's early political victims has always worried about how power might magnify Rove's already frighteningly adept political skills. Pete McRae went to prison for being only marginally associated with the kind of political work that takes place in Texas politics every day. An allegedly Rove-fueled investigation, conducted by an overeager FBI agent, convicted McRae and Deputy Agriculture Commissioner Mike Moeller of, essentially, not being very good supervisors. They got 18 months in federal penitentiaries.

"I've always worried about what Karl might do with real power," McRae said. "When you have a guy like this, and he has the power of the entire U.S. government at his disposal, I think you can expect some unsavory things to take place. Look at what he got done while he was nothing more than a campaign manager for an unknown candidate from rural Texas."

War, of course, is something more than unsavory. But it is the context for showing how Karl Rove's influence has worked on the national stage. While this book, *"Bush's Brain,"* was an attempt to tell the country about Rove's background, and how he might function as a White House advisor, events since its initial publication have only served to confirm that he has not changed, nor has his level of influence on the president diminished. Karl Rove is simply painting on a larger canvas, and doing so with the same eye for detail that marked his rise in Texas.

In the case of Ambassador Joseph Wilson, all of the "Karl Rove Has Been Here" signs are scattered up and down the thoroughfare of that scandal. In the rationale of Rove, it was okay for Wilson to travel to Niger to check and see if Saddam Hussein and Iraq had tried to purchase yellowcake uranium. That was not Wilson's sin. The Ambassador agitated Rove when he did not keep his mouth shut about his findings. Wilson reported his conclusion through proper protocol and governmental channels to both the CIA and the State Department. And he assumed, wrongly, that was the end of the affair. There was no basis to the Niger uranium claims. The documents purportedly showing the purchase were proved false, and rather easily.

The administration, presumably with Rove's guidance, has been very effective at putting a cap on intelligence that contradicted Bush administration allegations about Hussein's efforts to acquire weapons of mass destruction. Vice President Dick Cheney, often with former Congressman Newt Gingrich in tow, met almost daily with intelligence officials at CIA headquarters in Langley, Virginia. Analysts have said that the message was made clear, whenever they delivered reports that contradicted what the White House wanted: go back and look for what was "really" there.

"They wanted us to cook it," one operative said.

They also wanted them to keep their mouths shut. At least one national correspondent for a major publication has said every call made to an intelligence analyst, an operative, or a scientist, to ask about evidence contradicting the administration's claims on Iraq, was met with the same response: "We are not having this conversation." That was followed by the sound of the dial tone, or a dead phone line.

Faced with intimidation, a tactic Rove brought to the administration, people who actually knew the truth about Iraq's armaments, or lack thereof, were never allowed to come forth. As a result, aluminum tubes, marked by an Italian rocket manufacturer as a "Medusa 81" rocket body, were redefined as casings for a uranium gas centrifuge. There was an abundance of contradictory intelligence on these tubes, which clearly proved they could not be used in the construction of a centrifuge, but that data was effectively suppressed.

Similar pressures were operating when Ambassador Wilson returned with his report. He, alone among all voices in the Washington bureaucracy, was willing to confront the truth. Shocked by the fact that the president included the Niger yellowcake lie in his State of the Union speech, Wilson wrote an opinion piece for the *New York Times*, which indicated there was no substance to the claim. A week later, reporters were calling to ask about his wife's line of work. This is either a great coincidence, or the work of Karl Rove. Circumstantial, anecdotal, and historical evidence all point at the president's senior advisor.

The case is much too detailed to make convincingly in this brief narrative. One story from Texas, though, proves instructive. During the 1992 Bush/Quayle presidential campaign in Texas, Rove was a consultant reporting to Rob Mosbacher, Jr. Never one to surrender control, Rove began to complain to reporters that the campaign was a mess. In short time, political columnist Robert Novak wrote a column, which sounded, suspiciously, like Rove's whining over Mosbacher, and the campaign's operation. Novak has long denied that Rove was his source, and could certainly be expected to protect whoever gave him the information. Texas reporters, though, weren't the only ones who were suspicious. George H. W. Bush, who cannot abide disloyalty, fired Karl Rove for being the source of the leak. Bush, too, had heard the complaints out of Rove's mouth before they were published by Novak. Rove denied involvement.

Not surprisingly, journalists and political pros think Rove designed the leak strategy to blow the cover of Ambassador Wilson's wife. The purpose of this, of course, was to keep the lid on anyone who might want to also come out with contradictory intelligence, embarrassing the White House. The message was that anyone who messed with the Bush team might also find themselves and their families living at risk. While the leak strategy is classic Rove, it's just as likely he did not make the initial calls to reporters, though there have been reports that he made follow-up contact with some journalists. He almost always puts a layer of operatives between himself and the actual implementation of any plan of attack. All of the investigative roads can be expected to lead back to Rove, but, if past practice is any indication, they will wash out from a deluge of deception before they get to their destination. Rove has avoided the subject, but White House spokesman Scott McClellan has denied that Rove was the leaker.

The shock was not so much that a leak had occurred. What proved astounding was its blatant obviousness, the calculated meanness, its dissemination with the cool precision of an executive business plan. The Bush White House has been virtually leak proof—testament to fierce loyalties to the president and Karl Rove's absolute control. No one would have dared to leak information on a CIA agent without getting Karl Rove to check the "yes" box on the plan. To believe that Rove was oblivious to what happened requires complete abandonment of any knowledge of his past behavior in the arena of politics, or ignorance of his comprehensive involvement in the most minute of details in the Bush White House.

There is little value in believing whoever leaked the information will suffer actual incrimination for this cowardly act. In a nation at war, the Bush White House, or a senior official within the Bush administration, both of which are completely dominated by Rove, has allowed an agent of the U.S. government to be exposed. Even if the perpetrator were not Rove, a crime was most likely committed in the nation's most important public office. The fact that Valerie Plame has put her life at risk serving her country was apparently of no concern to the administration's leakers. Nor is the all-too-rich irony that she has been working in the area of weapons of mass destruction, undoubtedly having more impact on the safety and security of Americans than the Bush counselors who argued attacking Iraq would reduce our chances of being hit with such weapons. If Rove were ever fingered as treasonous, he most likely would argue that he had no idea Valerie Plame was undercover. Even if a record of calls exists, it will not prove what was said. It will only show that he dialed up reporters.

It will take more than circumstantial evidence and a vigorous critique by Democratic enemies to dislodge Karl Rove from his position of influence within the White House. Karl Rove will not go away.

President Bush cannot imagine a political life without him. Even if the investigation of the leaks begins to accumulate serious evidence against the senior advisor, the president will be more likely to build a protective wall around Rove than cut him loose. As maligned as the Bush intellect is, the president is smart enough to always "dance with the one that brung him." He knows there would be no second Bush presidency, if there were no planning, strategy, fund-raising, and nasty subterfuge by Karl Rove. For Rove to be ousted from the Bush White House, it would require Karen Hughes, Vice President Dick Cheney, and Colin Powell, to convince the president that re-election was not possible with Rove on the team. Bush, however, cannot conceive of a campaign without Karl Rove.

Bush's goal is re-election, the prize his father never won. Rove's vision is bigger—a fundamental, historic realignment of power in America.

Rove's ultimate wish is the establishment of a new Republican majority, much like the 30-year reign of the GOP a century ago that was built on a rising industrial elite. With the election of William McKinley in 1896, Republicans won six of the next eight presidential elections. It was an era of high influence and authority for the GOP, a period marked by conservative values and easy money and the Gilded Age crooks. Mostly, to Karl Rove, it was a period of Republican dominance that ended only with the catastrophe of the Depression and a new politicial realignment in America, this time producing a 30-year reign of Democrats from the New Deal through the Great Society.

In his collaboration with Bush, Rove sees the possibility of a permanent Republican majority in which the GOP controls the White House, both houses of Congress, the Supreme Court, and the vast architecture of the federal judiciary not just for a brief interval but for generations.

Meanwhile, the machinations of Rove have deep implications for journalism, politics, and international policy of the United States. In journalism, the leak has created a moral dilemma. There are reporters in Washington who could tell the FBI who called them with the leak. As soon as they do that, however, they will be finished in a town where the engines of journalism run on the gas from leaks. Fortunately, Rove has angered as many journalists as he has other political interests, and there is always the hope that, whoever the leaker is, one of those reporters will adhere to a higher ethic than source protection. Identifying a traitor in a time of war, someone who has exposed his country to danger is of greater importance than a solitary career in journalism.

Writing about Rove often results in accusations that his influence is being wildly overstated. Unfortunately, Rove leaves behind nothing but ephemera for anyone trying to prove his power. But the language and policy of the White House has shown Rovian texture in every endeavor of the Bush administration. What happened in Iraq was not a "war," but a battle. It is not to Rove's political advantage for the war to end. He needs a war time Commander-in-Chief during 2004 to help with re-election. Americans love their presidents the most during crisis, thus, Iraq is just a battle in a larger war on terrorism. In terms of positioning, Rove has also guided the White House in describing the current occupation of Iraq as the battlefront in the war on terrorism. Attacks on troops are consistently characterized as acts of terror, which, of course they are, and the American public is convincingly told that, "If we don't stop them there, we will face them in our own country." Under Karl Rove's message guidance, the White House's public relations campaign has sought to steer the national debate away from the lies and disingenuousness that led to the invasion.

As America moves toward a presidential election in 2004, few aspects of life in this country have not been affected by Karl Rove, and his profound influence on the president and his policies. He is the political mastermind of an administration that has preached compassionate conservatism, but has practiced something considerably different. If Karl Rove were not sitting in his corner office in the White House, there is an argument to be made that there might have been no war in Iraq; there would be underprivileged children still attending Head Start programs, which have been reduced or eliminated; there would be low-income families getting health care from the Children's Health Insurance Program, instead of going without because of federal cutbacks in funding; there may have been competitive bidding on contracts to rebuild Iraq instead of delivery of deals to Halliburton and other companies that are GOP fund-raisers; there would have been no California recall, which Rove engineered using a congressman from the state; there would be congressional districts in Texas with lines drawn to represent the interests of minorities; there might be a complete and honest report from the 9/11 Commission, if Rove had not approved redacting information to reduce political impact; there would be real accounting of Saudi Arabia's involvement in acts of terrorism; there might be real funding for Homeland Security's First Responders; and there would certainly be an independent counsel investigating who committed treason by leaking a CIA operative's name to a reporter; half of $87 billion requested for rebuilding Iraq might even have gone instead to implement full coverage health care for every man, woman, and child in America. Karl Rove has the kind of influence on politics and policy that Americans have never seen before, and are having trouble even acknowledging.

And sadly, that is not overstatement.

JAMES C. MOORE
WAYNE SLATER
Austin, Texas

Acknowledgments

All books are collaborations. They begin with authors sharing ideas and impressions with potential readers, friends, professional colleagues, or even sources. This process led the two of us to work together on a book about Karl Rove, a man we had known and written about since very early in his amazing political career.

We want readers to understand that what we have written here is neither an indictment nor an endorsement of Rove's skills. This is simply a story of a man who understands the American political process, quite possibly, better than anyone our culture has ever produced. He has used that knowledge to gain effective control in elections for his candidates. Frankly, we do not believe anyone has ever done it better. If one of the many very competent national political consultants had been in charge of the Bush campaign in 2000, rather than Rove, the current president would have ended up little more than an historical footnote, son of a former president who ran a failed race for the White House. Instead, he won, not just because of his own capabilities, but also through the genius of Karl Rove. Democracy has never before produced anyone like Karl Rove. History will not be able to ignore his importance. Just like a young artist with the gift of great prescience, a Hemingway or Fitzgerald, Rove knew from the beginning what he wanted to do and devoted all of his energy and intellectual development to this goal.

Obviously, this book owes much to Karl Rove. He gave up several hours of his time, driving down to Austin from the president's ranch in Crawford, to spend a sunny morning answering questions about matters he probably considered long ago disposed of. Pete

McRae and Mike Moeller, two casualties of Rove's strategic moves, also gave very generously of their time. Both spoke openly of a difficult time in their lives. The full measure of a political act cannot be taken without weighing human consequences. McRae and Moeller have long deserved to have their stories told. We hope we have done that here.

We are also indebted to the many fine reporters of the Texas capitol media corps. Their consistent diligence has provided a bounty of resources, which gave us a solid foundation for beginning our own work. When George W. Bush began his political ascension, and national journalists were looking at his background, their job was also made infinitely easier by all of the detailed reporting already conducted by Texas political writers, in and out of Austin. The work they have performed through the years has always met the highest of standards, and still does. Ask the president of the United States.

Other individuals, who are quoted but deserving of special note here, are Jesse Oliver, a Dallas attorney with a fine, analytical mind, who served as general counsel to the Texas Department of Agriculture; Buck Wood, an Austin attorney and political activist; Garry Mauro, former Texas Land Commissioner who ran for governor against George W. Bush; Reggie Bashur, Republican political consultant, a man who actually is a compassionate conservative and has the long-held respect of Austin journalists; Jason Stanford, a Democrat with equal parts courage, intellect, and conviction; Mark McKinnon, who is possessed of a valuable insight from both sides of the battle line; John Weaver, once a great Republican political consultant now a great Democratic political consultant; personal friend Paul Willcott, who isn't just the world's greatest undiscovered writer but is also the finest editor any writer might hope for; Pete Slover, who has the kind of relentlessness that always makes for great journalism; Chuck McDonald, for making sure people never fail to laugh at the absurdities of democracy; the late George Christian, former presidential press secretary and a man without enemies; *Dallas Morning News'* political writer Sam Attlesey for creating his own institution of political insight with an unsurpassed love of Texas and politics; Mike Toomey, who saw it all from the inside; Bill Miller, who represents both . . . ; Kim Ross, a lobbyist, gentleman, and leader; Brian Berry, who has worked closely with and admired the skills of Karl; Don Sipple, producer of political ads that helped in the Bush climb; Texas Senator Bill Ratliff and House Speaker Pete Laney, who take the term "public servant" very seriously; Governor Rick Perry, for his graciousness and insight; two of the finest political thinkers in America, Bruce Buchanan of the University of Texas and James Thurber of American University in Georgetown, their perspective comes from the neighborhood and not the Beltway; Texas State Representative Paul Sadler, who has single-handedly provided the intellectual force of will to improve Texas schools; former Texas House Representative Mark Stiles, for his honesty and integrity; Tom Pauken, a Republican on his own terms; Kenneth Boatwright, who found a good life outside of politics in the Texas Hill Country; Susie Galprin, whose help and recollections from Utah proved invaluable; Bill Israel, a journalist and scholar; Rossanna Salazar, a loyal Republican of the highest decency; Robert Bryce, author of *Pipe Dreams* and a man of considerable honor; Ken Vest for unflagging friendship and encouragement; Jimmy and Deb Denning for becoming family; compa Greg Groogan; brother Tim Moore, intellectual co-conspirator; John Hoblitzell for his assistance and knowledge of the mountain state; Chris Greta of the *Adranch* for his endless stream of promotional ideas; campaign television producer Catherine Herter and cameraman Cody Marcom; Ed Wendler, for endlessly serving his principles; the outstanding journalism of Bruce Tomaso, Christy Hoppe, David Elliot, Guillermo X. Garcia, Debbie Graves, Anne Marie Kilday, R.G. Ratcliffe, John Gravois, Robert Cullick, Mary Lenz, Ken Herman, Peggy Fikac, Jay Root, Bob Elder, Dave McNeely, Ross Ramsey of *Texas Weekly*, and Harvey Kronberg of *The Quorum Report*.

We also owe much to the national media working out of Washington, DC. Their language and insights framed George W. Bush and Karl Rove in a broader perspective and prompted fresh thinking for us. The product of their reporting is a resource often utilized in the creation of this narrative. We are also grateful to the Texas State Historical Archives, Texas A&M University, and the George H. W. Bush Presidential Library in Bryan-College Station, Texas. Additionally, the considerations and graciousness of the senior management at the *Dallas Morning News* were immeasurably critical to this accomplishment.

First thoughts of this book grew out of conversation in a tortilla factory in East Austin, temporary studios for an ill-fated Texas television news network. The story did not take on viability until several years later when we encountered Samuel Fleishman of Literary Artists Representatives. While other agents and publishers were disagreeing with our vision for a book about Karl Rove, Sam was carefully considering its potential and wondering if these Texas guys weren't onto an idea. He became our advocate and found just the right publisher and editor for the project. His friendship has become as valued as his counsel.

Bush's Brain was acquired by David Pugh of John Wiley and Sons, Inc. David's commitment to the project was no minor act of courage or intellect at a time when Karl Rove was still very much below the consciousness of mainstream America. But David liked our ideas and, even though he's a Brooklyn boy, he had those horizon eyes of a Texan and was able to see farther than other editors. He has stewarded this book through an expedited and diligent editorial process. We think the final product reflects his skill as much as ours.

Our thanks also go to Joan O'Neil, our publisher at John Wiley and Sons, Inc., who gave over resources and her own enthusiasm to speed this book to market; Peter Knapp and Elka Villa for their astute marketing efforts; Robin Factor and Todd Tedesco, who managed to turn a year-long production schedule into a few months and also make it work; Jesica Church and Mike Onorato, who have been tireless in their public relations efforts to tell the world about our book;

Nancy Marcus Land and her production team at Publications Development Company of Texas, and Helene Godin, whose discerning eye kept us on a proper course.

Our profoundest expressions of gratitude, however, are reserved for our families; our wives, Mary Lou and Dianne, and our children, Amanda and Todd. They've been believers for a long, long time.

All we ever needed was a chance.

JAMES MOORE AND WAYNE SLATER

Austin, Texas
January 2003

Contents

Part I
A Star behind the Clouds

Part II
Toward the Far Horizon

PART III
HISTORY MAKES MEN

"His master remarked to him more than once: There is nothing small about you, my boy. You are going to be a great man one way or the other, either for good or evil."

Plutarch, *The Rise and Fall of Athens*

BUSH'S BRAIN

PART
I

A Star behind the Clouds

Introduction:
Mr. Co-President

One of the penalties for refusing to participate in politics is that you end up being governed by your inferiors.

Plato

O n this particular evening, the aircraft had climbed to 35,000 feet, pulling away from a fog of cities and towns, which had blurred into a series of similar, forgetful events. The passenger cabin was dark, except for a few reading lights over the heads of reporters polishing scripts on their laptop computers. Far to the aft, a group of television photographers were sharing tiny, airline-sized bottles of gin and trying half-heartedly to keep down their noise level. One of them, a Texan, was spitting tobacco juice into a clear plastic bottle.

Usually, the candidate made his visits to the cabin earlier in the day. Tonight, however, George W. Bush worked his way down the 727's aisle talking softly and exchanging pleasantries with the few passengers still awake. Halfway back, the governor noticed long-time Texas television reporter Jim Moore sitting against a window and reading.

"Jimmy, my boy, how's it going for you out here?" he asked.

"I'm doing fine, Governor. How about you?"

He shrugged and then took the aisle seat, leaning across the empty middle spot in order to speak quietly.

Moore, like numerous Texas journalists, had reported on Bush long before his political ascension, but he rarely spoke to the governor about political issues outside of news conferences and interview sessions. The Texas governor and the TV reporter shared mutual interests in distance running and baseball.

"I don't know if I mentioned it to you, Governor," Moore said. "But I'm playing baseball in an over-forty men's league."

"What? Hardball? You kiddin'?"

"Nope, there's this league that is growing like mad and guys over forty are playing in baseball leagues all over the country."

"Oh, man." Bush looked up the aisle at the front of the plane, his eyes searching for nothing in particular. After about 30 seconds, he turned back to the reporter.

"You know, I still throw some? With the security guys. Usually just on the lawn outside the mansion. But, you know what, I think I can still bring it. It's kinda fun."

"Well, I sure love playing again," Moore answered. "I haven't played since high school."

"Yeah, I'll bet it's fun," the governor said, almost inaudibly.

There was a decided longing in Bush's downbeat response, a lament over the loss of something he had not acknowledged until that particular moment, crossing the dark American sky en route to a destination chosen, not by himself, but by family, friends, money, corporations, and destiny.

"Bet there's a lot of hamstring pulls," the governor said, smiling.

"Yeah, a few. Worries me."

"Well, I better . . ."

"Governor, just a second, before you go. I know this was a social call, and I don't want to interview you on the race. You know I don't get time with you the way the big newspapers and networks do these days, so I just wanted to ask you what you'd do if you lose this thing. What happens then, Governor?"

Bush settled back into his seat, put his head back, and exhaled gently.

"Oh, I don't know, Jimmy. That wouldn't be the worst thing that could happen. I guess I'd just go back to Dallas, watch a lot of baseball games, spend time with my friends and Laura and the girls, make a living, enjoy my life. Do what other people do."

"Simple as that?"

"Yep, that simple. Gotta get back up front and get some sleep. See ya tomorrow."

Long before he was afraid of losing the race for the presidency, George W. Bush was scared to death of winning. Gone from his life would be the solitary runs around the shaded trails of Austin's Town Lake, impromptu visits to his favorite Mexican food restaurants, the chance to slip off with wife Laura to a movie, going to visit old friends in Austin without a motorcade and security. The regular things that gave George W. Bush his appeal to regular people had to be sacrificed. As confident as his family and supporters were of the choice, the candidate remained tentative.

The Texan was a reluctant political warrior. The White House was not truly a dream of Bush's, just an assumed role foisted on him by circumstances such as his family and the expectations of his political party. The most likely motive was political restoration; to put the Bush name back into what the family viewed as its historically correct place after George Herbert Walker Bush was displaced by William Jefferson Clinton. The family wanted to avenge the father's defeat, and with considerable effort and the enormous political machinery of a national race, they did. But George W. Bush is an improbable president and there is sufficient reason to believe he would have chosen to follow a different path.

In his hometown of Midland, Texas, Bush came of age obsessed with baseball and protective of his mother, who had suffered the loss of a daughter to leukemia. Often, Bush gave up his afternoon baseball games to spend time comforting his mother while his father was away on numerous trips for his oil company.

One of his friends from his youth remains amazed to this day that Bush ended up in the White House.

"Of all the kids who lived in all the houses on our street, he's the last one I would have thought might become a president," he told a Texas reporter.

Bush had an innate gregariousness, though, and a powerful personal charm that helped him rise to governor of Texas and, eventually, president of the United States. Both of those characteristics run counter to the fierce, confrontational tactics needed to win primaries and the general election. No candidate can shake enough hands and go to enough rallies to charm his way to victory. Bush's instincts were always to make a new friend, not take on a political enemy. He also lacked the intellect or the curiosity to dip into the nuances of national issues surrounding the presidency.

How, then, does such a man become the leader of the free world? Sons of presidents do not get free tickets to the Oval Office. The children of presidents are more likely to express a disdain or keep a cautious distance from the pressures and politics they came to know through the service of their fathers. Voters do not expect the offspring to exhibit the same traits as their presidential parent. Otherwise, the logbook of American presidential service would be a carousel of recurring names, descendants of previous leaders.

Bush had some of the personal traits necessary to achieve national political prominence, but he was not capable of rising on his own. His attributes as a candidate—familial connections, money, personal affability, and a goal, regardless of whether it was his or someone else's—were still not enough. History requires a confluence of domestic and international currents and an expertise in the political arts. Fortunately, for Bush, long before he had even made

the decision to run for governor, the most important cog in his bur-
geoning machine was efficiently spinning in a way that made his
presidential race an inevitability, one he might not have been able
to resist had he tried.

George W. Bush had become a presidential candidate long before he even knew it.

Karl Rove, son of a Rocky Mountain geologist, peripatetic colle-
gian, saw in Bush the raw materials to create a winning candidate.
Rove, who was the first person hired by the elder Bush's presidential
campaign, had been involved with the family's political endeavors
for close to three decades. Intimately familiar with W's strengths
and handicaps, Rove readied himself for the moment of convergence between his own ambition of running a winning presidential
campaign and the political aspirations of the Bush family and its eldest son. When the battle was finally joined, Rove, more than his
candidate, altered the American political process in a manner that
will profoundly affect all future presidential elections.

"The thing that's unique, that's really different that I don't know
of a parallel for, is Rove is more of a mentor to Bush. He is the one
who has helped Bush to develop into the leading political professional in the United States."

University of Texas presidential scholar Bruce Buchanan also
believed that without Karl Rove, there would be no President
George W. Bush.

"He [Bush] wouldn't have had the vision on his own. He wouldn't
have had the game plan. He wouldn't have had the agenda. He didn't
have . . . here's a guy now who's making decisions about what the
United States needs to do and two years ago, or three years ago, he
didn't have the remotest interest in this stuff. And now all of a sudden he's the point man of the world."

The official history of the Bush campaign is that the governor did
not consider running for president until after he was re-elected to
Texas' highest office in 1998. The storytellers paint an image of Bush
confidante Karen Hughes walking into the office one optimistic

morning with a news story about a national poll showing the governor as an undeclared front runner. Karl Rove has said that it was
only after the 1998 election that "Bush began to think about it." In
fact, Rove, Bush, and the governor's family had been contemplating
his political future long before 1998.

In a joking admission, Rove said his pursuit of the presidency for
George W. began almost from the onset of his own consciousness.
After sharing the Karen Hughes' poll story with Norman Ornstein
of the American Enterprise Institute during a seminar in Washington, Rove was asked when he first began to seriously think about a
presidential campaign.

"December 25, 1950," he answered.

The day he was born.

For the journalists, friends, opponents, and clients who have
known Rove, the answer seemed less an overstatement than the af-
firmation of his obvious lifelong goal. Anyone who has spent any
time around Karl Rove knows he is obsessed with politics.

"It's a 24-hour a day conversation," said Bush media advisor Mark
McKinnon. "Part of it is just sheer brainpower. The guy's got an
extra chromosome. It's just sort of jaw dropping to spend any
amount of time around him and realize how much he can do and do
it well. I think most mortals would be able to do about a tenth of
what he does."

McKinnon's assessment is accurate. But there is also an inescapable sense that Rove has worked at crafting an image and a
mythology of his own. He is acutely aware that historians are likely
to decide that he played a greater role in Bush's success than political
advisors of previous presidents.

Consider the books Rove felt influenced his life's choices. He
has said that the first book he remembers reading is *Great Moments in
History*. Most elementary school boys were probably reading *The
Hardy Boys* or *Lank of the Little League*, but not Rove. And during the
campaign, he prominently passed around to staffers a political tract
he carried. The pamphlet, written by Michael Novak, was about

mediating structures in politics. Rove said the treatise helped him to realize he had to change the nature of the Republican party and foreshadow what was coming next. When the document went missing in the chaos of campaigning, he described it as, "a treasured volume from his youth." Rove also told a reporter that, in grammar school, he wrote an essay on dialectical materialism.

He has known his path from the beginning.

As a colleague pointed out, "The president grew up dreaming of becoming Willie Mays. Karl grew up dreaming of becoming a presidential advisor."

Karl Rove did not invent political consulting. Nonetheless, of the estimated 7,000 political consultants at work in America, he has turned into the franchise player, a man whose presence in an opponent's campaign can chill a Democrat's hopes. In political circles, his reputation occupies the gray ground between mythology and history, a locale of his own choosing.

"It's a great run," he said. "I was fortunate enough to be associated with some terrific people, both candidates and volunteers, and other people involved professionally in the campaign."

For all of his public pronouncements about being lucky, there are also a thousand stories about Rove's considerable political skills and focused ambition. They come from his admirers, his opponents, and Rove himself. Republicans and Democrats know that little they hear about the operative is implausible. They are convinced he has designed winning strategies for multimillion dollar campaigns on the backs of napkins and has, in his memory, at his immediate disposal, an encyclopedia of demographic data and voter turnout tallies from every major election of the last century. And yet for all of his ability to recall the most minute electoral detail and obscure historical reference, Rove often says he cannot remember generalities about controversial matters in his career and the campaigns he has conducted. This is not a tic in his impressive memory but a political technique to avoid culpability in the more questionable aspects of his politicking. To journalists who have reported on him, Rove's political genius and influence are clear, even if the precise details of his rise to power are not.

McKinnon, who was once a Democratic ideologue in Texas, underwent a conversion to George W. Bush Republican politics, and views Rove as a consultant in a class all his own.

"Karl Rove is the Bobby Fischer of politics," McKinnon has said. "He not only sees the board. He sees 20 moves ahead."

Karl Rove matters to all Americans, many who have never even heard his name. While the president chafes at the description of Rove as, "Bush's Brain," he can hardly deny that every policy and political decision either goes through, or comes from, the consultant. In political circles, there is frequent discussion, almost as a parlor game, of where Karl Rove ends and George Bush begins. The relationship between the president and Rove has transcended all of the traditional models.

"I think he's more in a position of grooming the president than in being a subordinate to the president, as I perceive it. It's pretty unusual," University of Texas political scientist Bruce Buchanan claimed.

Rove is shaping policy based on politics. He reads the polls and studies political trends and then argues for policies that point in the same direction. Asked to confirm the premise, Rove quickly turned the proposition on its head: politics is an instrument for accomplishing the president's policies, not the other way around.

"The politics at the White House is less about how does this impact us politically and more about how do you go about politically, go out here and make the case for this and who do you make the case to?"

Regardless, *Time* magazine's White House correspondent, James Carney, said, "Karl Rove is probably the most influential and important political consultant to a president that we've ever seen."

The relationship between the president and his guru ought to be, at a minimum, subject to intense scrutiny. Normally, the campaign consultant maintains a professional detachment as a hired hand,

someone who is able, unlike the candidate's volunteers and supporters, to step forward with unvarnished honesty. In Rove's case, there is
no such professional separation between him and his client. Bush and
his consultant are friends, peers, trusted confidantes, and admirers of
each other. The relationship is, almost by definition, co-dependent.
Neither man is able to operate independently and remain whole in his
political endeavors.

Bush is the product. Rove is the marketer. One cannot succeed
without the other.

The president's critics often overstate the case in efforts to discredit Bush. He is neither as intellectual as his circle of advisors
want the world to believe nor is he as dim as portrayed by Democrats. Opponents have frequently underestimated Bush's ability to
build coalitions and win the day for his arguments. But Rove was the
whetstone that sharpened Bush into a presidential device. In the
presidential campaign and in the White House, Rove's choices became the president's policies.

The inherent danger in an arrangement where the political advisor also drives policy is that the consultant is deciding what is
best for the next election cycle and his political party while the
president needs to be considering what best serves the country beyond election day. These two interests are frequently divergent
and in conflict. While the president does have considerable personal and political strengths, Rove has carried into their collaborations a rigorous intellect, superior political expertise, and capacity
for detail.

The end result is obvious: Karl Rove thinks it, and George W.
Bush does it.

That's the way it works. And it works well. Rove's political
strategies are steering administration decisions on domestic issues
and foreign policy. Karl Rove's political calculations have proved
more often right than wrong and, for a president interested in re-
election, a formula that sways a constituency or adds electoral votes
is something he cannot afford to ignore.

Karl Rove has turned his role into something grander than just presidential political advisor. While he has several White House titles, Rove is largely responsible for the politics that got George W. Bush elected, and remains instrumental in the policies that have resulted. His influence marks a transcendent moment in American politics: the rise of an unelected consultant to a position of unprecedented power. Secretary of State Colin Powell, for example, has influence over policy, but not a close, long-standing relationship with the president. And Bush's pal from Midland, Texas, Secretary of Commerce Don Evans has the friendship, but not the wide-ranging influence over policy.

Rove has both.

The influence of Karl Rove on the president may raise constitutional questions. But there is little doubt about the practical implications of his position. Rove has a more profound influence on American lives than most officeholders.

He is the co-president of the United States.

And Americans cannot deny his influence.

Rove's policy choices for the president are almost certain to have impact on individual consumers. If, for instance, the price of automobiles began to increase because of the cost of raw materials, Karl Rove's politics may be assigned the blame. The value of some types of steel will rise because of a strategic political move by Rove. In the 2000 election, Bush lost Pennsylvania while carrying West Virginia. Re-election has a greater probability if the president can win the electoral votes of Pennsylvania, the nation's leading producer of steel. Rove counseled the president to protect the industry's competitiveness on the world market and shore up support for the Bush campaign in Pennsylvania. According to Rove, the decision was also driven by a need to develop a bipartisan coalition to win fast-track trade promotion authority for the executive office.

"We're a group that wants to go as fast as possible," he said.

The president obliged, ignoring the hypocrisies of the decision. In spite of his support for a free market philosophy, embodied in the

North American Free Trade Agreement (NAFTA), Bush agreed to assess tariffs on imported steel. The duties keep the more expensively produced American steel on a price par with the less costly imports from nations like Japan. Steel import tariffs blatantly contradict the president's campaign speeches about free markets, but they tactically improve his re-election chances in key industrial swing states and also move votes in his direction for trade promotion powers. In the end, Bush may win a second term, and the purchasers of new automobiles may be making larger car payments—all the result of strategy and influence exercised by Karl Rove on the world's most powerful office, the U.S. presidency.

Karl Rove, a solitary citizen, unelected, now has the kind of power in government and politics never before granted to a private citizen. In Texas, where Rove's work transformed the state's power structure, those defeated by the consultant are apprehensive over how he has gathered his authority and how it might be abused.

Soundly drubbed by Rove and his client, George W. Bush, in the 1998 gubernatorial race in Texas, Garry Mauro is convinced Karl Rove and his tactics have corrupted the democratic process.

"Yeah, I think he's an evil man. See, when we [Democrats] had the U.S. attorneys and the FBI, we didn't go sit down with the FBI and tell 'em to go get somebody. Karl Rove thought that was always okay. And that's why I think he's evil. He corrupts the system in a basic way."

Before he reached the White House, Rove left some unsettling signs on the landscape of Texas politics. He is connected to an apparently fraudulent bugging incident in his own office. Publicity surrounding the story, perfectly timed for maximum political effect, the day of the first gubernatorial debate and one month ahead of the 1986 vote, appears to have turned the election. Rove's client, former Governor Bill Clements, won—defeating Democrat Mark White, who was seeking re-election.

An ephemeral Rove also shows up in the periphery of a federal investigation of the Texas Department of Agriculture. His client,

Rick Perry, who, ultimately, became the governor of Texas, was seeking to be elected agriculture commissioner, his first statewide office. Jim Hightower, the Democratic incumbent, was served with subpoenas the day he had planned for his re-election announcement. The subpoenas were based on files arguably delivered to an FBI agent by Larry Beauchamp, an investigator with the Travis County district attorney's office who had previously worked for Rick Perry's brother-in-law. Rove knew the FBI agent, Greg Rampton, from the earlier bugging investigation.

The day Rampton showed up at the Agriculture Department with the subpoenas, the Democrats of Texas turned their angry eyes to Rove.

Unfortunately, the political bullet meant for Democrat Hightower went wide of its mark, instead striking key administrators. Mike Moeller, deputy agriculture commissioner, and Pete McRae, another senior manager in the agency, were both indicted, along with three others, even though previous investigations by the state auditor and the U.S. Department of Agriculture found no violations of law. A compelling amount of narrative and files, some of it related to Karl Rove, built a significant case that the Texas Agriculture Department's executive staff were the objects of an orchestrated political assault. Exhibits not entered into evidence in the trial, along with other state and federal records that have never before been publicly revealed, are presented later in this book.

Rove has always worked best while hiding behind a curtain.

When the "Brooks Brothers Riots" broke out during the Florida recount of the presidential election, Democrats considered Rove the mastermind. Named after the "preppie" clothing of the protestors, the rowdy distractions at the recount headquarters were the result of the Bush campaign bringing in an estimated 250 people to disrupt the process. Documents released to the IRS 19 months after the election, show the Bush team spent over a million dollars to fly operatives into Florida and another million to pay their hotel bills. The effort also relied on a fleet of corporate jets owned by people like Enron chairman Ken Lay, a key Bush supporter, and Halliburton, where Vice President Dick Cheney had served as CEO.

Karl Rove, working with James A. Baker III, put it all together.

Episodes of dirty tricks, well-timed investigations, and electoral legerdemain, have turned Karl Rove into a political enigma. The idea that President George W. Bush simply does the bidding of his consultant is an obvious simplification. But it is just as foolish to ignore the manifest ways in which Rove has redefined the role of political advisor. The president may arrive at his own conclusions about politics and policy. But virtually all of the data, and its interpretation, are coming from Karl Rove. And the material, undoubtedly, points the president where his expert wants him to go on matters of both politics and policy.

In an evolutionary chart of the political consultant, Rove represents a new species of advisor. He is the product of the permanent campaign, the co-president, whose relationship with Bush, and his faithful guidance, have put him at the heart of power in a manner unknown to previous political consultants and U.S. electoral history.

Rove dismisses the notion that he is unique in American politics. He points to other precedents. But in virtually every case, past consultants have had a more circumscribed authority or, more typically, went away after their client took office. Not Rove. The consultant's role, based on his record, appears to be the business of getting the candidate elected, helping to steer policy while in office, assisting the officeholder's re-election, and using the second term to tee up the ball for the party's chosen successor. These are tasks that used to be the province of the candidate, who ultimately became the officeholder. The advent of the permanent campaign, however, a product of two decades of bitter presidential races, provided Rove the opportunity to alter the consultant's profile. He has created the *permanent consultant*. This new political creature brings with it implications Americans have yet to measure.

An amateur historian, Rove styled the Bush campaign after the work of Mark Hanna, an industrialist at the turn of the twentieth century. Hanna, who was more of an outside expert than a consultant, counseled William McKinley to ignore the post-Civil War influences on the electorate. His argument, which proved prescient, was that America was creating a new working class and economy as a result of industrialization and those people would vote on jobs and the future, not on associations lingering from the war. Similar visionary thinking by Rove, about the transformation of the Republican party and twenty-first century demographics, lifted his premier client to the White House and reconfigured the role of political consultant.

Rove's choice of Hanna as an icon to represent his efforts with Bush is more revealing than has been considered. An industrialist, Hanna was best known for resisting government efforts to break up the giant trusts being developed by corporate and mining interests. These financial behemoths were able to control labor and wages with oppressive power. Hanna turned to the trusts to raise a record $4 million for the McKinley campaign, which made victory impossible for his Democratic opponent, William Jennings Bryan. For Bush, Rove used the same tactic, generating cash donations from corporate America for the Republican, in an amount which was unheard of in the history of American politics.

Hanna treated labor seriously, but not equally. While arguing he was willing to talk to laborers to improve their situations, Hanna's concerns, like Rove and Bush, were for business, assuming if big companies did well, everyone else would, too. According to the *New York Times* in 1896, that is not the way things turned out.

"The secretary of the Cleveland Central Labor Union wrote that Mr. Hanna had wrecked the Seaman's union of the lower lake regions, that he had smashed the union of his street railway employees, and refuses to allow them to organize. Further, Mr. Hanna had assisted in destroying the mineworker's unions of Pennsylvania, and had tried to break up the carpenter's unions of Cleveland by employing nonunion men on his mansion at a critical time last Spring, when the eight-hour law was being put into effect."

This then, was Rove's example of whom you needed to be to get things done. And for Bush and Rove, it worked. Massive amounts of campaign money meant votes and then power. They won. But did democracy also lose something?

In the fullness of his accomplishments, Karl Rove has raised a new and disturbing question for American voters and their republic: Who really runs this country?

1

Battles and Wars

Self-confidence is the first requisite to great undertakings.

Samuel Johnson

Wayne Slater, Austin bureau chief of the *Dallas Morning News*, stepped outside of a rope line to make sure Karl Rove had no trouble finding him in the crowd. Until that moment, Slater had been inconspicuous among the supporters and journalists gathered on the airport tarmac in Manchester, New Hampshire. The correspondent assumed Texas Governor George W. Bush's senior strategist was certainly going to be present when his boss arrived on a charter flight from Iowa for the debate at WMUR-TV. He knew Rove wanted to discuss the story he had written for that morning's edition of the Dallas paper.

Slater hardly saw Rove approach. Whether from the chill air or his anger, Rove's face was pink as it hovered inches away from the reporter. His index finger swung like a saber across Slater's chest.

"You're trying to ruin me," Rove charged. "My reputation. You son of a bitch. It's my reputation."

"What are you talking about?"

Slater did not immediately connect Rove's anger with the story he had written for the paper that day. The intensity was out of proportion to what Slater perceived as a minor piece of reporting.

"That story, damn you. It's wrong. You're trying to ruin my reputation."

"Karl, everything I wrote is true."

"No, it isn't, you son of a bitch."

The two moved closer together, their coat lapels practically brushing, displaying the kind of overt anger that might abruptly turn physical. Slater reminded Rove they had previously discussed these matters, specifically, his dirty tricks as a young Republican.

"No, no, no! It's wrong."

Rove's finger was punching Slater firmly in the chest.

"Look, Karl, you forget it was me you kept calling about the FBI and the ag commissioner and what he was doing. You called me about the railroad commissioner's degree problem. You can say whatever you want to these other guys, but you can't deny this stuff to me. You were calling me. It was you and me, buddy."

Slater lightly touched Rove's chest with his index finger, as the consultant had done to him.

"Don't you touch me," Rove sputtered.

The extreme reaction did not make sense. Rove was fairly practiced at anger management and was more likely to slice up reporters with an intellectually condescending rebuke. Probably, the consultant was edgy because it was the day of the Republican Primary's initial debate. In Rove's mind, it must have seemed like the stars were lining up precisely as he had ordered. The Dallas story was a blemish on the face of Rove's beautifully executed campaign plan. There was no other explanation for his response. Two of Slater's colleagues watched in astonishment as Rove continued his rant, inches from the reporter's nose.

"You son of a bitch. You said I taught dirty tricks."

"You did, Karl."

"No, no, no."

"The *Washington Post* reported it, Karl."

Slater reminded Rove that he had never protested a profile he had written months before, which referred to the *Post* story.

"They said it. A newspaper said it, okay. But you wrote that I flat-out did it."

"Well, that's because you did."

"A newspaper said I did."

Rove knew that the story was certain to be picked up by a growing group of national reporters who, from now on, would simply state that Rove was a master of dirty tricks. In his view, nobody had ever proved he was involved in campaign skullduggery. A newspaper had reported it, yes, but his opponents based their belief that Rove had used dirty tricks on unsubstantiated allegations in a political race years ago as a young Republican.

Slater pressed the issue. Rove did not deny the dirty tricks as a young Republican, but he continued to insist the Dallas story went too far.

"You son of a bitch. You stay away from me," he hissed at Slater. "I'm not going to let you ruin my reputation."

Slater, left conspicuously alone between the rope lines as Rove abruptly stalked off, shrugged and moved toward the candidate coming from the plane. Less than a half hour later, inside the small general aviation terminal at the Manchester airport, he encountered Rove again.

"Hey, how's it goin'?" Slater asked.

"I'm fine," Rove answered.

Already, the strategist was moving on to more pressing matters. The confrontation with Slater was just another campaign event, part strategy, part emotion. Karl Rove has a fine eye for working journalists up to the edge, bullying and cajoling, and then pulling back. Rove had made his point. In the future, the reporter, and those in the campaign press corps watching from a few feet away, might exercise more caution when writing about him.

No doubt the Dallas story had set Rove's teeth to grinding over his morning coffee. He had absorbed a dozen newspapers that morning. Rove obsessively collected mountains of information and used it to create an arsenal of assault weapons against political opponents. This was his gift.

And also his curse.

Rove was incapable of ignoring the *Dallas Morning News* piece or the journalist who had filed the copy. Jumping Slater was on his list of tasks for that day, along with getting his candidate in a final state of readiness for his first national debate.

Rove actually had sufficient reasons to be upbeat and pleased with the status of his candidate's campaign on that December day in 1999. Governor Bush was arriving in New Hampshire for the debate after an inspiring trip through Iowa. People, drawn by simple curiosity as well as political inclinations, had turned out in large, enthusiastic numbers to see the Texas governor. But not much of it was spontaneous. Rove was at the controls and nothing, therefore, happened without his advice and consent. No one had ever run a presidential campaign as meticulously as Karl Rove. All of the tiny parts were under his command and made into a forceful, coordinated engine of influence. Hardly a soul in the four-county region surrounding Waterloo, Iowa, could have been oblivious to the Governor's tour through their farm country.

The energetic rallies with hay bales and music and the growing support for George W. Bush were not simply a democracy's response to the candidate's appeal. They were also the results of the plan being unfolded by Bush's senior political advisor. Rove was a strategist who was changing the process with his ideas. His gift, perhaps more than any political advisor in history, was the ability both to visualize the broad design of a successful presidential campaign and to manage its every detail.

"Karl just dominates this," said a Republican admirer from Texas.

"Who's writing the scripts? Karl. Who's sitting there editing the film? Karl. Who's overseeing the media buy? Karl. Karl says do this and you do it. That's how he did it at Karl Rove and Company in Texas, and that's how he'll do it electing somebody president of the United States."

A man whose round face and thinning hair suggest more of a mailroom clerk than one of history's most intense political minds, Rove was in the midst of executing a 50-million-dollar maneuver to make sure his candidate won the Republican nomination for president. And voters were behaving according to plan.

Rove's strategy for winning the nomination for Bush was simple and expensive. In each of the key primary states, he had built the most extensive political organizations of any previous presidential candidate; perhaps the most elaborate electoral operations ever seen in the primary locales. The first three contested states—Iowa, New Hampshire, and South Carolina—had hundreds of precincts and each one of them had a Bush campaign chair. While the ground troops were searching out the voters, air cover came in the form of saturation television and radio advertising. The machine Karl Rove had created and the money he had to operate—the most ever in the history of presidential politics—gave him the power to make a president of George W. Bush, or maybe even of a Des Moines plumber.

The managers of presidential campaigns have usually not held such a job before. The standard of performance allows few chances at redemption. You either win your first time out, or you are gone from the profession. Winners turn into gurus, who then focus their attention on more stately challenges within the White House, or they leave their candidate to the affairs of state and move into private business and become highly paid experts. Losers are not first choices for candidates making an initial run.

Karl Rove was not a loser, at least not back in Texas. But he had never managed a presidential campaign either. And among Bush family loyalists, there were some lingering questions about whether his successes in state elections translated to a grander national scale. Rove took little or no notice of his skeptics. They did not have his gift for seeing the inevitable outcome. They did not understand his ability to control the variables.

Rove watched it all unfold in his head, long before it took place in the voting booths of Iowa. Each element of the Bush Iowa operation was poised and ready for competition on caucus day. Rove knew how to make farmers come in from the cold fields and drafty barns, get in their pickups and drive the snowy country roads into town to vote for George W. Bush. The intuition and detailed planning that had marked all of his previous political wins was guiding him through the Republican presidential primary season.

Even the best make mistakes. Trouble was afoot in New Hampshire and Rove's finely tuned antennae were not picking up the signals. Iowa was a state where money and structure were a sound formula for predictable results. New Hampshire was more susceptible to a grass roots uprising. Candidates had almost enough time to shake the hand of each primary voter. The less complex dynamics were allowing Senator John McCain to surge in the state that hosted the first primary and Rove did not see the dark horizon. Mistakenly, the Bush campaign had misjudged McCain's frequent trips to New Hampshire during the previous August. In Iowa, Rove did not consider McCain to be a significant threat because of his opposition to federal subsidies for gasohol production from corn. McCain also lacked any type of field organization so critical in the caucuses.

Rove was overconfident. Two months from the New Hampshire vote, he was under the impression the situation was comfortably in hand. As his candidate campaigned across the state, Rove stepped up the media buy to a level that could not be matched by McCain. Tracking polls looked good and none of the intense background checks of Governor Bush by various media had led to damaging information. Rove felt he and his candidate had little left to do except execute the plan. The primary had become pro forma.

There were annoyances, like that day's story in the *Dallas Morning News*, but Rove dealt with such minor disturbances in an expeditious fashion. Put out the fire before it spreads. Protect the prize:

RIVALS AGAIN FAULT BUSH OVER RUMORS
Governor and Aides Deny Starting, Spreading Rumors
Wayne Slater

AUSTIN—The fallout over apparent attempts to smear GOP presidential contender John McCain has prompted comparisons with a similar dispute in Gov. George W. Bush's political past.

In recent weeks, the Bush campaign has been accused of—and has denied—spreading rumors that Mr. McCain may be unstable as a result of being tortured while a prisoner of war in North Vietnam.

Several Senate Republicans, among them party leaders who favor Mr. Bush for president, have been identified in published reports as being responsible for privately pushing the allegations.

Also, James B. Stockdale, a former prisoner of war in Vietnam who ran as Ross Perot's running mate in 1992, said he got a call from a friend close to the Bush campaign soliciting comments on Mr. McCain's "weakness."

The senators have denied engaging in such tactics, and Mr. Bush has distanced himself from the episode, saying he is running a positive campaign.

In 1994, in Mr. Bush's first race for governor, his campaign was accused of—and denied—fostering a whisper campaign in East Texas about Gov. Ann Richards' tolerance for gays.

The issue became public when Mr. Bush's regional political chairman, Republican Sen. Bill Ratliff of Mount Pleasant, was quoted criticizing Ms. Richards for "appointing avowed homosexual activists" to state jobs.

Mr. Bush said the senator was speaking for himself, not the campaign.

Bush spokesman Scott McClelland said Wednesday, "Governor Bush has always run positive, issue-oriented campaigns."

Chuck McDonald, who as Ms. Richards' spokesman blamed the Bush campaign in 1994, said this week that he sees some parallels with the McCain episode.

Mr. McDonald said Bush political operatives have a history in which supporters spread stories while the candidate stays above the fray.

"The Bush campaign in 1994 effectively used surrogates to spread any campaign message the campaign thought needed to be carried," said Mr. McDonald, now a political and business consultant in Austin.

Political scientists and consultants say hardball tactics are common as candidates seek to win an advantage over opponents. But Mr. Bush has sought to set his campaign apart, saying he won't engage in that.

Dan Schnur, a spokesman for Mr. McCain, said the Arizona senator doesn't know who is responsible for the whisper campaign. He said Mr. McCain plans to release hundreds of pages of medical records that will dispel any doubts about his fitness for office.

Bush political rivals Steve Forbes and Gary Bauer both have blamed the Bush campaign for the McCain attacks.

"There is no place for negative smear tactics against any candidates, particularly the type being used against Senator McCain," said Mr. Forbes.

Mr. McDonald said the architect of Mr. Bush's political campaigns is Karl Rove, a longtime strategist with an aggressive style.

"Clearly, Karl Rove has a formula, and everything in 1994, in 1998 Mr. Bush's re-election and this year fits within that formula," said Mr. McDonald.

Mr. Rove did not return calls for comment.

Mr. Rove, a colleague of the late GOP consultant Lee Atwater, got his start in Republican politics while a student in college.

In 1973, Mr. Rove organized conferences that instructed young Republicans on campaign dirty tricks, such as going through a rival's garbage to obtain inside memos and contributor lists.

As a Republican consultant in Texas over the last two decades, Mr. Rove has worked for most major GOP candidates seeking statewide office.

As consultant to Gov. Bill Clements in his 1982 re-election bid, Mr. Rove distributed a mock newspaper suggesting that Democratic challenger Mark White was drinking while driving when he had a wreck as a college student.

Mr. Rove was instrumental in 1990 in spreading information about an alleged contribution kickback scheme involving Democratic Agriculture Commissioner Jim Hightower. Mr. Hightower was never charged, but three aides were convicted on federal charges.

In 1992, Mr. Rove passed along information that state Railroad Commissioner Lena Guerrero, a rising star in the Texas Democratic party, had lied about graduating from college. The story hit the front pages of Texas newspapers and ended Ms. Guerrero's political career.

Asked about Mr. Rove, Bush spokesman McClelland said, "Governor Bush sets the tone of his campaign and has always run positive, issue-oriented campaigns."

Credit: Austin Bureau of the *Dallas Morning News.*

The Atwater and Rove approach for new political operatives, mentioned in Slater's story, was first reported in a 1973 *Washington Post* article. There was not much new in Slater's piece. The story, even in the estimation of the author, bordered on innocuous.

As Slater and other journalists traveling on the Bush Campaign knew, using operatives to attack opponents, leaking harmful information, or turning rumors into weapons, as was being done against McCain, was not a new tactic for Karl Rove. If traveling reporters did not know how Rove had used those tactics in the past, they did now. In campaigns at the state level, he had also used surrogates to blast opponents while his clients remained above the fray. A Rove candidate was always able to honestly argue that he was running a clean, issues-oriented campaign because Rove stirred up the dirt without involving his client. He made phone calls to reporters, supplied documents, and produced third-party groups with damaging allegations. This approach, already a template for the modern electoral campaign, was refined by Rove with a new precision.

After his confrontation with Slater, Rove left the Manchester airport in the governor's motorcade, a row of dark Suburbans chasing police cruisers with flashing lights through the snow and rock of New Hampshire. Anyone who knew him or had worked around him knew what Rove was thinking about. Certainly, he was looking ahead to that night's debate. But the heated exchange with the reporter must have still lingered in his mind. Rove knew the big picture was infinitely more important than a Texas journalist writing what he considered recycled copy. No one was allowed to damage the plan Karl Rove had been building for almost a quarter century, especially not a local reporter.

Rove understood that journalists were not so much opposition as referees. Dealing with them asked little of his great intellect. True political opponents, however, were a different kind of game, and Rove brought them down with the fervor of a natural predator.

"The playing field was always different for Karl," an adversary said. "There were no out-of-bounds markers for him. He'd do anything he had to, to win, even if that meant destroying your livelihood. A lot of times, it wasn't enough for Karl to just win. He had to crush you in the process."

The Texas political landscape was spotted with the blood of those who had been taken down by Karl Rove, and they, more than anyone in America, were confident George W. Bush was on his way to becoming president of the United States.

Karl Rove knew it, too. He knew something else, as well. This might not be only about George W. Bush. If he intended to play the role of high-profile political consultant, Rove needed to have answers for controversial matters in his own past. There were stories and allegations about things he had done. Eventually, reporters would hear about them. And then he would be the one answering questions. They were coming, no doubt about that. He just had to figure out what the answers were before he was asked. And hope his own past was of no risk to his candidate.

2

Timing Is Everything

The great majority of mankind is satisfied with appearances, as
though they were realities.

Machiavelli

For almost seven hours on a Sunday afternoon in 1986, security
experts swept two offices of the Bill Clements for Governor
campaign. They were looking for bugging devices but had,
thus far, found nothing. Convinced there were no illegal
transmitters in the main office, the two-man team moved to the
suites owned by Karl Rove, the governor's campaign strategist.

Gary L. Morphew, owner of Knight Diversified Services, and
Bruce Wayne Scott, one of his 60 employees, were conducting the
search. As evening approached, Scott said he stepped out of the offices to take a break, leaving Morphew alone with the job. Scott
claimed that when he walked back in, Morphew was unscrewing
switch plates from the wall and taking the phone apart.

"It wouldn't surprise me if we found a bug in this place," Scott remembered Morphew telling him.

Karl Rove and Company, a political consulting firm, was heavily
involved in the second gubernatorial campaign of Republican Bill

Clements. The private security company was called in to conduct the sweep because Rove and Clements' campaign manager, George Bayoud, had become convinced that proprietary information about their strategy had leaked to reporters, and the campaign staff of Democratic opponent, incumbent Governor Mark White.

"There have been a number of instances over the summer when sensitive issues about campaign strategy have become known," Rove said. "It's been eerie, too much on target, items that have been very closely held."

The 1986 campaign of former Governor Bill Clements, seeking to be returned to the Texas top elected post, was an important moment in Rove's professional career. Although Rove was not managing the effort, he was the general consultant, instrumental in developing strategy, and handling all of the candidate's direct mail. Winning this race was more critical to Rove's future than it was to Clements. Potential information leaks of campaign information could not be tolerated. Bayoud decided to call in security experts.

Scott said that after returning from his break, he continued his check of the space using a device called a Hound Dog, which is a field-strength gauge for measuring radio frequency transmissions. Scott reported nothing was registering on the meter.

"I'm not picking up anything on this, Gary," he said.

"I don't think you're doing it right," Morphew responded, according to Scott. "Let me show you how to reset, and then you can redo your sweep."

Scott said that after recalibrating the Hound Dog, Morphew left him alone in the room to finish the frequency scan.

This time, Scott located an electronic bug behind a picture frame above Karl Rove's desk, close enough to have picked up and transmitted all of Rove's phone conversations. Hidden on the frame of a red, white, and blue needlepoint of the GOP elephant, the transmitter had a short wire antenna and, according to later tests, was able to send radio signals up to a half mile in open air.

Scott said he called Morphew back into the room and held the picture away from the wall to reveal the transmitter. Morphew removed the device, opened the back with pencils, and flipped the power switch to the off position. Holding the transmitter by the antenna rather than the casing, he dropped it into an envelope, which he quickly sealed.

The bug was found at 7:40 P.M. on Sunday, October 5, 1986, and Jaime Clements, who is not related to the candidate, was the only Rove and Company employee in the building. Morphew and Scott informed Clements of the discovery.

"Turn it off and get it the hell out of here," Clements told the men, according to Morphew.

Morphew said he told Clements that authorities are not normally contacted when a transmitter is discovered. He said either he, or Rove and Company, could dispose of the bug. Scott later told investigators he was convinced Morphew did not believe the results of the sweep would be reported to law enforcement. The two men returned to their hotel rooms with the device.

Karl Rove, though, called the police. According to Texas Department of Public Safety (DPS) records, Rove contacted that agency a few minutes after 11:00 P.M. Sunday. He also phoned the U.S. attorney's office and the Travis County district attorney. The DPS's initial incident report said Rove claimed he was called by the FBI, and was told to secure the area. He said that bureau investigators told him they would be on the premises in the morning.

In the interim, Rove had Morphew and Scott come back to his office from their hotel and bring the device. Around midnight, two representatives of the Travis County district attorney's office arrived at Karl Rove and Company headquarters. They took possession of the bug and stored it in a safe at the DA's office in the Travis County Courthouse. Rove ordered the two private investigators, Morphew and Scott, to spend the night at his office. Morphew spent much of that time writing a statement about the discovery and disposition of the device, which he presented to the DPS the next morning. There were contradictions between Morphew's and Scott's description of events, including Morphew's denial he was ever alone in Rove's office.

By 9:00 A.M. Monday, DPS Commander Joe G. Murphy, and Assistant Commander Tommy Davis were leading a team of investigators on the scene at Rove's offices. They interviewed the two private detectives, Gary L. Morphew and Bruce Wayne Scott. Members of the DPS Narcotics Technical Unit examined the technology of the device and a crime lab technician performed forensic work, searching for latent fingerprints in the room. The DPS team also swept the office for other devices, but none was found.

As the state team carried out its investigation, FBI agent Greg Rampton arrived at Rove's offices. DPS commanders on the scene decided to turn the bug over to Rampton to have the federal labs in Washington, DC, do an extensive analysis of the device's operation and technology. A slender man with graying blonde hair, Rampton's name was to appear in Austin newspapers many times in coming years. Rampton eventually led investigations into nearly every statewide Democratic officeholder in Texas during his tenure in the Austin office of the FBI.

Rampton and the DPS officers talked with Rove, trying to determine who might have planted the bug. A company that maintained a security patrol at the site reported that it had responded to a burglar alarm a couple of weeks earlier, but there was no sign of an intruder and no problems since.

Rove had a quick and ready answer when asked about potential suspects, and it was, predictably, political. His perceptions were detailed in the FBI's incident report, apparently written by Special Agent Byron Sage a few days later, and relayed to the FBI director's office in Washington, DC:

ROVE AND CLEMENTS' CAMPAIGN DIRECTOR GEORGE BAY-
OUD DECIDED TO SEARCH FOR A "BUG" FOLLOWING A

TELEPHONE CONVERSATION BETWEEN THE TWO ON MONDAY, 9/29/86, WHEN THEY DISCUSSED THE POSSIBILITY OF LEE ATWATER, AIDE TO VICE PRESIDENT BUSH, BEING BROUGHT IN TO HELP THE CLEMENTS CAMPAIGN DURING ITS LAST 30 DAYS AND A DECISION TO INCREASE CLEMENTS' TV ADVERTISING BUY TO 650 GROSS RATINGS POINTS. ACCORDING TO ROVE, THIS INFORMATION WAS MENTIONED BY *DALLAS MORNING NEWS* REPORTER SAM ATTLESEY IN A CONVERSATION WITH CLEMENTS' PRESS SECRETARY REGGIE BASHUR ON 9/30/86 AND ATTLESEY SAID HIS SOURCE WAS HARRIS DIAMOND, A POLITICAL CONSULTANT TO CLEMENTS' OPPONENT, TEXAS GOVERNOR MARK WHITE. AS A RESULT, THE SEARCH WAS AUTHORIZED.

Bayoud hired Knight Diversified Services after talking with Jim Francis, who was an executive with Bright Banc Savings Association in Dallas. Francis had managed an earlier Clements gubernatorial campaign and had been an important political mentor to Rove. According to Bayoud, Francis asked the security officers at his bank for the name of a company that could do an electronic sweep of an office. They recommended Knight, and Bayoud arranged for the firm to check out campaign headquarters and, ultimately, Rove's offices.

"Checking my office was an afterthought," Rove said in an interview more than a decade and a half later. "Bayoud hired him to sweep the headquarters because the thought was it was in the headquarters. So, he was literally sent over to our office as an afterthought."

The notion that checking his office was an "afterthought" contradicted Rove's own recollections of the incident, at the time. Why would it have been an afterthought to sweep his office when Rove claimed that was the specific location where the private conversation took place? If there was a suspicion that the conversation cited in the FBI report was conducted in Rove's office, as he claimed, it certainly should not have been an afterthought to run a surveillance check of that location.

"Are you sure it [the conversation] wasn't on the phone?" he was asked, when questioned in 2002.

"Maybe it's on the phone. I can't remember. But it's something in my office. I can't remember what it was. But there's only one conversation where that number [gross ratings points] is discussed and it's in my office."

There does not appear to be any reasonable explanation as to why the security team was sent first to campaign headquarters and then to Rove's office when, by Rove's own recounting, the Clements' team was convinced the leak came from Rove's place.

The "afterthought," though, led to some forward thinking. Rove's instinct was to turn every circumstance into a political advantage. Before federal agents were out his door, he must have been developing plans to leverage news that his office had been bugged. Strictly from a commercial standpoint, the incident had the potential to be good for Rove's business. Any consultant good enough for somebody to bug his office was surely a consultant to be sought after for his wise counsel. More importantly, though, Rove used the discovery to point a finger at Democratic opponent, Mark White, and his campaign staff.

The only debate of the 1986 Texas gubernatorial race was to be held that night in Houston. If news about the bug spread widely enough, it might disrupt Mark White's debate preparations and overshadow any story lines critical of Rove's Republican candidate. Potential gaffes by Rove's client, Bill Clements—always a worry on debate night—might get secondary play in the next day's papers. The big story would be the bugging.

As October began, the Clements campaign was struggling. None of its issues had sufficient traction with voters and the incumbent governor, Mark White, was closing the gap between himself and his Republican opponent. Independent polls at midsummer had shown White trailing Clements by 20 points. By October, White cut this lead in half.

A member of the Republican campaign's group of advisors admitted their candidate was in need of an issue or a weapon. "Tactically, they ran a better campaign; they had better TV. I remember White attacked us all summer. And Clements didn't want to spend the money. And White basically caught up. So it was a close race. The tip-off was the Labor Day campaign. So Labor Day, we're just getting started and people are just starting to tune in. And then Clements has had enough, and he's starting to be the old guy again; he wasn't nice any more. He was tired. And that was in September. So by October, White had caught up."

Even to the uninitiated, it was clear the controversy over finding a secret listening device would help Clements. Hastily, Rove began to make plans for a news conference in his office. A reasonable number of TV crews showing up also meant that the early newscasts would be talking about the bugging, instead of the debate. Correspondents would not be previewing the debate, creating unrealistic expectations, talking about issues that might prove troubling for the Republican. Rove had to see this as an advantage for his client, whose proclivity for poorly chosen comments on a number of topics during his first term as governor had provided much embarrassment and news copy.

After reporters arrived, Rove laid out a tale of political espionage involving a hidden wireless microphone, secretly transmitting from his office. He got up and pointed at a framed needlepoint of a red, white, and blue elephant, the GOP mascot, on the wall. Rove explained that a transmitter, about the size of a matchbox, had been discovered attached to the frame of the needlepoint, only four feet from where he spoke regularly on the telephone. A long, curled wire trailed from the eavesdropping device, in a description provided by Rove, and fingerprint dust from investigators was clearly visible on the wall surrounding the frame.

"So, who do you think is responsible for this, Karl?" a reporter asked.

"Obviously, I do not know who did this, but there is no doubt in my mind that the only ones who could have benefited from this detailed, sensitive information, would have been the political opposition."

The air was acidic with skepticism as Rove told his story. Afterwards, reporters speculated whether the bugging was a political stunt pulled off by Rove or Republican operatives. The most dubious of the crowd was veteran political writer Sam Attlesey of the *Dallas Morning News*. Attlesey's detailed questions of Rove and the Clements' campaign managers had prompted Rove and Bayoud to hire the security firm. They claimed he had information from the Democrat camp that could have only come from the Clements campaign. In fact, the investigation by law enforcement eventually raised questions whether any such information was ever obtained unlawfully.

Attlesey was blunt at the news conference.

"How do we know you didn't just put it there yourself, Karl?" Attlesey asked. "You know, just so you could call a news conference and talk about it."

"Well, Sam, I guess you don't," Rove answered. "But it doesn't really make any sense for me to bug myself, does it?"

"How long do you suppose it had been there on the picture frame?" a television reporter asked.

"It could have been there at least for the past four days. But it could have been there, and likely was there, for a lot longer. I just don't know."

Rove apparently had been away from his office for the past four days. But one date he remembered exactly—the date he had last looked behind the needlepoint frame. August 6, he recalled. Rove said during the news conference that he had removed the piece of artwork from the wall on that date because he had considered replacing it with another picture but decided against the change. Even with a mind fueled by minutiae, the ability to recall a specific date from two months earlier about such an inconsequential act seemed, if not suspicious, at the very least, oddly precise.

As always, Rove's words during the session with reporters were very carefully measured for effect. Despite a sharp flurry of questioning, he never overtly accused the Democratic governor of doing anything illegal. His responses left open the possibility that someone in Mark White's campaign might have done this without the governor's knowledge—a rogue operative, maybe. At the same time, Rove did not discount the possibility that White might have been aware of the bugging. Consistently, Rove steered reporters back to the issue of who stood to benefit from a listening device being hidden in his office.

There was only one answer.

The media response was precisely what Rove might have anticipated. Representatives were present from each of the major newspapers in the state's four largest cities: the *Dallas Morning News, Dallas Times Herald, Houston Chronicle, Houston Post, Austin American-Statesman, Fort Worth Star-Telegram,* and the *San Antonio Express-News.* A full complement of television crews was also in attendance. The five and six o'clock newscasts on KPRC-TV, Houston, and WFAA-TV, Dallas, the two pre-eminent newscasts in Texas, led with live reports from their Austin correspondents. Also, KDFW-TV, Dallas-Fort Worth; KXAS-TV, Fort Worth; KTRK-TV, Houston; and KTVV-TV, Austin; sent reporter and photographer teams to Rove's news conference. Anchor lead-ins to the reports and promotional teases, on their early newscasts, were all characterized by borderline sensationalistic claims.

"Hours before the big debate in the governor's race, an illegal bugging device is discovered in one of the campaign offices. And one campaign worker says he knows who's to blame. That story's coming up on Channel Two News."

Inevitably, the story distracted from advance coverage of the debate and any reporting on issues confronting the state. Editors will pick a mystery over a policy discussion every time. The Karl Rove bugging, whether by design or coincidence, had all the elements necessary to bring greater attention to the gubernatorial election and, not coincidentally, to Rove himself.

The debate between Mark White and Bill Clements went on as scheduled, broadcast statewide, and no questions were asked about the bugging. But after the camera lights went off, reporters in the studio flocked to the two candidates to ask questions about the debate and the listening device.

"Well, I was surprised," Clements told reporters. "I was disappointed. I was shocked. I think that properly describes my reaction. I don't really have any comment about it at this time because I don't know anything about it."

Clements' carefully considered words allowed viewers of the late newscasts that night to infer he was "shocked" and "disappointed" in his opponent, Mark White. Clearly, Rove and the ex-governor had talked about the episode.

Suddenly faced with implications that he might be connected to the bugging episode, the incumbent governor, normally a subdued campaigner, stood before a battery of cameras, his face flushed with anger.

"I don't know anything about it, and I would hope they wouldn't suggest we had anything to do with it," White said. "Obviously, we didn't. I have no doubt there's no possibility that anybody on my staff would have anything to do with that. It's just ridiculous."

The bugging did do political harm. The late Matt Lyon, who was Governor White's speechwriter, later told his friend, Patricia Tierney Alofsin, that White got news of the bugging at precisely the wrong time.

"Mark White got word right before they went on for the debate. I know all this through Matt. Matt told me that Mark White was told all about this minutes before going on, and it just really rattled him. And he didn't give a very good performance. If you go back and look at that debate, it was terrible. It was really from that moment on that things started going not so well for Mark White."

Tuesday morning's papers, not surprisingly, gave the bugging story prominent play, overwhelming the coverage of the debate. The Republican and Democratic campaigns released operatives to put their spin on the story. The main media liaison for the White camp was Mark McKinnon, who some years later switched to the Republican party and joined the legions of Karl Rove admirers. More than a decade later, McKinnon became part of the Texas team that put Bush in the White House. On the day of the bug's discovery, however, his Democratic taproot was still deep in its political soil.

"If they found a bug, that's a serious matter. But if they are blaming us, it's a bunch of bull. It is outrageous and sad that Rove would suggest the White campaign would be involved in a matter like this. The entire matter is both bizarre and incredible."

Early indications, in follow-up stories, were that the Republicans intended to press hard and use the bugging as an issue to question the credibility and trustworthiness of the Democrats. Reggie Bashur, Clements' media spokesperson, told Anne Marie Kilday of the *Houston Chronicle* that the bugging of Rove's office was a sad milestone for Texas politics.

"Whoever thought Watergate-style politics would come to the Lone Star state? It's happened. It's Texasgate."

Bashur's comments were an indication the Republicans planned to use the Rove bugging incident to grind down the White campaign. They had a controversial issue they could use to batter the Democrat. Why wouldn't they use it? And use it every day. But something happened to cause Rove and his team to go quiet on the bugging.

The investigation ended up making suspects out of Rove, the Republicans, and their security experts, instead of the Democrats.

3

Perception Is Reality

Son, always tell the truth. Then you'll never have to remember
what you said the last time.

Sam Rayburn, Former U.S. House Speaker

Things were not happening the way they were supposed
to for Karl Rove. The security company hired by the
Clements campaign had damaged his reputation. The way
the firm handled the discovery of a bug in Rove's office
had led to an endless assault of questions from lawmen, reporters,
and Democrats. While Republicans were referring to the bugging as
"Texasgate," privately, professional security experts and even some
of the official investigators came to refer to the incident in a decidedly less ponderous fashion: Questions about the way Knight Diversified Services and the Clements campaign handled the situation
prompted the nickname, "Goobergate."

Suddenly, and without explanation, Republicans dropped the
controversy as a campaign issue. Whatever the early political advantage, a series of bungled decisions began to make people doubt the
Republicans more than the Democrats.

A Republican campaign operative, who assisted the Clements team, still has questions about the affair. Who hired the security company, and why? Why didn't Rove, and the Clements team keep pushing the controversy when it was so obviously creating a drag on Mark White's campaign?

A Republican operative was baffled.

"And we got this firm out of Fort Worth. And I asked why did you go to Fort Worth? And, it's, well, they discovered it. So, I'm buying this, hook, line, and sinker. And we're pushing this four, five days. And the next day, I wake up, all right, listen. And . . . says, well listen, we may want to tone this down. And I say what? And Karl says that's enough, that's enough. And the tracking shows the Mark White advance stalls, and actually reverses. We did a great job."

The most troubling aspect of the case, however, for both law enforcement and the Clements campaign, was the disposition of the electronic device after the Hound Dog meter had found it. Even an amateur sleuth would have thought to leave the bug in place, feed it phony information and then wait for a source to use that false material. Although there were discrepancies among law enforcement agencies about the range and the power of the bug, none showed it to broadcast beyond a half mile. Rove's office, which sat on a limestone ledge above Shoal Creek, was bordered on the south by 15th Street, one of Austin's busiest thoroughfares, and to the west by Lamar Boulevard, a main north-south artery, as well as the open space of Pease Park. North and east there are a handful of residences. There were not an overwhelming number of doors to be knocked on by law officers. Whoever might have been monitoring the transmissions, it appeared, could have been easily discovered within that sparsely populated half-mile radius.

When Morphew removed the bug from the wall frame, he eliminated the best chance of finding the interloper. His actions became the subject of dispute by political interests and law enforcement agencies. Morphew's decision on how to handle the bug had the effect of turning him into a suspect and making resolution of the case nearly impossible. In his statement to investigators, Morphew said he was ordered to get the device out of the office by Rove employee Jaime Clements.

Clements denied that.

"I told them to do what it is they do," Clements told reporters, who began calling him repeatedly. "I certainly do not recall telling them to turn it off and get it out of the office. I never even knew if or when it was turned off."

Morphew disagreed with Jaime Clements' characterization of why the bug was taken back to Morphew and Scott's hotel room.

"I removed that device at the direction of their people," he told the DPS and FBI. "I did nothing illegal or wrong."

Morphew, and his colleague on the sweep, Scott, also found themselves in disagreement over the facts. Scott told the FBI that Morphew was in Rove's office alone for a period of time before Scott returned and found the bug. Morphew vehemently denied that version of events. Scott, who had no background in electronic countermeasures, agreed to a polygraph exam. According to the FBI, his results were, "satisfactory."

Under pressure from the Clements campaign, Morphew also said he was willing to sit for the lie detector. However, when arrangements were made for the test, he changed his mind and refused for what he called, "personal reasons." Morphew said he would consider the test only after he had spoken to some people. He did not identify those individuals.

"I have no legal or moral requirements to take it. I don't have to, and I am not going to," declared Morphew to the *Austin American-Statesman*.

Two weeks later, Texas newspapers were still writing about Morphew's decisions and the episode in Rove's office. In an interview with Guillermo X. Garcia of the *Austin American-Statesman*, Dave Logan, a former federal investigator from Dallas, was among the most critical of Knight Diversified Services.

"I can tell you that just about any professional would have handled the situation different. An investigator who is paid good money should be able to advise the client about options, the legalities involved, who enforces the appropriate criminal statutes, how to preserve the scene as evidence, things like that. I damn sure would not have removed it to a motel room without even contacting authorities, the FBI, which has the jurisdiction."

Results of the FBI lab work in Washington only added confusion. According to tests, the battery was a six-volt with 5.8 volts of remaining power. The life of the battery, however, caused the greatest problem for investigators. Maximum battery life was 10 hours. Obviously, this was evidence that whoever had placed the bug was someone with recurring access to change the battery, or someone who did not care if the device transmitted, only that it be found. Equally troubling, the residual life of the battery, at 5.8 volts, was irrefutable proof that the bug had been put in place and turned on the same day it had been discovered.

McKinnon, the Republican convert and compatriot of Rove's in the Bush presidential campaign, implied during the 1986 campaign that Rove had planted the bug himself by referring to the Watergate break-in of 1972. "It seems to me the Republicans are the ones who have experience at this kind of stuff. I think this whole thing stinks, and I think that the wind is blowing from the Clements campaign. The Clements campaign has been asking who has the most to gain from this, and I would suggest that it's the Clements campaign."

Publicly, at least, there was one issue on which both the White and Clements campaigns concurred. Both sides felt removing the bug had been a mistake.

"I don't know why they took the bug with them to the hotel," Rove said. "But I am not going to second guess them. I believed it would have been useful to feed the bug information to see where that information surfaced."

McKinnon agreed.

"Why didn't they just leave the damn thing on and really put out some disinformation, and catch whoever it was red-handed?"

To reduce suspicion that their campaigns were complicit, Rove and Bayoud volunteered to submit to lie detector tests, as did Democratic Governor Mark White and his campaign staff. Investigators, however, never took any of them up on their offers. Officially, law enforcement looked at both operations and came to no conclusion. The FBI report, however, casts some doubt over Rove's and Bayoud's motivation for having a security company conduct a sweep.

The oft-repeated story from Rove and Bayoud went like this: Information from a privileged, confidential telephone conversation they had on September 30, 1986, had gotten into the hands of *Dallas Morning News* reporter Sam Attlesey. During that call, the two said they discussed raising the Clements' media buy to 650 gross ratings points—a measure of how many people would see the commercial—as well as hiring consultant Lee Atwater for the final 30 days of the gubernatorial race. Attlesey first heard the information from Harris Diamond, a political consultant in Virginia, retained by the White campaign. Clements' staffers then told several Texas reporters that the only way Diamond could have acquired such information was through the bug in Rove's office.

"That's a bunch of bullshit," Diamond told R. G. Ratcliffe of the *Fort Worth Star-Telegram.*

Regardless, it was the pretext Rove and Bayoud used as a reason to have the campaign headquarters on Congress Avenue, and Rove's office checked for security leaks.

According to Rove, during an interview years later, his suspicions of a leak were prompted by the confidential discussion with Bayoud of ratings points for the media buy. During that private conversation, Rove said, he gave the wrong number to Bayoud.

"Later that day I see Bayoud, I'm on my way to the Austin Club, and I say, 'George, I got the number wrong, the real number is X,' and then later that afternoon Bayoud calls me and says, 'I got a call from Sam or somebody about the number.' Well, I had misspoken the number. It's not like that was on a piece of paper anywhere that could have been circulated by anyone else. I literally say the number wrong. I say it right on the street. I correct it on the street. I say it's not what the number X was. Here's the real number. And so Bayoud then calls me that afternoon and says this is sort of weird that number you gave me this morning and says, in essence, 'Did you call anybody?'"

Clements' press liaison Reggie Bashur said he was asked by reporter Sam Attlesey whether the Governor's campaign planned to hire Charlie Black, who partnered with Lee Atwater, and if it intended to increase its advertising buy that week to 650 gross ratings points. According to Bashur, Attlesey told him he had been informed of the Charlie Black decision by Harris Diamond, the Democratic consultant working for Governor Mark White. Bashur didn't know about the Black hiring, so he asked Bayoud how it was that an operative for Mark White knew about the move.

When he was interviewed by the FBI, Attlesey said that Diamond never made any mention of "gross ratings points" or Lee Atwater. He spoke only in general terms of the firm in which Atwater was a partner, Stone, Black, Manafort and Atwater. Diamond also used the dollar figure of $650,000.00, not "gross ratings points." Diamond told investigators he got weekly canvassing reports from the Sawyer-Miller Group in New York City, which was producing television ads for the Mark White campaign. Sawyer-Miller staffers called television stations in the 20 Texas markets to determine how much advertising was being purchased by the Clements campaign.

As it turned out, the secret information from the Clements camp might not have been so secret after all. There was no discussion about Atwater, but about Charlie Black and his political firm. As for the purchase of television time, that information was readily available, although Rove disputes that.

"We haven't placed a buy at that point. We're placing the buy. It's not fully placed. Whatever it was. There's no way anyone could have fully deduced that number."

The FBI's incident report on the Rove bugging has never before been published. The document, written in all capital letters, blatantly contradicted Rove's rationale for having an electronic sweep performed in his office:

DIAMOND ADVISED THAT SOMETIME BETWEEN 9/26/86 AND 10/3/86 HE WAS TOLD BY THE SAWYER/MILLER GROUP THAT CLEMENTS HAD INCREASED HIS BUY FROM 450 TO 700 GROSS RATINGS POINTS FOR THE FIRST TIME. DIAMOND LATER RAN INTO ATTLESEY AT A LOCAL RESTAURANT AND MENTIONED IT TO HIM. ACCORDING TO DIAMOND, ATTLESEY ASKED HIM TO TRANSLATE 700 POINTS TO DOLLARS AND DIAMOND FIGURED THAT AT A RATE OF $70,000 TO $80,000 PER 100 POINTS THAT THE WHITE CAMPAIGN WAS PAYING 700 POINTS WOULD TOTAL $500,000 AND THE ADDITIONAL RADIO ADVERTISING TIME CLEMENTS WAS BUYING WOULD AMOUNT TO $150,000, GIVING A TOTAL OF $650,000. THIS IS THE FIGURE HE GAVE ATTLESEY.

Transmitted to the FBI director in Washington, investigators reported to the agency that it was easy to acquire the information through public sources. The FBI quickly concluded that neither Harris Diamond, nor anyone else, needed a hidden microphone to pick up details on Rove's media buy for the Clements campaign. All anyone needed was a telephone.

Determining how Diamond learned of plans to hire Charlie Black also did not require great detective skills, according to the FBI. Governor Mark White's pollster, Dick Morris, who later worked for President Bill Clinton, told Harris Diamond that Black had been asked by the Clements camp to join them for the final month of the race. Morris and Black frequently shared professional information because they served together as consultants on other campaigns. In the autumn of 1986, Black and Morris were working together on a U.S. Senate campaign in another state. Morris, who made himself available to both Republicans and Democrats, had access to information from both parties.

Five minutes after Charlie Black told Morris he had been approached by the Clements campaign, Morris called the White campaign with the news. No illegal listening device was necessary. Dick Morris told them. Not a hidden transmitter. Again, the FBI investigation doubted Rove's allegations that the detail came from a bug:

... IT APPEARS THAT THE INFORMATION THAT THE CLEMENTS CAMPAIGN STAFFERS FELT WAS CLOSELY HELD WAS, IN ACTUALITY, KNOWN BY THE WHITE CAMPAIGN THROUGH LEGITIMATE SOURCES AT ABOUT THE SAME PERIOD OF TIME. THE SIGNIFICANT FIGURE OF 650 GROSS RATINGS POINTS WHICH VICTIM ROVE GAVE GEORGE BAYOUD ON 9/29/86, WAS COINCIDENTALLY SIMILAR TO THE $650,000 FIGURE DERIVED FROM 700 GROSS RATING POINTS BY DIAMOND AND GIVEN TO NEWS REPORTER ATTLESEY.

So how did the bug end up in Karl Rove's office? Democrat Mark White's staffers believe Rove was the culprit. But because of the transmitter's short battery life, that means Rove had to have slipped clandestinely back into Austin, early Sunday morning, from his campaign trip, plant the bug, and then race back to Dallas. Unlikely, unless he had put it in place before leaving and an accomplice turned it on Sunday at Rove's direction. Maybe one of Rove's business or political opponents did it. The short battery life, though, suggested they would have had to breach security on a daily basis to keep the bug transmitting. And there's no evidence anyone had broken into Rove and Company headquarters. The battery's six hours of usefulness and the lack of any evidence indicating a break-in is a strong clue that, whoever planted the bug had easy, recurring access to Rove's office.

Only deepening the mystery, Rove has recently offered another possibility, something that has not ever turned up in any of the law enforcement agencies' incident reports. Rove might be suggesting a new theory to increase the confusion surrounding the bugging. In his political career, he has frequently used a tactic of offering numerous plausible explanations for events and circumstances. The method makes it more and more difficult to arrive at the truth. In this case, Rove has created a new suspect, a new plausibility, and he has taken another step in moving suspicion away from him and the campaign he was running when his office was bugged. "The other thing is that we do know, this was a back loading dock area, and there was an unexplained visit by a white panel truck, to the loading dock a few days before. A few days before, there is a white . . . the neighbors . . . people who live around there report having seen someone emerge from the back office with phone equipment hanging off their belt in a white panel truck, saying they were there to work on the phone system. Nobody, nobody, ever worked on the phone system."

Of course, if someone were going to tamper with the phone equipment illegally, it's not the least bit likely he is going to be walking out the door into the daylight with electronic tools hanging off of his belt. The building was small, with only a few clients, and masquerading as a phone technician would have been impossible. Rove did not tell this story at the time of the bugging, possibly because it could have been so easily refuted. Besides, if there were people in the neighborhood who witnessed this, why were they never questioned by police? There are no names of nearby residents or any other trace of this story in any of the official reports.

Suspicion, publicly, kept getting aimed at the surveillance company.

The reluctance and, ultimately, the refusal of Morphew, owner of the security firm, to take a polygraph exam also made him a key suspect. A few Republicans came to believe that Morphew planted the bug himself, and then revealed its location to bring attention to his security company, Knight Diversified Services. Finding a secret listening device inside the headquarters of a high-profile political operation like Rove's might enhance Knight's reputation, particularly with inevitable widespread media coverage.

Even though he has consistently denied involvement in the bugging through the years, one of the Texas DPS investigators still thinks the evidence points to Morphew.

"I wouldn't quite call it an old policeman's intuition. But we had everything but a confession from the guy," said Tommy Davis, lead DPS investigator on the bugging. "We're pretty certain he was the one. We just didn't have enough evidence to prove it. I think he probably did it to make a lot of money, thinking he'd get attention and business out of it all. We don't think the guy ever realized the police would be called."

Davis, who became the commanding officer of the entire Texas DPS, believes there is no reason to think Rove had a hand in the matter. "Karl's a lot smarter than that," he said.

A Texas Republican party insider who was closely involved in the 1986 campaign is still wondering what might be the truth. "Did Karl know about all this stuff, or didn't he know about it? The bug was in his office. I don't know if they discovered it or Karl discovered it. It's a good anecdote in the play-for-keeps department. Either [the Clements campaign] knew when they hired them that they would find it, or it was possible they [Knight Diversified Services] were promoting their own deal. We were very eager. Because we were in trouble. Mark White was winning that election, and we had to do something, and we jumped at what we thought was something."

As for Rove, he has repeatedly found himself at the periphery of unexpected, campaign-shaping events, but nothing ever links him directly to those events. It became his motif. There is no crime, just a victim. Evidence is gone before acquiring substance. Rove must have known that various advertising companies acquired information on campaign media buys on a regular basis. How could he not know that this was readily accessible, under the law, to anyone who went to the trouble to contact television stations? Or that his competition, Governor Mark White's campaign, was using its media firm to gather the material on the Clements' buy?

Rove has insisted all along that he was never a suspect in the case. But an FBI source in Washington, speaking on condition of anonymity, said, from the beginning, the suspects were obvious and Rove was, indeed, at the top of the list. According to this person, who was close to the investigation, agents were immediately suspicious of Rove and the Clements campaign because of the timing and the technical specifications of the device and lack of evidence of a break-in. This investigator said all of those details made the bugging look like an inside job, which meant, in his assessment, that someone in the campaign planted the bug or they were working with the security firm to make sure a bug was discovered.

"We were completely aware of the dynamics of all of this. It was the day before the debate. It was toward the end of the election and it could affect a lot of things. It all pointed in an obvious direction. We just did not have time to prove it. There were more important things going on in Texas at that time. It's interesting that all of these individuals have continued to evolve politically, after this happened, all of the way up to the White House."

The source said he was convinced the U.S. attorney for the Western District in Texas closed down the case because she feared it would ultimately implicate the Clements team. He described Republican appointee Helen Eversberg as the most political U.S. attorney he had ever encountered in law enforcement.

Sixteen years after it happened, Rove was asked who he thought was responsible for planting the transmitter in his building.

"I have no idea. Look, there are a lot of weird people running around in politics, particularly in Austin, Texas, in the seventies and eighties. There are just a lot of crazy people."

Polls from the 1986 Texas gubernatorial election show that ubiquitous news coverage of the bugging altered Mark White's political fortunes. The steady increase in his support came to a quick stop, and then began to decline. Mark McKinnon, the Rove adversary turned associate, was told of the impact.

"The numbers show that when the bugging came out, he just stopped."

"He?" McKinnon asked.

"White."

"So, it worked."

While describing the incident as one of the great, ongoing political mysteries that was never solved, McKinnon did not credit the bugging with changing the course of the election. He said that Mark White was defeated by a superior campaign on the Republican side, the careful plan of Karl Rove.

Whatever the residual skepticism over the bugging incident, the affair had faded into the haze of Texas political lore until the 2000 presidential race. George W. Bush and, to a lesser extent, his chief strategist were suddenly the objects of great scrutiny. With a few exceptions, feature stories on Rove gave little or no attention to the bugging. Instead, they concentrated on making a case for the political wunderkind, his brilliance and vision, his command of the field of battle, and the Rove willingness to do whatever was necessary to win. He was careful who he gave interviews to, scrupulous to avoid u-turns into areas that did not advance the cause of his candidate.

Journalism was another campaign element he managed brilliantly. Rove liked reporters but never enough to completely trust them. Rarely chatty with journalists, he succumbed, one evening while campaigning, to convivial talk about his chosen profession. Conversation centered on a movie involving political consulting, which had captured Rove's imagination. Directed by Sidney Lumet, the film *Power* is about a high-profile, very successful political strategist, who travels around the country on private jets, winning campaigns.

The lead character, played by Richard Gere, lives in a pricey Manhattan high rise, deftly manipulates the media, and determines the fate of candidates across the nation. Almost every change of setting begins with a private jet landing in a different city or showing a camera perspective from inside the plane, looking down on the next destination.

Rove loved the film for its absurdities. "I mean what was important to me was, what was unbelievable, the guy flies around in his own private jet. Everybody pays him 25 grand a month, his offices are sleekly paneled in a New York high rise, he has an unbelievably attractive secretary, who he has sex with in the shower, I mean, you know, that's what I remember, I don't remember the other stuff."

In his enthusiasm for the movie, Rove either overlooked or forgot the pivotal moment in the story's plot. Gere's character, who is managing several campaigns, is talking on the phone in his production studio. As he approaches the video monitor to view a tape, while still conducting his phone conversation, he notices the picture flutters. He backs away and the screen stabilizes. Stepping close to the monitor again, he holds up the phone, and the picture, once more, flutters. The character immediately realizes that radio signals coming from his phone are causing distortion on his television screen. Unscrewing the cover on the mouthpiece, he finds a wireless transmitter, a bug.

The movie showed up in theatres early in 1986, months before the illegal electronic device was uncovered in the offices of Karl Rove and Company.

Asked about that coincidence, Rove said he had watched the movie on a VCR, many years after its release, and was probably not paying attention when the bugging scene was on.

"That's why it was probably on a VCR because, you know, I don't know about you, but I put the VCR in there, and I get phone calls or go get a . . . but I literally do not remember that part."

The discovery of the bug in *Power* is the revelation of the entire movie. Every scene, each development of the story, prior to finding the bug, is a construction designed to add impact to the time when Gere unscrews his phone's cover, about halfway through the film.

The remainder of the plot is a product of how the bugging has affected the campaigns of Gere's clients and his own professional life. Rove had to have been powerfully entranced by the depiction of charter jets and $25,000-a-month retainers not to notice the movie's biggest, most important scene.

If Rove's campaigns are characterized by anything, it is his attention to detail and an exquisite sense of timing. There is an exact moment to attack and a right time to talk issues. He lays out a schedule and plotline with the same eye for detail as a movie producer. So the release of the film *Power* with its pivotal scene about campaign espionage just months before a similar episode played itself out for real in Rove's office—leveling the campaign of Democrat Mark White—had the look of extraordinary coincidence, at the very least.

A federal grand jury in Austin was presented all available evidence in the real-life bugging involving Rove. Gary L. Morphew confirmed to a Dallas reporter that he received a "target letter," notifying him he was the object of an investigation. The goal was to resolve the matter in October 1986, prior to the November 4 election, but the deadline proved impossible to meet. With the election approaching, U.S. attorney for the Western District of Texas, Helen Eversberg, issued a statement exonerating both campaigns.

"At this time, we have no reason to believe that anyone on Governor White's or Governor Clements' staff was involved in the bugging," she said.

Three months later, at approximately the time Rove's client, William P. Clements was being inaugurated, federal investigators conceded they did not have enough material evidence to indict anyone.

An inter-office memo from the DPS in February 1987 noted that Morphew had refused to take a polygraph and that he "remains the primary suspect."

"At this writing," the memo added, "all investigative leads have been exhausted and it appears that no criminal charges are forthcoming. It is herewith recommended that the case assignment be designated 'closed.'"

Morphew should be no more of a suspect than Rove. His life, though, has followed a markedly different trajectory. Knight Diversified Services went out of business and Morphew leads a hardscrabble existence as a rancher on a small piece of scrub and mesquite in the remote reaches of Commanche County, Texas. During the presidential campaign, Morphew was asked again about the bugging by reporter Pete Slover of the *Dallas Morning News* and denied again he had any role in the incident.

One summer night about a year after the bugging, Rove may have offered a glimpse of the facts. Political consultant John Weaver had invited Rove and his wife, Darby, to dinner. The Weavers had been friends of the Rove's for a long time. Weaver had worked on Clements' campaign, and now that Clements was governor, he and Rove had moved on to other projects.

Democrats and Republicans were working together to bring the Superconducting Supercollider to Texas. The giant atom smasher was the most important scientific project in the country and the campaign to bring it to Texas transcended political party.

Matt Lyon, the defeated governor's speechwriter, and his friend, Patricia Tierney Alofsin, were also invited to the small dinner party. At one point in the evening, Tierney Alofsin recalled, the subject of conversation turned to the bugging.

"Of course, Rove knew Matt had worked with Mark White. And there was some discussion about it. And Karl all but came out and said, 'I did it.' He was proud of it. It was sort of like, 'We really messed you over, didn't we?'"

Tierney Alofsin thought how odd it was to be sitting there so long after the fact, after all the fulsome denials and the wreckage it had made of White's campaign—and now Rove, grinning and ebullient, was acting as if he wanted to take credit for it. She considered getting up and leaving, but did not.

"I don't remember the exact words, but I remember being shocked," she said. "It was like those cases where people murder people, and then they leave clues because they do this fabulous murder, and they want the police to know they did it. It was that sort of thing. He was so proud of it.

"What came across to me, whether it was that he did it and wanted us to know he did it, or that it happened and he wanted to take credit for it in some way, it came across the same: 'Wasn't I a clever boy?' That's the way it came across. He left the impression, 'wasn't I clever, and didn't it work, and let me rub your nose in it.' It was so amazing I couldn't believe it."

All successful people are susceptible to moments of rambunctious ego. Political operatives are conflicted by the nature of their profession. If their ideas and implementation work, they do not get to take credit. The candidate wins. Not the consultant. Maybe Rove did not plant the bug. But his own behavior, new information from investigators, unheard of versions of the story offered by Rove, and simply the timing, makes it hard to disconnect him from culpability in the incident.

Whenever he deconstructs campaigns of his past, Rove always talks about luck. He is consistently lucky. But how much luck can a political operative have? His office ends up being bugged and it gets discovered the day before the only debate of the campaign? Not even lucky Karl Rove is *that* lucky. And the bug is discovered in the same year that a movie about a political bugging is released and Rove wants people to believe that, too, is just coincidence.

Lucky Karl.

Whatever happened, it did not stick to him, even though, over the years, fingers have slowly pointed back in his direction. Rove has claimed that situations arise and he uses them to create better campaigns. But there is greater plausibility that Rove is responsible for generating the environments that provide advantage to his candidates. He never got publicly accused in the bugging of his own office. But it's hard to look elsewhere for the perpetrator, especially using Rove's own standard of, "Who had the most to gain?"

Karl Rove did.

And Karl Rove remains a primary suspect, regardless of his arguments to the contrary.

Several other mysterious things happened around Rove as he worked his way toward the White House.

And some wrecked careers and changed Texas politics forever.

4

Suspicions and Clues

Politics is supposed to be the second oldest profession. I have
come to realize that it bears a very close resemblance to the first.

Ronald Reagan

When the phone rang, Bob Boyd later told colleagues,
he was shocked to hear the voice on the other end of
the line.

"Bob, this is Ken. Ken Boatwright."

"Uh, yeah."

As a consultant to the Texas Department of Agriculture, Boyd
could not have expected to get a phone call at home from Ken
Boatwright. Boyd was a supporter of Democratic Agriculture Commissioner Jim Hightower, which placed him in political conflict
with Boatwright, who had decided to run against Hightower as a
Republican.

"We need to talk about some things, Bob," Boatwright said.

"Well, okay, then. Go ahead. Let's talk."

"No, I don't want to talk about this on the phone. Can we meet
somewhere?"

"Uh, I suppose."

The previous autumn, September 1989, Boatwright had also been working for the Texas Department of Agriculture as the Director of the Seed and Grain Warehouse Division. After a senior staff meeting with Commissioner Jim Hightower, Boatwright announced the following morning that he was resigning his position. In a matter of days, he became a declared Republican candidate for Texas agriculture commissioner, hoping to unseat his former boss, the Democrat Hightower.

Boyd and Boatwright made arrangements on the phone to meet at Jim's, a restaurant on the north side of Austin that summer evening of 1990. Before leaving home, however, Bob Boyd called his attorney to ask what he thought of the decision to talk with Boatwright. Boyd's consulting contract with the Texas Department of Agriculture (TDA), as well as the agency itself and senior aides, had been the subject of recent audits and investigations. His lawyer warned Boyd to mostly listen because it was possible Boatwright was wearing a wireless microphone.

The next day the agriculture consultant recalled, in great detail, his conversation with Boatwright.

"I just wanted to let you know that I am sorry all of this happened."

Boatwright was referring to investigations of the TDA by the U.S. Department of Agriculture (USDA), the state auditor's office, and the FBI.

"I never meant to hurt, y'all. I just wanted to get Hightower. This thing has taken off in a direction I never wanted it to go."

Boyd left the restaurant convinced that his former colleague had been leaking information to political adversaries of Texas Agriculture Commissioner Jim Hightower.

At the agency, Boatwright had been a supporter of Hightower as well as his handpicked successor, Deputy Agriculture Commissioner Mike Moeller. Slightly round of face and sandy haired, the stocky

Boatwright was considered pleasant and hard working during his tenure. Hightower had promoted him to division director.

Boatwright's antipathy, however, might have stemmed from a promotion he did not get. Hightower, always astute to political winds, had hired as a deputy commissioner, Sheila Jackson Lee, an African American from the state's largest urban region. She had no experience with farm and ranch issues but did have enormous political potential. Jackson Lee went on to become a member of the Houston city council and then the U.S. congress.

Boatwright likely thought he should have gotten the job. The perceived slight certainly gave him a motive to run against Hightower and spread negative details about the TDA, if he wanted to choose such a course of action.

There were a limited number of entities, political and governmental, that might have been able to use information from Ken Boatwright, assuming he had knowledge to share of any improprieties. The state auditor's office, USDA, and various law enforcement authorities would have all been interested in potential crimes. Harmful words about Jim Hightower were also valuable to the Texas Republican party. When Boatwright was considering resigning and running as a Republican against Hightower, he contacted top Texas GOP operatives and organizers.

Karl Rove was the Republican in charge of the campaign who was most interested in defeating Jim Hightower.

In a recent interview, Rove claimed not to remember Boatwright, until he was reminded of his brief candidacy.

"I remember him saying, 'I know bad things. I'll unveil bad things. But I have to have a promise of a job,' and I was, basically, polite and said, 'Thank you, very much, but no can do.' He struck me as an odd character."

Rove and state Republican leadership had already picked as the party's nominee for agriculture commissioner the handsome rancher from West Texas, Rick Perry. Anything Boatwright knew about irregularities inside the agency was of immense value to Rove and his client. Republicans were eager to defeat Hightower, a populist with oratorical powers, who was instrumental in keeping Democrats in control of state government. Even though Rove said he dismissed Boatwright, his insider's knowledge was exactly the type of information that Rove routinely used in campaigns against political opponents.

In retrospect, Rove has remained insistent that Kenneth Boatwright was of no consequence to the Republicans or the campaign of Rick Perry.

"I think I had one or two phone calls with the guy. He tried to seek a meeting, my recollection of which is now distant. He was clearly not a guy who was credible and dependable. He had a sort of price that he wanted to have paid for unannounced, undescribed things and I said get this guy out of here."

In a news release he issued on November 27, 1989, Boatwright implied he knew there were matters amiss at the state agriculture department and that he thought investigations being conducted, and written about in newspapers, would prove revelatory.

"It is possible that this flap is only the tip of the iceberg and many more charges will likely surface during the next few months following the state auditor's report."

In leaving his job to campaign, Boatwright had abandoned 16 years of friendships and professional associations he had developed while working at the agency. If he had information, the Republicans and Karl Rove must have wanted it. But they did not want him, and they offered nothing in return. A month after making known his intentions, Boatwright came to grips with the fact that the Republican party was promoting Rick Perry as its candidate. He withdrew from the race when he was able to raise only $6,100.

After his apology to Bob Boyd that early summer night in 1990, Boatwright found himself adrift, not just politically, but also emotionally. He sat down and wrote a series of suicide notes. A few were left behind as he got into his late model GMC pickup and drove eastward. Near the Waller County line, outside of Houston, Boatwright brought his truck to a stop on the bank of the Brazos River. The river, running dark and muddy, as always, was moving swiftly toward the Gulf of Mexico. In the black of a muggy Texas night, Ken Boatwright disappeared.

Hamilton County Sheriff's deputies called Waller County authorities when Boatwright's wife, Nika, informed them that her husband had threatened to kill himself by jumping off a bridge over the Brazos. When his truck was discovered the next day, Waller County Sheriff Randy Smith led a rescue team in a five-day search of the river. Smith refused to provide great detail about the suicide notes but did say Boatwright had indicated he was going to kill himself because, "he didn't want to go to jail."

"The information we received indicated he was in the river," Smith said.

A few days before Boatwright disappeared and deputies dragged the river for his body, Karl Rove was in Washington, DC, talking to reporters. In casual conversations at a fund-raising reception, Rove told journalists that Texas Agriculture Commissioner Jim Hightower and several of his aides "face the possibility of indictment in June or July."

Hightower's campaign director, Geoff Sugerman, was livid. He asked *Houston Chronicle* reporter Robert Cullick, "How the hell does Karl Rove know that? Is he getting information straight out of the U.S. attorney's office or the federal investigators supposedly working on this case? Or is he making it up?"

Cullick's article, headlined, *"Worker Who Left Suicide Notes Allegedly Told of Improprieties,"* was the first connection between Boatwright and the ongoing probe of TDA and Hightower. The Hightower camp issued a statement to the Austin press corps, which was the campaign's perception of how the developments all fit into a single fabrication, initiated by Boatwright and refined by Rove.

"The Perry campaign and the Justice Department have been relying on a troubled ex-employee to make its case against us. We said all along these were false accusations. Now we learn, sadly, these are the accusations of a troubled mind."

Journalists, briefly, thought they might get some answers to the emerging controversy surrounding TDA. There was one person who might clear up a lot of things. In Waller County, the search for the body of Boatwright was called off when he surfaced at a mental clinic in California. His disappearance had been staged.

"I have a lot of questions for Mr. Boatwright," Waller County Sheriff Randy Smith said. "You have to presume by what happened that he wanted to disappear."

If, however, Sheriff Smith did get a chance to interrogate Boatwright, what he discovered from that questioning has never been revealed. Reporters also were frustrated in their attempts to contact Boatwright. After his family went to pick him up in California, Boatwright's phone was disconnected and his brother said the former agriculture agency official would have no comment.

Then, Boatwright disappeared again, this time from public life.

He took with him any information he had on how Karl Rove might have been involved in pushing the investigation of the agriculture department to help Rick Perry.

And whatever role Rove might have played in the development of Boatwright's own unhappy destiny.

In the Travis County district attorney's office, Larry Beauchamp was launching his own investigation. He had called the office of the inspector general at the regional headquarters of the United States Department of Agriculture (USDA). An assistant inspector got on the line and fielded a request from Beauchamp. As an investigator with the Public Integrity Unit of the Travis County district attorney's office, Beauchamp was a member of a marginally funded and understaffed operation tasked with watching over government agencies and elected officials. He asked for records related to a USDA probe of Texas Agriculture Commissioner Jim Hightower and his operation of the Texas Federal Inspection Service.

A year earlier, questions had been asked about credit card expenditures of Hightower and members of his staff, who were involved in running Texas-Federal. Established as a quasi-federal government operation, the inspection service was self-supporting and administered by the Texas Department of Agriculture. It was designed to grade produce and was funded with fees paid by growers. As part of a decades old cooperative agreement with USDA, Texas ran the operation and money generated from the service covered the expenses of managers. Credit cards used by Texas-Federal employees were paid out of an account that was not subject to standard state audits. Problems for the operation began when a Texas-Federal employee had suggested to Washington that there might have been indiscretions in how those credit cards were used.

Those problems became political when Karl Rove's client decided to run for agriculture commissioner.

Although USDA's internal audit of Texas-Federal found that "there are no apparent violations of federal laws or misuse of federal funds," Larry Beauchamp was seeking files from the final report. The records were likely to disappoint him or any other investigator. A summary, written by the regional inspector general, said, "The agency is very pleased with the program being carried out by Texas-Federal, in terms of quality and accuracy of the fruit and vegetable inspection work, proper application of federal fruit and vegetable standards, responsiveness to industry needs, and related programmatic priorities."

Beauchamp's curiosity, though, was probably not driven by the findings of the audit summary but what details might have been turned up in the process. Neither was Beauchamp without a possible political motive for his call. Before joining the Travis County district attorney's staff, Beauchamp had worked as an investigator for the district attorney in Haskell County, Texas, a man named Joseph Thigpen. Thigpen's sister Anita was married to Rick Perry, who, one month prior to Beauchamp's call to USDA, had announced he was switching to the Republican party and contemplating a run for agri-culture commissioner against Jim Hightower.

Beauchamp had become friends with the Perrys, who also came from Haskell County, and he was, quite possibly, looking for infor-mation in the USDA audit that might help Perry in a potential cam-paign against Hightower. Beauchamp, like everyone else involved in Texas politics, must have been aware that Perry had a campaign consultant who knew how to use detrimental material. Karl Rove had been credited with leading the successful re-election of Repub-lican Governor Bill Clements. Even if Beauchamp did not find evi-dence in the USDA report that might lead prosecutors to launch their own investigation, there still might be documents and evi-dence that would prove valuable in a political campaign. Rove would know what to do with it. Campaigns did not need to prove allegations like auditors and lawyers.

Almost a year later, when he was confronted about his political affiliations and possible reasons for contacting USDA, Beauchamp did not shade his anger.

"To question my intentions and integrity on that is really offen-sive to me," he told *Austin American-Statesman* reporter David Elliot.

Beauchamp may have been acting on his own initiative but he did have political connections to the Republicans. Karl Rove, who had stepped in to guide Rick Perry's political future after the rancher left the Democratic party, was also the head strategist for Republican Governor Bill Clements. Both Clements and Perry would be pleased by the demise of Agriculture Commissioner Jim Hightower. He was Perry's Democratic opponent in the coming election, if Perry chose to run for agriculture commissioner, and Clements had long despised Hightower for his nontraditional approach to agriculture.

A populist, the diminutive Hightower, who was never seen in public without a cowboy hat and boots, began pushing stricter pesticide regulations and hormone-free beef. The Texas chemical industry, no minor influence in the state, expressed its displeasure to Governor Clements, explaining that it made a decent amount of money producing pesticides for crops and hormones to stimulate beef growth.

Outside of Austin, the Texas Farm Bureau, historically of a Republican bent, began calling for Hightower's resignation. Leaders of the organization tried to recruit former Dallas Cowboys' running back Walt Garrison and Texas Rangers' pitcher Nolan Ryan to consider running as Republicans against Hightower. Both men declined to engage in the political fight.

When that didn't work, the GOP and the Texas Farm Bureau tried something else. Six former members of the Texas Farm Bureau, whose filing fees were paid for by the association, were recruited to run against Hightower in the Democratic primary. It was a political strategy of divide and conquer. If any member of the six-pack managed to get Hightower into a runoff, he might defeat him in the primary and effectively allow Perry to win the general election.

"It's a continuation of the now eight-year assault on me by this extremist leadership of the Farm Bureau insurance gang," Hightower said. "They pretty much admitted they are Republicans. They've certainly never been active in the Democratic party. And they are using our primary just to harass me."

The tactic looks remarkably like a strategy used in the 2002 congressional race in New Mexico.

The chairman of the Republican party of New Mexico publicly declared that he was approached by a figure associated with the national GOP, who asked him to offer $100,000 to the Green party. Money was available to the Green party candidates if they filed in two congressional contests where Democrats were running close with Republicans. John Dendahl, who had been Republican party chair in New Mexico for eight years, refused to identify the person making the offer but said, "it was a proposal of substance."

Karl Rove had already proved adept at using surrogates and like-minded associations to accomplish his ends. There's no evidence that

Rove was directly connected to the New Mexico idea, any more than there is evidence that he engineered the Texas Farm Bureau's six-pack. But it is inconceivable that the Texas Farm Bureau acted on behalf of Rove's client without his approval in 1990 and equally unlikely that the Republican party acted without his knowledge more than a decade later in New Mexico.

Rove moved operatives and surrogates around like a skilled chess player.

Larry Beauchamp, while not officially a part of the Perry campaign, could have been acting as a Rove surrogate. Beauchamp did not need authorization to launch his own investigation of the Texas agriculture department. It was common practice for investigators of the Travis County Public Integrity Unit to gather information when they heard allegations.

The requested files were forwarded to Beauchamp with a note that said, "We did not investigate this matter due to the absence of a provable federal violation." But Beauchamp may have had his own plans for the material. When asked by a reporter if he had turned them over to the FBI, he said, "It's possible."

A federal investigation of the Texas Department of Agriculture, Commissioner Jim Hightower, and the Texas Federal Inspection Service had the potential to change the political landscape of Texas and feed Karl Rove's dreams. Nationally, leaders of the Republican party despised Hightower. During a keynote speech at the Democratic National Convention in 1988, Hightower kept referring to George Herbert Walker Bush as "Georgie."

In his most quoted line from the Atlanta meeting, Hightower said, "George Bush is the kind of guy who wakes up on third base and thinks he hit a triple."

Hightower had also been traveling the country spitting out acerbic barbs at the revered Ronald Reagan, as well. Ridiculing Reagan's intellect, he said, "Ol' Ronnie Reagan's idea of a good farm program is *Hee Haw*."

Hightower's rhetorical skills were not the only annoyance. The attention he had begun to receive as a populist orator, particularly as a result of his Democratic National Convention speech, had him thinking he had a shot at knocking off Republican U.S. Senator Phil Gramm of Texas. If, however, Hightower chose to run for re-election to agriculture commissioner instead of taking on Gramm, and Rove then was able to bring Hightower down with a Perry candidacy, Rove would be doing a favor for his party and the Bush family who he had been involved with since the early 1970s.

It would also serve a greater plan Rove was already formulating.

The task was hardly a simple one. In spite of Bill Clements' re-election, Texas was still a state where Democrats were in charge. They were proficient fund-raisers with sound organization and conservative policies. As 1990 approached, Democrats did not expect Rove and his party to gain more than a precarious foothold.

Pete McRae, who worked for Hightower at Texas-Federal, said Democrats were confident and Rove's machinations did not cause them great concern.

"At that time, there were no reasonable hopes for them. All of our incumbents were well financed, much better than the opposition. The likelihood of a state rep like Rick Perry beating an incumbent like Hightower was considered highly remote. And not just by us but by the Republicans, too."

And then things started happening.

In the span of three days, political infrastructure began to deteriorate for Texas Democrats. On Halloween morning of 1989, Bruce Tomaso of the *Dallas Morning News* started a series of stories about credit card usage by agriculture department staffers doing Texas-Federal work.

The next morning Larry Beauchamp made his call to the USDA, seeking records of the agency's audit of Texas-Federal.

Forty-eight hours later, Kenneth Boatwright, the former agriculture department division director, who worked for Hightower, announced his candidacy, implying corruption was afoot within the agency.

And Thomas Wall, the USDA official contacted by Beauchamp, also took a call from an Austin FBI agent.

"And I furnished him the exact same type of information that I furnished Mr. Beauchamp," Wall said.

The agent, who went on to lead the federal investigation of Hightower's office, was Greg Rampton. Stationed in Austin beginning in the late 1970s, Rampton launched a round of investigations into Texas state officeholders, who were all Democrats. As one of his first projects in the state capitol, he was part of Brilab, an FBI sting operation, which was designed to determine if elected officials would accept cash bribes in return for favorable political considerations. Speaker of the Texas house, Billy Clayton, was indicted in the case and later exonerated. Participants in the trial remember Rampton, a devout Mormon, sitting quietly in the back of the courtroom, reading his Bible. Clayton, acquitted, yet politically mauled, was gone from public life after the next legislative session.

"I'd heard about Rampton," said Austin lawyer Buck Wood, who was also indicted and acquitted in the Brilab affair. "I was told he was a mad dog against Democrats."

Sandy-haired and bespectacled, Rampton presented an unremarkable countenance and a fierce law enforcement zeal. In 1988, the office of Texas Land Commissioner Garry Mauro became his target.

"He showed up in my office with 18 agents," Mauro recalled. "And they walked in, they demanded their subpoena had called for computers. We had a computer set up for them and stacks and stacks of files. They walked in and they had a regressive analysis. They had a list of people and this program where you could type in people who had given you contributions and you could show through regressive analysis that they had, which is very sophisticated, you were supposed to be able to show they got higher appraisals and faster turnaround times. Only problem is, they didn't. It took 'em about an hour to figure it out."

Rampton did not pull out of Mauro's office until six months later and he left the case open for two years, though there was never any proof of illegal behavior. What prompted him to take on the land commissioner's agency has never been clear, except to Mauro.

"You gotta understand, Rampton had a basic concept. Nobody gave a political contribution unless it was quid pro quo and that was against the law, so every political contribution, you give me, [Rampton] enough time and I'll prove an illegal connection. And what he did to me was, he decided if you gave me a political contribution you would get special treatment in the Veterans' Land Board."

Mauro has continued to believe that Rampton came to his office at the prompting of Karl Rove.

"You think Rove sent Rampton to your office?" he was asked.

"Oh, there's no doubt in my mind."

"You think he did?"

"No doubt in my mind. I don't think there's any doubt that he [Rampton] and Karl had lunch on a regular basis and had telephone calls on a regular basis. I think it was fairly common knowledge and they did it in public so it wasn't like they were that secretive."

Byron Sage, the special agent-in-charge of the Austin office of the FBI for 12 years, defended Rampton. He said there was never anything political about the agent's work, and if there had been, it would have not been tolerated.

Another Texas Democrat, fearful Karl Rove may complicate his business, talked about his particular theory related to Rampton and Rove on the condition his name not be revealed.

"He worked for Gramm at one time, didn't he? And Gramm and Rove are both Republicans and wanted Hightower out of the way, just in case he did choose to run against him. And to please the Bush family, Gramm appointed the U.S. attorney for Texas, the assistant U.S. attorney in Austin reported to the Gramm appointee. Don't you think it's possible that there were conversations that ran in one direction, maybe with Gramm suggesting the agriculture department allegations were worth looking into, and it ended up with the U.S. attorney in Austin talking to the FBI in Austin about the whole thing? Anyone who thinks things don't work like that in Texas is naïve."

Assistant U.S. attorney for Austin, Dan Mills, told a lawyer for the agriculture department that he had been instructed by his superiors to "concentrate on making cases involving elected officials."

The officials were all Democrats.

Even if there is no substance to the political conspiracy theory, connections did exist for Rove to use. State auditor, Larry Alwin, who had a professed dislike of Agriculture Commissioner Jim Hightower, had ordered an audit of Texas-Federal. His actions were based on a letter he received from the USDA, suggesting the Texas auditor take a look at the very same expenses USDA had said were not inappropriate. Reporter Bruce Tomaso of the *Dallas Morning News* had apparently been tipped to this communication because a USDA letter to him is an answer to a formal request he filed for records related to the USDA's investigation.

The state auditor's own report was a few months away from completion when details were leaked to Tomaso. According to staffers at the Dallas paper's Austin office, Rove was always calling with leads and ideas for stories. Though he was not the source to make first contact with Tomaso, Rove could have easily arranged for the auditor or an intermediary to get advance information of the final report of the state audit of Texas-Federal into Tomaso's hands. Eventually, Tomaso said, Rove did begin contacting him with information.

Although Tomaso's first story was about the federal government's audit conclusions of a year earlier, which the USDA had said were "not provable violations of federal law," he launched a media follow-up frenzy. Dozens of articles about the credit card expenditures by Hightower and his staff ran in papers around the state over the course of the next few weeks.

USDA Questions Billings by Hightower, Deputy

Bruce Tomaso

Texas Agriculture Commissioner Jim Hightower and his top deputy have billed thousands of dollars in travel and meals to a state-and-federal crop inspection program, including many credit-card charges that "appear to be highly questionable," according to records of the U.S. Department of Agriculture.

The charges include costly meals at some of the finest restaurants in Austin, and hotel and dining tabs from around the country. All were billed to the Texas-Federal Inspection Service, a cooperative, quasi-governmental agency established in 1959 to provide crop inspections to Texas growers.

The service, whose traveling inspectors are supervised by the Texas Department of Agriculture and the U.S. Department of Agriculture, is supported by fees collected from growers.

Many of the bills accrued by Mr. Hightower and Deputy Agriculture Commissioner Mike Moeller, however, appear to have little to do with crop inspections, according to federal investigators.

"The charge-card use by Mr. Hightower and Mr. Moeller appears questionable," David Lewis, director of compliance for the U.S.D.A.'s Agricultural Marketing Service, wrote to Texas State Auditor Larry Alwin on June 22.

"Certainly, many of the charges cannot be expected to relate to the work of the fresh fruit and vegetable inspection program in Texas."

Mr. Moeller and a spokesman for Mr. Hightower, who was out of state, defended the credit-card charges Monday and suggested that the U.S.D.A.'s allegations were politically motivated. Mr. Hightower, a populist Democrat, has been a vocal critic of farm policies under the Reagan and Bush administrations.

Credit: Staff Writer of the *Dallas Morning News*, October 31, 1989, p. 1a.

The lengthy piece went on to include a denial from a Texas Agriculture Department spokesman who said it was just a case of Washington Republicans trying to stir up trouble for Commissioner Jim Hightower. Tomaso's listing of credit card charges, however, did look incriminating for Hightower and two of his top assistants, Deputy Agriculture Commissioner Mike Moeller, and Pete McRae, administrator of Texas-Federal. According to Tomaso's story, Hightower had spent more than $4,000 on his card in just under two years. A number of meals, exceeding $100, had been charged in Austin and Dallas, Texas; San Francisco, California; Washington, DC; Venice, California; and Fargo, North Dakota.

Political rancor against Hightower and his agency increased by an order of magnitude after the publication of Tomaso's story.

The general counsel for the agriculture department, Jesse Oliver, was certain the initial stories were prompted by Karl Rove to set up the Perry campaign for success.

"In terms of how it worked for him, [Rove] it boils down to him having the right contacts and he expanded his tentacles. He could gather information and use it to his candidate's benefit. He's like a rat sniffing out information all the time and piecing it back together to figure out where the food is."

Regardless of who had initiated the contact, a link had been established to reporter Tomaso. Once the first story broke, Rove had no reason to be overly cautious in leaking to Tomaso and providing him leads and tips. The controversy was now part of the public political discourse and Rove could help the journalists cover the story and still ask for source protection. He began frequent conversations with Tomaso and other Austin journalists, pointing them in directions that served his goals.

"I can't tell you for certain Karl was the only one driving that agriculture department story," David Elliot of the *Austin American-Statesman* said. "But I dealt with him a whole, whole lot, several times a week."

A few key reporters began to get leaks about subpoenas before they were even served to witnesses.

When the *Dallas Morning News* hit the Texas streets on November 13, 1989, the political problems for the agriculture department began to be compounded by legalities. The headline was, "Ag Agency Contracts Questioned." The subheading pointed out, "Beneficiary a Backer of Agricultural Official." The official was Mike Moeller, Hightower's political understudy and anointed successor to campaign for the office of agriculture commissioner. A few years earlier, Moeller supporters had formed a political action committee (PAC) called Building Texas Agriculture. While the PAC did fund general purpose interests in Texas agriculture, the eventual, unstated goal was to transition the organization and the money into the expectant candidacy of Moeller.

The chief fund-raiser and one of five board members for the Building Texas Agriculture PAC was an agency consultant. Bob Boyd, along with his associate Russell Koontz, had been involved with the Texas Department of Agriculture since the 1950s. Boyd, in particular, had been providing Hightower with a bridge to the more traditional political influences in Texas agriculture. His help, however, had gone uncompensated. With a wife at home suffering a debilitating disease, Boyd was having difficulty handling her medical bills and, therefore, decided he could no longer work for free.

"I actually engineered this thing," Pete McRae said. "He came to me and said he needed to make some money. I told Hightower we needed to do something for Bob, put him on a contract or something."

The timing for execution of the agreements could not have been worse. Boyd's deal was arranged only weeks after the political action committee was formed. Boyd and Koontz also were known by both political parties to have spent years traveling the state and raising money for previous agriculture commissioners. They did their fund-raising while also serving as employees of the agency. The men claimed they had always been careful not to solicit political contributions while doing regulatory work for the department. Nonetheless, they did have discussions about political donations on the same day with the same people they had been talking to about TDA business. Frequently, the solicitations came over dinner but they also occurred on the premises of the business, which was being regulated by TDA.

Under the contract with Texas-Federal, Boyd and Koontz were to advise the state on methods for improving inspections and enforcing seed laws, as well as weights and measures.

The two men also had other unstated goals.

Boyd and Koontz intended to function as regulators and political operatives, doing their TDA business while picking up a check or two for Jim Hightower. This was the way agriculture agency business and politics had been performed for decades. The new twist to their endeavors was that they wanted to generate cash for the Building Texas Agriculture PAC because they knew, in addition to providing scholarships and promoting agriculture, it would eventually set up Mike Moeller's campaign to succeed Hightower.

Tomaso's story that November morning in 1989 said that Boyd got nearly $20,000 "while he was working to promote the political career of Deputy Agriculture Commissioner Mike Moeller." Moeller, a burly wall of a man, who came from a Texas ranching family, defended the consulting deal with Boyd.

"If he is not the most competent consultant we have ever had while I have been working here, he is very near the top. He is a personal friend of mine, no question about that. But what he does on his own time, in terms of raising money for various causes, is his own business."

Unfortunately, for Moeller and McRae, who had arranged the contracts with Boyd's company, the consultant was not raising money on his own time. Boyd was criss-crossing the state with Bill Quicksall, the executive director of Texas-Federal, and when they were finished with their regulatory discussions with growers and agri-business people, Boyd took up solicitations for donations. The two had worked out a prearranged verbal cue, which meant it was time for Quicksall to leave the room while Boyd pinned down a political gift.

Boyd began rounding up money for the Building Texas Agriculture PAC, telling donors the funds were to be used for scholarships and promoting Texas produce. By most accounts, he was honest and informed donors the money might also be used to help Moeller run for office after Hightower stepped aside. Moeller's political ascension, however, had collided with Hightower's change of plans.

Hightower had decided to run for re-election, for a third term.

But his campaign was off to a bad start. And everyone on Hightower's team thought it was because of a relationship Karl Rove had with an FBI agent. Reporters, like Debbie Graves of the *Austin American-Statesman*, kept making calls to the agriculture agency asking about personal appearance subpoenas before the documents had ever been delivered. Hightower's staff suspected collaboration between Rove and agent Rampton. Whenever Graves called, according to former staffers, she always had the names of people who were to be subpoenaed before the individuals had even been notified.

The information being leaked to Graves could only have come from a few places. A source on a grand jury or in the U.S. attorney's office would have had the details provided Graves. But leaking it would have put at grave risk a federal investigation and the legal careers of all involved, confronting the leaker with potential federal criminal charges like obstruction of justice. The FBI and Rove were the other possible sources of leaks. Rampton would have been taking a bigger chance than Rove by getting material to reporters. Rove remains the most likely source, letting out information he may have been given by Rampton during the course of the investigation.

Appearing before the State Senate Nominations Committee several years later, Rove was questioned about a possible relationship with Rampton. The hearing was related to his confirmation as a regent to East Texas State University.

Democratic State Senator Bob Glasgow submitted Rove to a series of questions. Pete McRae, who, by then, was a former administrator of Texas-Federal, wrote them for the senator. Glasgow, who lacked context and detailed familiarity with what he was asking, seemed to be trying to get Rove to admit he had schemed with FBI agent Rampton in a series of investigations of Democratic state officeholders. Rove, acutely aware of the time line of the FBI probe, almost kept things straight, until he began talking about his work in Rick Perry's campaign.

"I do know that I became involved in the campaign of Rick Perry in November of 1989. At that point, there was already an FBI investigation ongoing of the Texas Department of Agriculture, prompted by stories, which had appeared in August and September, I believe, in the *Dallas Morning News* regarding the use of Department of Agriculture funds."

Rove's answer ruins his credibility. If he was, indeed, aware of the ongoing FBI probe of Hightower in November 1989, he knew about it a month before the Department of Agriculture had been informed by subpoena. Moreover, Rove's assumption that the newspaper stories prompted the investigation was just that, an assumption—unless he knew it directly from the FBI.

Rove's descriptions of his encounters with Greg Rampton have varied through the years. There is no doubt the agent and the consultant interacted but how much is unclear. Before the Nominations Committee, Rove's answers appeared inconsistent and almost Clintonesque when he was asked about Rampton.

"How long have you known an FBI agent by the name of Greg Rampton?" Senator Glasgow asked.

"Ah, Senator, it depends. Would you *define* know for me?"

"What is your relationship with him?"

"Ah, I know, I would not recognize Greg [Rampton] if he walked in the door. We have talked on the phone a var . . . a number of times. Ah, and he has visited in my office once or twice. But we do not have a social or personal relationship whatsoever."

As unremarkable as Rampton might have been as a physical presence, it also was difficult to believe that the agent had been in Rove's office for a conversation, and now, less than a year later, Rove would not be able to identify him. One gift Rove possesses is a keen memory, so good he regularly recalled the most minute details of history or the exact date he contemplated taking a picture off his office wall.

Interviewed during his White House years about a possible relationship with Rampton, Rove made it sound as if there was never more than a solitary phone conversation between himself and the agent.

"I don't recall whether I called Rampton or he called me. I have a vague recollection that he called me to say, if you know of anything, let us know."

Frequently, Rove has appeared to exhibit selective recall. His political memory is legendary. In the same interview where Rove suggested there was nothing more than a phone call, he later considered the possibility he may have met with Rampton.

"I can't remember if it was a meeting or a phone call. I met him somewhere, along the way, but I can't remember. The whole idea that I had control over the FBI . . ."

At least once, Karl Rove did meet with FBI agent Rampton, and he remembered it. In 1990, President George H. W. Bush nominated Rove to the Board for International Broadcasting and he had to fill out a sworn document for the Senate Committee on Foreign Relations. Under Part E of the questionnaire, identified as Ethical Matters, question number five asked, "Have you been interviewed or asked to supply any information in connection with any administrative or grand jury investigation in the past eighteen months?"

The answer was the first definitive proof that Rove had, in fact, consulted with FBI agent Rampton, and from a strictly technical perspective, it contradicted his sworn testimony to the Texas Senate. Rove's answers on the Rampton question have ranged from "may have met him once, somewhere" to "talked to him on the phone once or twice" to "may have met him along the way somewhere."

This sworn answer to U.S. Senate Committee on Foreign Relations gets close to the truth.

"This summer [1990] I met with agent Greg Rampton of the Austin FBI office at his request regarding a probe of political corruption in the office of Texas Agriculture Commissioner Jim Hightower."

Whether Rove's information launched the investigation or he simply ended up assisting an eager FBI agent will likely never be known.

The FBI, though, had not yet formally begun its probe in November 1989, and Pete McRae was already worried. He knew how bad things looked to the average newspaper reader. If they knew as much as McRae, it would be even worse. He was troubled over how Karl Rove was likely to use information in the newspaper stories. And just as concerned by what Rove did not yet know and what he might do when he learned it.

Whatever Pete McRae and Mike Moeller were thinking, they still had to have been cheered by the release of the state auditor's report. While charging that Texas-Federal had been run with "an absence of effective control," the December 1, 1989, summary, according to Auditor Larry Alwin, "generally corroborated" the agriculture department's claims it was doing nothing improper. Alwin was relatively critical of the relationship between the Texas Department of Agriculture and the Texas Federal Inspection Service but his findings did not imply there was wrongdoing.

The day the report was issued there was a celebration in the executive offices of the Texas Department of Agriculture. Hightower, Moeller, and McRae all had reason to be pleased with the outcome. First, USDA had cleared them with "no provable violations of federal law" and now the Texas state auditor had carefully checked their operations and had found nothing improper.

"We were drinking a beer and just cackling," Pete McRae recalled. "Jesse [Oliver, TDA legal counsel] said, 'You know, we really ought to let these guys win one of these things, once in a while.' We had won every issue over the last couple of years. We beat the Chemical Council's attempt to shut us down through Sunset Review, and now we had come out clean after two audits at the state and federal level."

They thought they had kicked down Republican schemes to harm Hightower and the agriculture department.

"That was the pivotal thought," Jesse Oliver said, "that we had won, beat them on the issues, and now they had to go back and lick their wounds. We didn't know that they wouldn't quit. We just didn't realize that whoever was doing this thing would come back again and again to come after us."

But they were coming. And Karl Rove wasn't just one of them. He was their general, the battle tactician and leader.

And he didn't like to lose.

5

A Number Two Mexican Dinner with One Taco Missing

Men occasionally stumble over the truth, but most of them pick themselves up and hurry off as if nothing had happened.

Winston Churchill

The story of the auditor's report of the Texas Department of Agriculture had barely cleared the front pages of Texas newspapers when State Representative Rick Perry announced he was a Republican candidate for agriculture commissioner. Two months earlier, Perry had abandoned his Democratic background and switched to the GOP during a high profile news conference with U.S. Senator Phil Gramm. Before talking with reporters about his campaign against Hightower, Perry had told a rural newspaper that Kenneth Boatwright, his opposition in the primary, was planning to withdraw and support him.

Hightower's campaign staff searched in vain for Karl Rove's fingerprints on Boatwright's decision to quit.

During his session with reporters, the Haskell County lawmaker also implied that he knew more problems were ahead for Hightower. Even though the USDA and the Texas state auditor had refuted allegations of illegalities by Hightower, Perry said, "USDA officials are not through looking at those expenditures yet, and I think we've just seen the tip of the iceberg on those expenditures."

How could Perry have known? Was Karl Rove speaking with the FBI and telling Perry what he was learning from the investigation?

Perry's pronouncement used the same phrase as Boatwright when he issued a news release about his own candidacy. It made Hightower's staff think Rove had written the statements for both men.

Hightower hardly had reason to care about Perry's declarations. The agency had just gotten a clean bill of health. He had the power of a two-term incumbency behind him, and was rising in national prominence within the Democratic party. His party had good candidates at the top of the Texas ballot, and even with bad newspaper stories; there was no reason to think Perry had much of a chance. Hightower had scheduled his own announcement for re-election at a farm rally in the panhandle town of Dawn, Texas, for two weeks after Perry's event, December 18.

FBI agent Greg Rampton also had plans for December 18, 1989.

Unannounced, Rampton arrived at the offices of the Texas Department of Agriculture and asked to see Hightower. He was not in the office. Instead of delivering it to Hightower, the agent handed a federal grand jury subpoena to an aide. The document requested contract and personnel records on consultant Bob Boyd.

Hightower's team immediately suspected Karl Rove's involvement, especially since the Rampton visit was the same day as Hightower's scheduled announcement. They believed the delivery of the federal court subpoenas were timed for political effect, to cover up news of Hightower's announcement.

"I do know he played a role in it," Mike Moeller said. "I don't think there's any question about that. And I think Rampton was willing to let him play a role. I think he wanted to know what Rampton was hearing, in some cases, before Rampton heard it. They shared information."

Things were not the way they appeared, according to Rove. His client, Rick Perry, Rove said, was just a lucky guy, Rove recalled in 2002.

"I will just tell you this, the Rick Perry campaign for ag commissioner, the myth has grown into the manipulation of the world intelligence, total conspiracy theory. This is the world's most fortuitous human being. Talk about being in the right place at the right time."

Maybe. But somebody was talking to reporters.

By January 12, the first reporter's inquiry on the investigation came from Debbie Graves of the *Austin American-Statesman*. Graves contacted the press office of the Texas Department of Agriculture (TDA) wanting to know about rumors of an FBI investigation. She had the names of people who were to be subpoenaed.

"Debbie Graves had inside knowledge about the first personal appearance subpoenas," Pete McRae said. "She called and asked to talk to specific people at the ag department who had gotten them. Only trouble was, they hadn't gotten them yet. She called days before they were even delivered."

Although nothing had been publicly released about a federal probe, reporters seemed to know where to look for information and what to ask for. On the same day that Graves called the ag department, January 24, the Texas comptroller's office received open records requests from the *Austin American-Statesman* and the *Dallas Morning News*. Both papers were fishing in the same pond. They wanted payment documents and relevant materials related to Bob Boyd. Who steered them there and told them to ask about Bob Boyd? Was it Rampton or Rove or someone inside the grand jury?

Agent Rampton had already asked for the same records. He spent February 1990 expanding his investigation while publicity about it was also on the increase. Rampton informed numerous people inside and out of the Texas Department of Agriculture he wanted to interview them. The questions were all characterized by an attempt to acquire information on work performed by Bob Boyd and Russell Koontz and any records of how they were compensated. During these interviews, Rampton made it abundantly clear he thought the two men were not doing any work under their consulting agreements and had spent their days raising money for Hightower, the Building Texas Agriculture political action committee (PAC), and Mike Moeller.

The story of the investigation, which first broke in the newspapers, followed Rampton and Rove's theme. The *Dallas Morning News* Austin bureau correspondent Christy Hoppe interviewed Commissioner Hightower about $6600 he had received in campaign contributions. According to her sources, Boyd solicited the money while he was on agriculture department business. Financial disclosure reports from the Hightower campaign showed that the donations came a day after the visits by Boyd.

Mike Moeller read the *Dallas Morning News* article by Christy Hoppe and was incensed. As if TDA did not have enough troubles with stories about credit card usage at Texas-Federal and now they were giving ammunition to Karl Rove and Republican Rick Perry. The deputy agriculture commissioner expected to get hammered even harder by these latest allegations concerning the behavior of Boyd.

And that's what happened.

Rick Perry, who was under the managerial guidance of Karl Rove, began making even greater use of the investigation as an issue. Perry's campaign put out a statement saying, "The problems at TDA are spreading like the fire ant problem. In both cases, the commissioner has done little to squelch the spread."

Mike Moeller just wanted to make sure there was no further damage.

"I am the one who called in Boyd and Koontz and said, 'What in the hell is going on?' I told them to stop it and stop it now. That turned out to be the end of it. It did stop."

The negative stories in the newspaper, however, did not stop.

Thursday morning's paper in Austin, the day after Christy Hoppe's story was published in the *Dallas Morning News*, carried a huge banner headline across the top of the front page: Hightower Consultant Investigated. Debbie Graves, the reporter who had made several calls to the agriculture department asking about unconfirmed reports of an FBI investigation, wrote that a federal grand jury was looking into misuse of public funds. Graves said that unnamed sources had confirmed the U.S. government was trying to determine if consultant Bob Boyd had been paid to raise campaign funds for Commissioner Jim Hightower and the prospective race of Mike Moeller, before Hightower had decided to seek a third term.

One of the unnamed sources in Grave's piece, an agri-businessman, said Boyd "coerced" him into making a donation to Hightower: "I was furious. But I felt I had no choice. A few people told them to go to hell."

According to Graves' story, "one source who has talked to the FBI said seed dealers were told: 'You give us $1000 or we'll put you out of business.'"

Reporters were consistently getting information about the investigation before the agriculture department and the individuals being investigated. Additionally, employees of the agriculture department were being solicited to provide insider information. According to Moeller, numerous agency workers were approached and told that, if they had allegations to make, they should take them to Karl Rove. Rove was accused of screening employees' stories and deciding which ones were to be taken to the FBI.

Agriculture agency officials also thought Rove was behind the leaks and was working with an old Republican ally, the Texas Farm Bureau.

The Texas Farm Bureau was one of Hightower's biggest political opponents. As politically inept as the organization was, it still knew the value of a controversy. The Texas Farm Bureau had been used as a surrogate in a number of Republican causes in Texas politics and its fevered disdain for Hightower and his policies made it inevitable the group would enter the latest fray, especially since it had invested $18,000 in filing fees for six candidates to run against Hightower in the March primary. Even before Hoppe's story about strong-arming tactics by Hightower associates, the Texas Farm Bureau was trying to get an investigation launched.

Vernie R. Glasson, executive director of the Texas Farm Bureau, wrote to the organization's national director in Washington, DC, on February 7, 1990, exactly one week before Hoppe's piece in the Dallas paper. In his letter to John C. Datt, Glasson wrote, "What we need is some kind of full-scale (or otherwise) investigation into State/Federal relationships between USDA and the Texas Department of Agriculture."

The text of his letter indicated that Glasson had been tipped by somebody that the FBI was already hard at work talking to TDA employees.

"I understand there might be some kind of investigation underway. What would help is a February 15 or so (prior to March 13) announcement, or leak to Texas Press (particularly, the *Dallas Morning News*). We are confident there are many skeletons in the closet and they need to be rattled."

Making something happen before March 13 was important because that was the day of the Texas Democratic Primary and the Farm Bureau's six candidates were running against Hightower.

Attorneys for the TDA cited the letter as proof that Karl Rove's tentacles were reaching across the state and deploying his operatives. The letter, in some respects, is what Texas political operatives describe as "classic Rove." If there are enough institutions and people involved in an effort to discredit and leak, there is no way to pin the blame on him. If nothing else, the Farm Bureau letter's date is proof that someone had informed the organization of an FBI investigation long before the public had been made aware of any probe.

One week after Glasson suggested a leak, Hoppe's story showed up in the Dallas paper.

In the Democratic Primary, though, the Farm Bureau tactic failed and Hightower easily defeated the "six-pack." But the organization's pleas to Washington had an impact.

Glasson's letter may have served to solidify federal support within the George H. W. Bush administration for the FBI probe of Bush family nemesis Hightower. Executive director of the American Farm Bureau Federation, John C. Datt, wrote to an assistant secretary of agriculture, attaching Glasson's letter. Datt said, "The Texas Farm Bureau needs to have this matter fully investigated to determine what has been going on in the Texas Department of Agriculture as it relates to the federal/state commodity inspection and grading program."

The matter was being "fully investigated" by FBI agent Greg Rampton.

In conversations with attorneys for some of the agriculture agency staffers, Rampton said he had become aware of "sham contracts." According to numerous agriculture department workers, Rampton threatened obstruction of justice charges against people because they were all hiring lawyers before agreeing to FBI interviews. Before the investigation had concluded, many employees of the agriculture department had accused agent Rampton of questionable tactics. Several said they were accused of perjury, tampering with evidence, and obstruction of justice, often just for demanding they be allowed to have an attorney present when questioned. At one time during 1990, almost all of the defense attorneys in Austin had at least one client from TDA. And all of them were charging Rampton with improper use of his authority.

Special agent-in-charge of the bureau's Austin office, Byron Sage, said he thought interview subjects simply misinterpreted Rampton.

"There are a lot of different ways to conduct an interview. I can see where someone might feel threatened. But I'm certain Greg never did anything to openly intimidate people. It just was not his style. This guy was one of the best investigators around and was strictly by the book. And I worked with a lot of good ones during my time with the bureau."

Rampton has spoken about his role in the agriculture department investigation on only two occasions. Mary Lenz of the *Houston Post* was able to get Rampton on the phone and asked him if he thought he was being used to play partisan politics and discredit Democrats.

"That's like saying, 'When did you stop beating your wife?'" he told Lenz. "I can say that never entered the picture at all."

Years after the investigation of Hightower's office had concluded, columnist Molly Ivins spoke with the agent about consistent allegations from Hightower and Democrats that Rampton was collaborating and sharing information with GOP operative Karl Rove.

"Let me think. I couldn't recall talking to him on that particular case at all. If there was a conversation we had on that case, I can't recall it. He was not an integral part of that case. I don't even remember bouncing anything off of him as somebody who was familiar with politics in Austin."

The quote meant that either Rampton or Rove was confused, had a bad memory, or was simply lying, because in Rove's sworn statement to the Board for International Broadcasting, Rove said he "met" with Rampton. Also, in his testimony before the Texas Senate Nominations Committee, Rove conceded that he had talked with Rampton a few times, possibly in person.

The apparent contradictions may not mean anything more than the fact that political attacks are always hard to prove. Often the evidence is circumstantial. TDA officials always assumed that Kenneth Boatwright had started it all by providing information to Rove and Rampton. And Boatwright's call to meet Boyd at Jim's Restaurant, where he appeared stressed and offered a rambling apology, only served to confirm that assumption.

After coverage of Boatwright's faked suicide, the federal investigation of the Texas Department of Agriculture fell off the pages of state newspapers until September, in the heat of the election campaign, when FBI agent Greg Rampton turned up at the secretary of state's office. Signing his name and affiliation on the office register, Rampton asked for copies of campaign contribution

reports for Hightower and Democrat Bob Bullock, the state comptroller who was running for lieutenant governor. It was inevitable
that reporters, who were constantly checking with the secretary
of state on campaign funding issues, would see Rampton's name
and find out that he had copied finance statements for the two
Democrats.

Bullock called it a "gut job."

"Nixonian dirty tricks," Hightower charged. "They've caught us
with our pants up. He [Rampton] didn't want those campaign reports. He wants the headlines."

The chairman of the Texas Democratic party issued a statement
seething with resentment: "The recurring leaks of purported FBI investigations of Democratic candidates during election campaigns is
highly questionable and repugnant. The Republican Justice Department seems determined to politicize the FBI, one of our most respected institutions.

"Such abuses are bad politics and worse government. The Republicans don't have to take my word for it; they can just ask Richard
Nixon."

In spite of all he had done prior to visiting the secretary of state's
office, that singular public act increased agent Rampton's profile and
caused intense scrutiny of the FBI's endeavors. Some of the state's
newspapers began to editorialize in Hightower's favor. But it was
not sufficient to save his political career.

Republican Rick Perry upset Hightower by about 50,000 votes.

Perry, who became the governor of Texas when George W.
Bush was elected president, passed off the glory to his consultant,
Karl Rove.

"He did everything. He says, 'Here's who to hire. Here's who
not to hire. Here's how to run the campaign.' He showed me a plan
and pointed to it. Lots of numbers. He points to it. He says, 'You'll
stay pretty much underground until this point.'"

Not surprisingly, the defeated Hightower campaign also credited Rove. Pete McRae has cemented his belief that Rove did not

just make Perry a viable candidate, but also was closely involved with the federal investigation and FBI agent Rampton.

"I'm one hundred percent convinced. My experience is in Texas politics and how it works and what the stakes are. Rick Perry could not have won that initial race in '90 against Hightower without hitting a home run ball. It was Karl's job to make sure that happened."

While Hightower lost the political election, he escaped the federal probe. None of the agriculture department staffers, including those at the Texas-Federal, was willing to cooperate with agent Rampton and give him evidence, possibly implicating Hightower.

And they paid for their loyalty.

On January 8, 1991, only days before Rick Perry was sworn in as the new Texas agriculture commissioner, federal indictments were returned against Deputy Agriculture Commissioner Mike Moeller, Texas-Federal administrator Pete McRae, executive director of Texas-Federal Bill Quicksall, and agriculture department consultants Bob Boyd and Russell Koontz.

Taking office after the indictments became public, Perry hired an ethics advisor to help the agriculture department undo any damage incurred by the federal investigation. The man he named to the job was Larry Beauchamp, the investigator for the district attorney who had also worked for Perry's brother-in-law. Beauchamp's request of USDA records, and his subsequent admission that it was "possible" he turned them over to the FBI, may have been what prompted the federal probe.

The next summer, Tom Smith, executive director of the government watchdog group Texas Public Citizen, was asked by the Austin paper to comment on Beauchamp's tactics and his relationship to Perry.

"This begins to appear as if there was a concerted effort to influence the outcome of an election by starting investigations and rumors. This is one of the oldest tricks in the 'How to Win an Election Handbook.' It is beyond belief that all of these events are coincidental," Smith said.

Contacted in 2002, Beauchamp refused to talk about any possible involvement in the investigation of TDA. "I don't talk to the media," he said. "And I don't want to be in any book."

The closest Karl Rove ever came to acknowledging the possibility of his own involvement or the Perry campaign's was during brief comments to John Gravois of the *Houston Post*'s Austin bureau. Rove conceded it was "conceivable" someone in the campaign may have been feeding allegations and information to the FBI, but he was not guilty of the tactic, he insisted. Anyone who did such a thing, Rove claimed, did it independently and there was no campaign official involved.

Regardless of his claims to the contrary, there is no plausible way Karl Rove did not take part in the federal investigation of the Texas Department of Agriculture. His sworn statement that he met with FBI agent Greg Rampton is an indication of likely participation. If the federal agent was conducting an unbiased probe into the Texas Department of Agriculture, why did he need to speak with the political operative trying to unseat the Democratic office holder? At a minimum, Rove and Rampton being together has the appearance of impropriety and unfairness. And his several versions of denial have never sounded true. Of course, there was no reason for Rove to decline to take part in Rampton's work.

He had much to gain by helping out.

The trial was also a series of miscalculations, and surprising rulings. The case did not reach the federal court of Judge Sam Sparks of Austin for two and a half years. Five TDA officials were indicted under a law that appears to have been designed to prevent local officials from hiring friends to provide kickbacks on federally funded projects.

Before the docket date, Russell Koontz suffered a stroke and Bob Boyd had a heart attack and underwent surgery. Judge Sparks agreed to sever both men from the case because they were not able to assist in their own defense.

Strategically, the defense team began by making what some legal experts said was a mistake. As the trial opened, arguments were made that the prosecution of Moeller, McRae, and Quicksall was political and ought to be dismissed. Unfortunately, the judge said the time to present such claims was when the indictments were returned. According to the court, if a motion had been filed seeking to quash the indictments, a full hearing could have been held on political allegations. Judge Sparks said no political evidence was to be introduced, which meant that the defense could not call Karl Rove, Farm Bureau officers, USDA officials, anyone from the governor's office, the state auditor, or Republican party operatives to testify.

The case became legal instead of political.

"I told Mike Moeller to not ever let his lawyers forget this is a political case and a political prosecution and don't let them turn it into a legal fight," said Austin attorney and Democratic activist Buck Wood. "They didn't do that."

Testimony began on September 22, 1993, and, at first, it looked favorable for the three remaining defendants. In spite of key government investigator FBI agent Rampton, Pete McRae felt most witnesses were "stumping the prosecution's asses." Then Assistant U.S. Attorney Dan Mills began calling owners of agri-businesses who claimed to have been shaken down for political money by Boyd and Koontz. Eleven growers and processors took the stand and described how the two men pressured them to donate to the Building Texas Agriculture political action committee and Hightower's re-election campaign.

McRae later came to refer to those 11 witnesses as "the parade of horribles."

"I had a little hope when one of the biggest growers in South Texas got up there and said, 'Pete and Mike are good guys. The two guys I don't like are those two old sons-of-bitches who come around and shake me down. I don't like that a bit.'"

McRae's hopefulness turned to sadness when Bill Quicksall took the stand.

The former executive director of Texas-Federal was asked about the scheme involving himself and Boyd, how they traveled together to raise money while doing state regulatory work. Prosecutor Mills got Quicksall to confirm the two men had a prearranged signal that meant it was time for Quicksall to leave the room and wait in the car while Boyd made his case for a political contribution.

"That's kind of like driving a getaway car for a couple of bank robbers, isn't it?" Mills asked the witness.

"Uh, yeah."

Pete McRae threw up his hands and buried his face. He knew they were doomed. Defense attorneys immediately protested that Quicksall, whose hearing was failing, had not understood the question.

The jury took two days to convict all three men of conspiracy and bribery charges.

McRae maintains he is not guilty of anything but bad judgment.

"I know we made some bad decisions. But we were convicted of running a kind of shakedown operation to help Moeller and Hightower. And we just did not do that. We had no idea of the way Boyd and Koontz were operating."

During sentencing, Judge Sparks sentenced Moeller and McRae to serve 27 months in federal prison. Quicksall was given a year.

The sentences were handed down on Friday, November 19, 1993.

Karl Rove was busily preparing George W. Bush's first run for governor of Texas.

The highway out to Kenneth Boatwright's hometown runs just west of the Balcones Escarpment, a topographical rift that has broken Texas into two pieces. Geologists call the formation the place where the South ends and the West begins. Route 281 skirts the eastern edge of the Edwards Plateau, where the trees are toughened live oak and mesquite. The landscape appears to be in a constant, painful transition.

By going home to Hamilton County, however, Boatwright found his own permanence, away from government and politics. His house is a modest wood-frame structure on the corner of two patched blacktop roads. A plastic department store play scape sits in the backyard near the metal storage building and a large cottonwood tree reaches back over the rooftop, shading the home against the push of the Texas summer heat. The narrow lane leading up to the drive is bumpy and patched from the sun busting up the dark asphalt.

On weekends, Boatwright plays golf on a hardpan course in the Texas Hill Country, teeing off not far from where cattle stand and watch from a rocky ridgeline. During the week, he commutes to Lampasas, where he has become a schoolteacher.

But Kenneth Boatwright has still not completely solved his own mystery.

When he was asked about his staged suicide, Boatwright said it really did not have anything to do with the agriculture department or politics.

"I was just going through divorce is all. And I had some financial problems. We got all that taken care of."

At first, the former agriculture department official denied ever meeting with political consultant Karl Rove. After some prompting had refreshed his memory, he was able to recall dealing with Rove.

"Yeah, he contacted me, I think, or he had somebody contact me. I went by there and talked to him. He got in touch after I pulled out of the race. He was asking for support for Perry. I met with Karl one time, in his office. It wudn't even five minutes."

When he was told he had been suspected of being a source for the FBI, Boatwright laughed.

"I think it's ridiculous they would think I had any info. I never gave any information to Karl or the FBI."

As he finished his thought, Boatwright changed his mind and said that, in fact, he had spoken with Rove and the FBI after all.

"Most of the time, it wudn't anything I ever told them that could have been any help to them."

The critical key to Moeller and McRae's suspicions related to Boatwright is meeting with Bob Boyd. Moeller said Boyd called him after the two met at Jim's Restaurant in Austin and Boyd described Boatwright as apologetic for what was happening to his old friends. Boatwright first said he never had been to any meeting with Boyd. Then he was given the name of the restaurant, and he suddenly remembered.

"Oh yeah, sure. But, you know, I wudn't apologizin' for anything. I had heard so many rumors floatin' around sayin' what all I had done and I was just tryin' to get rumors straightened out that I had not done that at all. We did meet. But it wasn't to apologize. I wanted to get some things straight. They thought I had turned some evidence over. I had been contacted, but I couldn't help that."

For Boatwright, all of that was a long time ago. But something put him through a great deal of mental and emotional duress; otherwise he would not have faked his suicide and admitted himself to a mental health clinic in California. Maybe it was nothing more than divorce and financial problems. He is remarried now, and happy. And he finds the stories of political conspiracies kind of funny.

"Makes for good readin', though, dudn't it?"

Defense attorney Gerry Spence had reached a critical moment in the Ruby Ridge trial. In 30 years of criminal defense, the famed Wyoming lawyer had not lost a case. And he was not going to have this nationally prominent prosecution be the first time he failed.

Spence was defending Randy Weaver, whose wife and son had been shot by federal agents when they tried to arrest him at his mountain cabin. Weaver and a friend had been charged with killing a deputy marshal while resisting arrest.

Some of the government's evidence had bothered Spence. In particular, he could not figure why one bullet casing from the scene had appeared so pristine. The shell came from a Ruger Mini-14 and Spence had dubbed it "the magic bullet." He was convinced an FBI agent, or someone else trying to protect the government's sharpshooters from prosecution, had planted it there. When he suggested his theory, the FBI said it was impossible.

A few days earlier, Spence had called to the stand Special Agent Greg Rampton of the Boise, Idaho, office of the FBI and had questioned him about a series of photographs, which the agency had admitted into evidence. Rampton was called back to the witness stand after the U.S. attorney informed the court that some of the evidence in a few of the photos from the crime scene had been staged.

Spence was about to prove the FBI was manufacturing evidence.

"You knew before the trial that the pictures I had were reconstructed when I cross-examined you the other day, isn't that true?" he asked Rampton.

"You never asked me about that and I tried to stick with the questions you asked me," Rampton replied.

After Rampton's admission that the FBI had doctored evidence, there was little else Spence had to do to make sure his client was acquitted.

One of Rampton's colleagues in the bureau told the government prosecutor before the trial began, two months earlier, that the photos were re-creations of the crime scene. The pictures did not show the evidence where the FBI found it, according the government's own lawyer. The government had screwed up. Shell casings were removed too quickly. Agents replaced them and then "reshot" photos of the evidence.

The prosecutor had not informed the court of that fact until the trial was nearing conclusion. Rampton's testimony meant the government's case against separatist Randy Weaver had no possibility of winning a conviction.

Agent Rampton had been transferred to Boise, Idaho, after concluding an investigation involving agriculture department employees in Texas. Even before the defendants—Mike Moeller, Pete McRae, and Bill Quicksall—were convicted; Texas Democrats had been accusing Rampton of being the Republican party's pet FBI agent. He had conducted enough investigations of Democratic officeholders that two Austin attorneys, Buck Wood and John Hannah, had filed a one-inch thick pleading with the Department of Justice to have Rampton transferred out of Austin.

He was.

Wood said it was because he and Hannah had built a convincing case against Rampton, that he was persecuting Democrats, cooperating with Republican operatives like Karl Rove, and leaking information about personal appearance subpoenas to reporters before the documents had ever been delivered.

"That's a bunch of crap," said Byron Sage, former special agent-in-charge of the Austin office of the FBI. "Greg did a great job in Austin. He and his wife wanted to get their kids back closer to family in Salt Lake City. They were Mormons. He wanted to go to Boise, and let me just tell you, if you've done something wrong at the bureau, you don't get transferred to the place you've requested."

Sage, who ran the Austin office while Rampton was stationed there, described Rampton as "one of the most professional agents" he ever worked with.

Sage refused to talk about anything related to the agriculture department investigation or any other work that might have been conducted by the FBI during his tenure in Austin. He was, however, willing to defend Rampton as a "top professional."

Except for when the FBI is reconstructing evidence at a crime scene?

At Ruby Ridge, Rampton admitted on the stand that the FBI, in a case where he was a key agent, was involved with what he had once accused employees of the Texas Department of Agriculture of doing; tampering with evidence and obstructing justice. No one in the FBI, however, was charged or tried.

"These are phony and reconstructed photos we've had in our possession the whole time," Spence told the jury.

After Rampton's testimony, Spence was so confident the government had failed to prove its case he did not even bother to present a defense.

The jury acquitted Randy Weaver.

In August, just over two months after the trial had concluded, the U.S. attorney for Idaho's district retired. Rampton was never mentioned specifically but Maurice Ellsworth said his office had faced "significant problems" in dealing with the FBI over evidence in the Ruby Ridge case. Similar criticisms came from the chief deputy U.S. Marshal for Idaho, Ron Evans, who labeled as "unprecedented" some of the tactics prosecutors had to use to accomplish their work in the face of FBI obstacles. U.S. Attorney General Janet Reno said the agency's performance was under review.

None of this had any effect on Greg Rampton's career. He was transferred again, this time to Denver, where he rose to special agent-in-charge of the Denver office.

During his tenure in Colorado, Rampton led the FBI's Y2k project to seek out millennialist groups and domestic terrorists. When gun rights activists and conservatives claimed the government's Project Megiddo was making a move on their constitutional rights, Rampton went on a radio talk show to defend the bureau and calm down critics.

The agent was poised, handling adversarial calls with the polish of a seasoned political candidate.

"I think that there's, in general, a healthy skepticism about anything the government does; and, unfortunately, that can sometimes hinder the truth. A wise man once said, 'Truth is always in short supply, but invariably supply exceeds demand.' So I think we have to be very careful about our skepticism, and, hopefully, that it will lead us to the truth, and not away from the truth."

FBI agent Greg Rampton retired from the Denver office of the bureau as a special agent-in-charge.

If anyone in the taxpaying public calls the Denver office to inquire of Rampton's whereabouts, they are informed he left no forwarding address.

6

The Confirmation

The truth is mighty and will prevail. There is nothing the matter with that. Except it ain't so.

Mark Twain

The plane cut a straight line across the winter sky. After leveling out at 35,000 feet, the Gulfstream was already moving over the dark bottomland of the upper Mississippi valley. All of the Bush campaign staff onboard had reason to be optimistic. A few, undoubtedly, were staring out the window at the brittle February landscape of Iowa and Illinois. Atop the jet stream, the aircraft slipped easily eastward toward Manchester, New Hampshire. Before the landing gear squawked across the runway in New England, the Bush team had completed the psychological transition from dreamers to believers. This, they had begun to realize, could actually happen.

Iowa was behind them, in the dark; victory only hours old. Texas Governor George W. Bush had just won his initial test in the race for the Republican nomination for president. Knowing the news value of the moment, Bush and a key advisor, Karen Hughes, had invited a select group of writers to join them on the candidate's private jet. Taking seats in a lounge area at the back of the plane, Frank Bruni of the *New York Times*, Judy Keene of *USA Today*, Glenn Johnson with the *Associated Press*, and Wayne Slater from the *Dallas Morning News*, were strapped in for the quick run to the northeast. The governor was hoping to attend an indoor rally at 3:00 A.M. in a Manchester airport hangar, celebrating his Iowa win.

Uncharacteristically, Karl Rove, a man in constant motion, appeared to be dozing at the front of the aircraft. Lying in the leather seat of the Gulfstream, eyes closed, his legs were stretched out before him. Rove seemed almost serene, not at all the kinetic, combustible force that had confronted reporter Wayne Slater two months earlier on the tarmac in Manchester. There was no longer any reason for him to be jittery about the campaign's prospects in the Iowa caucuses. Bush had won. After two years of preparation, building a financial network, courting the party elite, cultivating a mounting presence in the media, creating the persona of front-runner, after years of meticulous groundwork, Team Bush had finally won its first official victory of the 2000 presidential campaign. Rove had delivered, as promised.

Out the window, a circle of moon hung just above the wing. It was past midnight in the heartland. In two weeks, the cranky, independent-minded voters of New Hampshire were to hand the governor his head in the primary, the big test in his quest for the presidency. In the afterglow of Iowa, though, Bush was jazzed, lumbering through the tiny cabin with an adolescent exuberance. Inexplicably, he was wearing plastic ski shades and orange ear plugs, feeling his way along, identifying people by touching faces and heads.

"Logan," he announced, delighted by his correct identification of travel aide Logan Walters. Then, laying hands on someone else, he assumed the caricature of a tent-show preacher.

"Heal!" he declared.

The adrenaline was pumping, and Bush was relieved and excited that he had bested the Republican field. The GOP front-runner for more than a year, he had been catapulted to the lead by his name and a mountain of campaign cash. It was not until Iowa, though, that he had actually won an election, the first event of the presidential season. His father had finished second in Iowa in 1988, but he had won the nomination. In the warm glow of the jet, with his wife sleeping nearby and his most loyal aides around him, Bush allowed himself to think, for one forbidden, delicious, rogue moment, of the end game in which he was to retake the White House for the Bush family.

"This was a big moment today," he told the four reporters. "It'll be eclipsed by the next big moment, then the next big moment, leading up to the biggest of all moments."

Sitting among the journalists in the rear of the plane, Bush was momentarily pensive. Wayne Slater reminded the governor there was a long road ahead.

"What if you lose?" Slater wondered aloud.

Bush's face grew solemn, thinking about his father, who had won the White House only to be turned out for a second term.

"I won't like it. I've seen a great man lose more than once. I know full well life goes on, but I don't want to lose. I don't think I will lose."

In the window of the jet, lights speckled the broad farmland below. Bush turned back to the reporters after gazing at the fleeing dark.

"Sometimes, there are forces greater in the process, things that are totally out of my control. I don't know what they will be. But I know so far we're running a campaign that, if there's a chance, we'll win. This is a very well run campaign, a great team. The strategy seems to be working."

Adjacent to him, eyes closed, sat the man responsible for that strategy. Smiling, Karl Rove's thin hair was tangled in disarray, his shirt disheveled. Stuck to his forehead and braced by his glasses was a card he'd pick up from somewhere. It bore the word "Press," one of the many forces to be managed along the way to victory.

"Fabulous," he said, a favorite word in the Rove lexicon when things were going well.

More than anyone, Karl Rove had gotten Bush to this point, and everyone knew it. He was the genius of the campaign, the tactician, and the guru. Everyone described him as brainy, the brainy Karl Rove, who spouted voter statistics and arcane political data like a geyser. When he had arrived in Texas to set up shop, there were no statewide Republican officeholders. Twenty years later, Republicans sat in every state office from governor through Supreme Court, and most had been Rove clients.

In George W. Bush, though, lay the instrument of a larger plan. Rove had worked for the father at the Republican National Committee in Washington, where he first met the son. Later, in Texas, he became chief political advisor to the younger Bush, preparing him to run for governor, steering the politics of his administration and developing the blueprint to win the White House. In Bush, Rove had seen the perfect vehicle for his ambitions to become the single most influential political figure in Washington.

"To Karl, the man with the plan," Bush had written on a photo that hung in Rove's office years before the presidential race.

They were complimentary figures, Bush and Rove, each offering elements the other lacked. Rove was cerebral; Bush never liked going too deeply into the homework. Rove had an encyclopedic mind and a gift for campaign arithmetic; Bush had engaging people skills, a knack for winning over opponents with pure charm. If Rove approached politics as a blood sport, Bush's instinct was to search out compromise and agreement. They offered each other a perfect counterbalance.

They also shared some important traits. Though they came from different academic backgrounds, Bush was the product of Yale; Rove never graduated from college, each harbored a deep suspicion of the gratuitous intellectualism of the Ivy League. Bush saw in Rove extreme loyalty, which the family valued above all other things. In Bush, Rove saw an aspect of his own personality, a relentless focus and self-discipline. This man could be president, Rove concluded early on.

Rove may have already realized, in this odd place, seven miles in the sky over America, he was slumbering in the seat adjacent to the next president of the United States. The road was long and getting longer. Still, he had directed the governor's race, helped develop the agenda, managed the policies of the Bush administration, and cleared every political appointment. He had been the architect of Bush's re-election, organizer of the early presidential money machine, and tactical genius behind a political field operation that was to deliver the Republican nomination for president. Along the way, he had damaged the reputations of political enemies and assisted the fortunes of friends, and understood, probably down to a cellular level, that his dream was unfolding perfectly.

"Bush is the kind of candidate and officeholder political hacks like me wait a lifetime to be associated with," he told a reporter.

Ahead lay victory and the White House. From the moment the Bush team moved into the West Wing, Karl Rove extended his considerable influence over the affairs of the office. Taxes, tariffs, the Middle East. Nothing was able to escape his political prism. Congressional leaders, corporate America, political consultants, journalists, and all people of influence came seeking Rove's advice and guidance. The man with the plan, in the end, did not only affect the affairs of political Washington, but also the lives of every American.

"Fabulous," Rove said, extending his legs further. "Fabuloso."

They were well into the race and the campaign was clicking for Rove and his candidate. Sure, there were some things out there yet that might cause him or the governor some problems. But reporters weren't asking. So, he wasn't telling. Besides, nobody had any proof that Karl Rove had done anything in Texas, except run winning campaigns. And all of the tactics he deployed in Texas, the things he had learned from those campaigns, Rove intended to deploy in the biggest contest of all: the race for president of the United States.

PART

II

Toward the Far Horizon

7

Never Young

His talent was as natural as the pattern that was made by the dust on a butterfly's wings. At one time he understood it no more than the butterfly did and he did not know when it was brushed or marred.

Ernest Hemingway

The White House meeting went late so President George W. Bush invited a couple of aides to join him for dinner in the dining room. Afterwards, he brought out cigars and the three of them—media chief Mark McKinnon, political advisor Karl Rove, and the president—sat around the table under the soft curl of cigar smoke and talked. It was just months since Bush was inaugurated, and the chandelier in the State Dining Room cast a golden light over the crystal and the remaining plates of the chocolate tumbleweed and poached pear dessert.

Andrew Jackson had been in this room. And Woodrow Wilson. And Truman. And the Roosevelts, especially Teddy. During the Civil War, Abraham Lincoln had carried the agonizing weight of the job into this very room. Nobody knew this better than Rove, a conspicuous student of history. This was a room rich in power and precedent.

It seemed only natural that the talk among the three—sitting alone now—turned to the subject of presidents and kings and leaders on the world stage. Of influence. Of power.

"Let me show you something," Bush said brightly, pushing a button.

Four attendants in white jackets instantly appeared.

"Yes sir, Mr. President. Is there something we can get you?"

The president paused.

"Uh, sure. A glass of water would be good."

The attendants turned crisply and left the room with purposeful dispatch.

Bush looked over at Karl and smiled.

"Now *that's* power."

They had arrived, the president and his guru—Bush through a strange arc of circumstances, Rove according to plan. If George W. Bush had pursued politics almost as an afterthought, Rove had set his sights on the White House almost from the beginning. Bush seemed to glide into this seat of power; Rove labored ferociously to achieve his goals. They were, in so many ways, inverse images of each other.

Bush had come from a political family and was remarkably apolitical. Rove was the reverse. While Bush was the prodigal son at Yale in the 1960s, the affable master of the beer blasts at the DKE house; Rove was 3,000 miles away building his debate-card collection at Olympus High School in Utah. They were worlds apart, and if Bush was pursuing an unsteady trajectory, Rove was strictly on target. Rove always knew he wanted to go to Washington, and now here he was, here under an amber-dark portrait of Lincoln in the State Dining Room, at the right hand of power. Karl Christian Rove.

"There were no ifs, ands, or buts. He was going to be in politics, one way or the other," recalled high school classmate Randy

Ludlow. "We did discuss it. We just knew that he was going to go to Washington."

Long into their collaboration, Bush autographed the photo—"To Karl Rove, the man with the plan"—which Rove framed and hung on the wall as a measure of their relationship. That was the heart of his genius, getting people where they wanted to be. Bush called him Boy Genius, among other things. Austin political types addressed him as Groovy, a play on the word guru, which delighted Rove no end. Groovy as in . . . *cool* . . . which was comical because Karl was never cool and he knew it—not cool like the high school jocks or the frat rats in college or the elegant money men with faces burnished from golf weekends at Palm Springs who sailed along the gilded edges of Republican politics.

He wasn't one of them.

He was the brain playing three-dimensional chess, the guru— the man with a plan as far back as he could remember, as far back as Utah and high school, where his obsession with politics began.

Karl Rove moved through the hallways of Olympus High in the late sixties like a thunderstorm, full of noise and electricity. He was going in all directions at once, pieces of motion, everything flung out in all directions, arms, hands, mouth—mostly his mouth, which moved in an avalanche of words. Rove was always talking. He had opinions on everything, which he shared generously: on McNamara's prosecution of the Vietnam War, on defects in New Deal liberalism, on food in the cafeteria and the class schedule, on deoxyribonucleic acid, and military conscription, and an inevitable cure for the common cold. He had an opinion on every subject, every day, and on this day the subject was Karl Rove, candidate for president of the student senate at Olympus School, Salt Lake City, Utah.

He passed through the halls, reviewing the campaign posters, both his and those of his opponent, John Sorensen. Sorensen was junior class president, one of the Mormon kids, smart and popular and confident of victory. Rove was an ace debater who carried into the arena of high school a spindly body in Hush Puppies and horn rims. There was never a day, classmates remember, that Rove did not wear a coat and tie. He was, by his own account, a "big nerd, complete with the pocket protector, briefcase, the whole deal." At the same time, there was something oddly compelling about him, friends remember. He had a kind of energized personality that transcended, even then, his nerdy nature.

Classmate Rick Higgins considered Rove completely confident.

"He never doubted where he stood. He established his position and, by god, that's where it was. Karl had enormous focus, he just zeroed in and was extremely tenacious."

He was also bright, scary bright.

"He was so smart and so able to communicate with people that he was like a magnet," recalled classmate Glenn Hargreaves.

The student senate was the governing council for the student body. It organized student forums, arranged assemblies, debated school issues, and passed resolutions to improve things at Olympus High. About two dozen students made up the senate, representing homerooms and school organizations. The president, elected by the student body, set the agenda and presided over the meetings. In other words, the president of the senate was at the heart of every issue on campus. This was politics and Karl Rove loved politics.

When the day came for the assembly where candidates were to formally present themselves, Rove was ready. He had analyzed what it would take to win—three parts preparation, one part surprise—and had put a plan in effect. He was always the man with the plan.

"He was task-oriented," recalled Rick Higgins, a high school classmate.

"It didn't matter how much it took to become prepared, he was better prepared than anyone else. That was the goal. That's what he did."

Rove had recruited a core of supporters and plastered the walls with posters. He had methodically pursued student support, in the hallways, in classrooms, at the long rows of lunch tables in the cafeteria. He pitched himself furiously, promising great things. It was hilarious how serious he was about a school election.

Sorenson, Rove's opponent in the race, understood more clearly in hindsight.

"You have to remember high school is basically a popularity contest. Karl is extremely bright. He was on the debate team, could basically debate anything and win any argument. He could debate that the sky was black when it was blue and he could debate it was blue when it was black. And he would succeed."

As for Sorensen, he was the candidate of experience, the junior class president. He was rail-thin with a thatch of blond hair and a ready smile—the perfect candidate. Those running for office tried to do something to catch people's attention and prompt them to vote for you.

Sorensen decided to make a play on his name.

His name was John so he pulled a mock outhouse into the hall. Wrapping up his campaign appeal, Sorensen turned and pretended to flush, and to the sound of a flushing toilet and the rising chant—Vote for John! Vote for John!—he walked triumphantly around the gym floor, toilet paper dangling from his pants, and accepted the cheers of the crowd.

"Everybody went crazy," he said. "I thought, hey, I've got this in the bag."

Walking off the floor, though, Sorensen noticed something odd. Someone had removed the doors to the shop, to create a wider entrance to the gym. Outside, although he couldn't see it at this moment, was his opponent, preparing for entry. Years later, in a political memo that launched the Republican takeover of Texas, Rove outlined for a political candidate what it takes to win. He quoted Napoleon: "The whole art of war consists in a well-reasoned and extremely circumspect defensive, followed by rapid and audacious attack."

That's what he was doing in a high school contest.

Suddenly, into the gymnasium came Karl Rove in the back of a Volkswagen convertible, a pretty girl on each side. He was sitting up on the back seat in coat and tie, waving his arms broadly like a candidate in a parade. The car wheeled around the gym floor. He was both the candidate and someone mocking the conventions of candidacy. He waved wildly, grinning, thin and geeky, his eyes blazing with delight behind enormous horn-rim glasses. The place erupted.

Sorenson understood, in that moment, he was not going to be elected.

"Well, obviously, you could tell who was going to win. I knew I had lost."

In everything, Karl Rove always wanted to win. He was a gyroscope, spinning around on a single point, and that point was politics. When he was 9, he chose sides in the presidential race between John Kennedy and Richard Nixon. He chose Nixon.

"The little girl across the street I can remember beating the hell out of me in 1960 because I was for Nixon and she was for Kennedy. She had a couple of years and a few pounds on me, and I can remember being on the pavement," Rove later told a reporter for the *New York Times*.

His sister, Reba Hammond, said Karl was consumed by politics at an early age. While other kids had posters of rock stars or sports figures on their walls, he had a poster above his bed that said, "Wake up, America."

Reba said politics enthralled him. "He was always going to be president."

She told journalist Miriam Rozen the family used to rely on Rove's photographic memory for evening entertainment.

"The game was, 'See if you can stump Karl," she said in an interview published in the *Dallas Observer*. His older brother Eric would read a passage from a book Karl had read the week before. The challenge was to guess which word his brother had intentionally left out.

Growing up, Rove's family moved around a lot. His father, Louis, was a mineral geologist and was away from home much of the time working. The household was not particularly happy. Louis and Reba Wood Rove argued, and by the time Karl was in his teens, his parents split. The family—two sisters, three brothers—moved from Nevada to Salt Lake City just as Karl was entering high school.

Salt Lake City was not where he was first introduced to politics, but it was the place that incubated his obsession, and Republican politics in particular. The conservative city sat on a landscape dominated by two monuments—the copper dome of the state capitol and the spires of the Mormon Church. God and church and state. There was no easy way to determine where one stopped and other began. The church was the dominant religious, political, and social force in Utah and divided the community into two camps: the majority who were Mormons and the minority who were not.

Every day at Olympus High, the Mormon kids trooped across the street to the Latter Day Saints seminary for a class in religious instruction. The Mormon Church built seminaries near public schools so students would choose seminary as an elective. Once a day, the Mormon students stepped off campus for seminary, while Rove and the rest—the Mormon kids called them the gentiles—stayed behind. He spent a lot of time in the library, reading and building a prodigious set of debate cards.

Very early at Olympus High, Rove knew he wanted to be part of the debate team. Debate was a perfect melding of two things—words and opinions—and he had plenty of both. The star of the debate team his sophomore year was a senior named Keith Roark, who became a lawyer and ran unsuccessfully in 2002 for attorney general in Idaho, as a Democrat.

Roark was president of the debate club and captain of the debate team. He seemed to be everything Rove was not—at least not yet—confident, self-possessed, and physically impressive.

Rove latched onto him immediately.

"I didn't think of him as a great debater at that point in time. He was a little guy, diminutive with glasses half as big as his head. A classic towhead. He had a very high, irritating voice and something of an immature manner. But it was pretty clear he was focused. What struck me then, and still strikes me now, was the fact that when I first met him, he was a dyed-in-the-wool Republican. It was somewhat peculiar, even in conservative Salt Lake City, for anyone of his age to be so deeply interested in politics."

Roark noticed something else, too. Rove was obsessively well prepared.

"His card file was twice the size of anybody else's."

Debaters kept their arguments on 3 × 5 cards, which they carried about in shoeboxes or metal containers. Rove had the most impressive collection of debate cards at Olympus High. If his teammates had a shoebox filled with cards, Rove carried two, which he plunked down on the table in an ominous display of force.

By his senior year, the arsenal had swelled to 5 or 10 boxes. Rove figured that if two or three boxes unnerved an opposing team, why not something truly overwhelming? Why not a table full of cards? Why not buy them by the thousands and wheel them in on handcarts? Why not throw the fear of God into the enemy before the debate even began?

The thing was, the thing nobody knew was, that the cards were mostly fake.

"We went out and bought thousands, if not tens of thousands, of debate cards," said debate partner Emil Langeland, now a lawyer in Salt Lake City.

"Everybody was using 3 × 5 debate cards. And we decided we'd better have 4 × 6—a little bigger than the next guy. And we had shoeboxes, a table full. We would come in and set up those boxes with file cards in them, color-coded, with tabs sticking up, and there were literally thousands and thousands of them. And you know what? There wasn't a thing on 99 percent of them.

"If they gave us a 4 × 4 table, we'd make it a 4 × 8 table and we'd stack this information—what appeared to be information—on the table. We'd lay out all these papers. The reality was that the core of our attack or strategy was on 20 or 30 cards. We never used much more than that. But we'd just hand truck them in, then go back out into the hall and hand truck another set in and set them up on the table almost to the point where you couldn't see us. It was all psychological, to psych out your opponent."

Rove didn't just want to win; he wanted the opponents destroyed. His worldview was clear even then: There was his team and the other team, and he would make the other team pay. He would defeat them, slaughter them, and humiliate them. He would win by any means, but he would win.

"Debate was a big deal when we were in high school. The competitive debates were in the classroom, so the debate team would literally travel from classroom to classroom, all day long, with whoever the opposing debater was from the opposing team. Kids at school would actually watch this debate, so you got a fair amount of visibility," said Cary Jones, a Salt Lake City lawyer who was a fellow debater in high school.

"What would happen is, say, East High School or another Salt Lake school's debate team would come to your high school and for four periods—social science, English, whatever—there would be a debate. Kids would stand up in class with judges in the classroom, typically parents or whatever. And you literally spoke before every student in the school, maybe five times a year."

The best debaters could argue every side of every issue with both evidence and conviction. Rove's junior year, the subject was the Miranda warning.

"Resolved: Congress should establish uniform regulations to control criminal investigation procedures."

Rove was equally adept at arguing the affirmative—the Miranda warning is a linchpin of freedom and liberty—and the negative—the law handcuffs the police and jeopardizes our safety.

Along the way, he developed some tricks.

One was the house of cards, which he used with some regularity. Rove closed the debate by pulling from his suit pocket a dozen playing cards and, as he recalled the arguments of the opposing team, he balanced the cards precariously on the table. Then, he paused.

After a beat, Rove seized on some errant fact, some soft point in the opponents' presentation, and in a dramatic flourish, pulled out a card to send the other team's whole argument tumbling to the table.

Fellow student Eric Kiesler said the moment was as engaging as an athletic event.

"When Karl was done, the crowd was fired up and cheering. The crowd reaction was comparable to having one of our sports teams win the state championship. It was amazing."

Once, Rove put on sunglasses and carried a cane, pretending to be blind as he built his case, fact by fact. He stumbled about the room, leading the student audience away from the flaws of his opponent's argument and to the logic of his own, out of the darkness and into the light. Finally, his audience persuaded, he pulled off his sunglasses and threw down the cane.

"Now you see!" he declared triumphantly.

"It was theater," according to classmate Mark Gustavson.

Senior year, the topic was compulsory military service. The draft. Few subjects had such power at that moment on high school and colleges campuses. The boys of Olympus High, like those everywhere, were nervously aware of the sharp divisions caused by Vietnam and the how American involvement in that distant war was about to affect their lives.

"We were all so worried about being drafted," said classmate Rick Higgins.

The war was front-page news in the *Salt Lake Tribune* every day, on the network news every night. In January 1968, communist forces launched the Tet offensive on Hue and other major South Vietnam towns. By February, General William Westmoreland had requested 206,000 more troops. At home, there were draft card burnings and antiwar protests.

While Rove was in high school in Utah, a future president, Bill Clinton, was finishing Georgetown University and then moving to England to attend Oxford as a Rhodes scholar. He escaped the draft and, in the famous ROTC letter, outlined his reservations: "The draft system itself is illegitimate. No government really rooted in limited, parliamentary democracy should have the power to make its citizens fight and kill and die in a war they may oppose, a war which even possibly may be wrong, a war, which in any case, does not involve immediately the peace and freedom of the nation."

Curiously, Rove's view at the time was not so different, according to classmates. Rove had doubts about the war—which after all, was being prosecuted by a Democrat, Lyndon Johnson. In any case, he felt government had no right to require citizens to serve in the military.

He and classmate Mark Gustavson sat by the huge windows in the cafeteria discussing the issue.

"He was opposed to compulsory service. He felt we don't need the damn government telling us what to do. We can do it on our own."

According to Gustavson, Rove had reached his conclusion not from the left, but the right—as an expression of libertarianism. Supporting the war was equivalent to supporting big government and the intrusions of big government, especially the bloated, post-New Deal government of LBJ and Hubert Humphrey and the rest of the liberal Washington establishment. Whether guided more by the apprehension of being drafted or a commitment to individual liberty—Rove was no fan of the war, or at least the draft.

He brought this passion to the topic of compulsory military service, winning debate after debate in classrooms of receptive draft-age young high school students. He used what he called the "Mom, apple pie, and flag defense," meaning the position of the true American patriot. It was a fine piece of rhetorical jujitsu, friends remembered, which allowed Rove to reconcile opposition to the draft with conservative principle.

"I think there was a flag behind Karl. He brought in some cherry pie one day and handed out pieces of cherry pie to everyone. It was one of those one-upsmanships that would make the opponent think, 'where the hell do we go from here?'" said Gustavson.

There is a picture of Rove with the debate club in the 1969 high school yearbook, his senior year. He is seated in the first row and around him are his fellow debaters, mostly young men in spectacles and open-collar shirts. Rove is in a suit and tie. He is wearing an exuberant grin and is perched like a bundle of potential energy, as if he wants to burst out of the picture. Next to him, with her hand placed lightly on his knee as if to keep him from moving, is the faculty advisor, Diana Childs. She has the look of a teacher weary of trying to contain a hopelessly excitable terrier. Rove's mouth is open. Even here, at the moment the camera takes the picture, he is talking.

In the section highlighting student body officers, there is also a shot of Karl Rove, president of the student senate. It says: "Talking, reading, talking, writing speeches, talking, talking, talking—sometimes brilliant, sometimes verbose. Coming or going, constantly on the move. A doer instead of a watcher; vitally concerned, ever-debating, a mighty funny, never-stopped-to-ponder kind of guy."

Eldon Tolman's history class was made for students who liked to talk. Tolman wore a bow tie and glasses and he had a large, bony forehead and the imperious glare of a headmaster. He prodded students to talk in class, pushing and baiting them to express their views and then to defend them. He was a New Deal Democrat, an unreconstructed liberal. Tolman taught advanced placement history and government classes. He encouraged discussion, but Rove tested his limits. Once, he and a fellow student were so vociferous, refusing to shut up, that an exasperated Tolman ordered them both out of class.

Still, he saw instantly in Rove something he valued, a student passionate about the art of politics.

"Mr. Rove," Tolman announced one day, "it will be easy for you to get an A in this class, but to get an A you must join a campaign. I care not which."

It was an offer Rove could not refuse. He went down to Republican party headquarters and signed up as a volunteer for the re-election campaign of Senator Wallace Bennett. He ran errands, erected lawn signs, knocked on doors, and distributed campaign literature. Around Halloween, he passed out pamphlets that said: "The Great Pumpkin says Vote for Wallace F. Bennett." It occurred to him how a message could be so simple, yet effective. He hung around the executive director's office a lot, interjecting himself into discussions about phone banks and political mailings. He became a regular habitué at GOP headquarters, a skinny little 17-year-old— "130 pounds, soaking wet," a friend said—with little experience and lots of ideas.

Randy Ludlow, another high school volunteer, said Rove wanted in on the big stuff from the beginning.

"Karl was down at campaign headquarters day in and day out. They would be strategizing and Karl would come up with different ideas and plans. They'd send him off to get coffee and donuts."

At school, Rove wore his Republicanism on his sleeve. One day at assembly, he introduced Governor Calvin Rampton, a moderate Democrat, with a jab at his politics.

The moment was startling.

Rove was trying to be funny, as if introducing a political peer. But he was a teenager and the governor was a guest and, according to some in the audience, it apparently occurred to everyone except Rove that he was no equal to a political figure who had been governor since 1965 and who was to become one of the most popular chief executives in Utah history, winning re-election twice. The photo of the event in the yearbook showed Rove accompanying an

exasperated-looking Rampton, looking all the world like a man trying to escape his escort.

Whatever his charm to some people, Rove was irritating to others.

"He annoyed a number of students," recalled Mike Gustavson.

Rove did not get the best grades in school. He was not among
the top 3 percent, not a member of the National Honor Society. But
he wielded a facile rhetoric, which he used like a weapon.

"Karl was a little guy but you didn't mess with him because Karl
had a very sharp tongue," said classmate Chris Smart, now the editor of a weekly newspaper in Salt Lake City. "If you were going to
give Karl some crap, you knew it was coming back at you. He was
quick-witted and had a quick tongue."

He larded his conversations with facts and figures, imposing
some historic framework on whatever point he sought to make. And,
students still remember, he was enormously condescending.

"You know so much, you tend to lecture people. And sometimes
that wasn't effective," said classmate Rick Higgins.

"To be overbearing with the facts and all your enormous knowledge sometimes backfires. It's almost like he would bully with that.
Most of the guys who teased Karl admired him very much. It was just,
'Karl, for heaven's sake, nobody needs to know about the Revolution-
ary War and how it influenced the Vietnam era.' But he'd insist on
telling you. He'd continue to go through it, he'd finish his thought."

Rove also had plenty of thoughts about Democrats, especially
those like Hubert Humphrey. When classmate Mark Gustavson
wrote a column in the student newspaper condemning both the pro-
testers and the police at the 1968 Democratic National Convention
in Chicago, Rove complained about it in Tolman's class. Tolman,
seeing this as a teachable moment, asked what the police should
have done in the face of massive protests.

"Not assault and commit criminal acts against people in the
street," Gustavson declared.

Rove leaped into the conversation, denouncing Tom Hayden
and the Weathermen and the Students for Democratic Society. He

acknowledged that the police shared some responsibility for its response, which seemed excessive. But the blame, he said, fell where it so often did, in Rove's mind—with the Democratic party. The Democrats were at fault. Humphrey was to blame because he had acted too late in condemning what was going on in the streets, he had shown no moral leadership, no political courage. Rove had reduced the police riot in Chicago and the right of free speech and the whole wrenching national debate over Vietnam to a political formula, which he wore as a button on his lapel: "Nixon's the One."

The first time Rove saw a presidential race close up was that year, when Richard Nixon, George Wallace, and Hubert Humphrey all campaigned at the Mormon Tabernacle. Wallace's visit to the vividly white environs of Salt Lake City brought an unsettling racist appeal.

"Wallace was the first time I saw bigotry," Rove said. "Wallace was just ugly and vicious and mean. I will never forget the roar of the crowd when he said, 'If they lay down in front of my car, it'll be the last time.' The crowd just roared in hatred. And it astonished me."

The visit by the vice president was a particularly memorable moment. His entourage arrived at the Mormon Tabernacle late in the campaign, under a bright Western sun. It was hot, September 30, the final weeks of the 1968 presidential contest. And here came Hubert Humphrey—Happy Hubert—into the rarefied air of Republican Utah, into the prim heart of the Mormon Church. Rove was exuberant at the prospect of seeing a national political candidate in the flesh, even if it was the enemy. He was excited to see the apparatus of a national campaign, how a candidate entered the hall, the swarm of the press, the positioning of the Secret Service.

Tolman wanted his entire class to see the speech, so he commandeered a school bus to transport everybody. The class arrived early and was to take a spot near the back of the Tabernacle, squeezed in among a crowd of thousands. But first, the students milled about outside for a while as the school buses arrived and streams of staid and proper Mormons made their way into the building. This was perfect because Rove had decided before leaving that he would not just attend the speech; he would launch a protest outside.

"Karl and I immediately got into trouble with some Democrat supporters outside the Tabernacle," Gustavson said.

For one thing, Rove had printed up and distributed buttons, which he was wearing proudly on his suit coat. They said "Hubert Humphrey" with a line drawn through the name, and he pinned them on his lapel, turned upside down in the universal sign of distress.

Gustavson described reactions to Rove's approach as fairly predictable.

"I remember an older woman coming up, first accosting Karl and then me, blowing her stack at us for being disrespectful young people who were there to disrupt everything."

Rove was delighted. He stood in the bright sun in his suit and tie, a stone's throw from Temple Square, and shouted contempt for the policies of Lyndon Johnson and his henchman, Hubert Humphrey. Somebody yelled at Rove and he yelled back.

"Nixon's the one!" he shouted. "Nixon's the one!"

"There was a banner or two or a sign," Gustavson said. "We were loudly advocating against Lyndon Johnson's war, his revised New Deal politics and economics. The Democrats were down there in force and vociferous. It was quite a Hyde Park scene, very loud, very strident public debate outside Temple Square. It was great. We were giving them hell."

Rove said he cannot recall the protest.

In Salt Lake City, after the speech at the Tabernacle, Humphrey went to a television studio and told a nationwide audience that he favored halting the bombing of North Vietnam. The Humphrey camp was seeking to distance their man from Johnson, and polls in the succeeding weeks indicated that he was closing the gap with Nixon, but not quickly enough.

In Utah, Republican Wallace Bennett won election to his fourth and final term as senator. Democrat Calvin Rampton buried his opponent for governor nearly two-to-one. And the *New* Nixon—

Rove's candidate—took Utah with 55 percent of the vote and carried a narrow national victory to Washington where, a few years later in the political wreckage of Watergate, Rove first met George W. Bush, the man who was to take him to the White House.

The thing that seemed so odd to some of his classmates was how wedded Rove was to the Republican party, how he had attached himself so early to the hoary apparatus of the party.

"I always viewed the Republican party as the party of my parents. And who wanted anything to do with that?" said classmate Cary Jones.

But there was something in the party that appealed to Rove, something solid and stable. The strong and muscular message—defense of home and hearth, discipline, order. The Democrats were the party of giveaways and lassitude. All around him was division. Salt Lake City was divided between those who were Mormon and those who were not. The nation was divided over Vietnam. His home was coming apart. His father was away much of the time and even when his parents were together, they argued. In a city where the prevalent influences were political and religious, his family was neither. He grew up in an apolitical household, without religious mooring.

Friend Mark Dangerfield told a reporter that it seemed to bother Rove that "he was raised in a completely nonreligious home."

His father, Louis, took a job in California with the mineral department of an oil company, and commuted. The plan, so far as Rove knew, was that the family would move to Los Angeles, but that never happened. In December 1969, his father came in, his parents fought, and Louis turned around and left for good. It was Christmas Eve. By the time he entered college, his parents were divorcing. Rove was 20 before he learned that Louis was actually his stepfather. He never knew his biological father. After the divorce, his mother moved to Reno and, some years later, she killed herself.

When Keith Roark came home from Vietnam, he picked up a copy of the student newspaper at the University of Utah and saw Karl Rove's name. Roark, the captain of the high school debate team Rove's sophomore year, had volunteered for the draft, joined the Army and gone to Vietnam. When he returned, he enrolled at the University of Utah. And it was there on campus in 1971 that he sat down with the campus newspaper one day and saw the name of Karl Rove, president of the University of Utah College Republicans.

"I was amazed that in the two years I had been gone, how many people who sort of had Republican leanings had become fervent anti-Nixon, anti-Republican. But not Karl Rove. Antiwar sentiment, even at the University of Utah, was rife. We're talking about the era of huge antiwar protests and hippies and marijuana and communes and alternative lifestyles. And Karl, as far as I know, never even winked in that direction. He set a course that he never wavered from, not even momentarily."

Chris Smart remembered how the hierarchy of interests that occupied so many young men at the time—skiing, girls, and drinking beer—was not a priority with Rove.

"We were trying to get one of our parents' cars, trying to score some beer, trying to score some cigarettes, trying to score girls. And Karl was not doing that. We just wanted to get drunk and get laid and be kind of grown up in that way. Karl, I think, was trying to be grown up in an entirely different way."

Rove was almost standing alone at a time when his generation was gathering for political effect. He didn't belong with the partiers. And the protestors weren't his kind, not even the comparatively innocent version of Students for Democratic Society (SDS). His first day on campus, Rove saw a huge banner hanging off the student union that said: Smash the State and the War. Dance Friday night. 25 cents. Sponsored by SDS.

"A more benevolent face of radicalism," Rove said, recalling the episode years later. The only fit for him was the conservative politics of Republicans. Even in Utah, though, Rove was unique—a conservative young man in a screaming, youthful world of political outrage.

As a freshman at Utah, Rove got involved with something called the Hinckley Institute, which offered students an opportunity for internships both at the state capital and in Washington. The institute was an adjunct of the political science department on campus. It was created by Bob Hinckley, an old New Dealer who overcame a palpable resistance by the administration to the study of practical politics with a check for $250,000 for creation of an institute. His motto: Every student a politician.

When J. D. Williams first saw Rove his freshman year, he knew he had a live wire. Williams was the director of the Hinckley Institute, a venerated professor with a strong progressive streak—"My mortal gods are Thomas Jefferson, Franklin D. Roosevelt, and Martin Luther King."—who became the second academic liberal to take Rove under his wing. Since the founding of the institute in 1965, Williams had not seen a student so interested in the application of practical politics. Rove threw himself into his internship at the Statehouse and in Washington.

"I always felt a little guilty about the fact that he got so carried away with these political activities that he never graduated," said Williams, now professor emeritus.

Rove never got a college degree. He attended several colleges and eventually taught at the University of Texas, but the lure of practicing politics always outstripped his studies.

During the antiwar years, there was no tougher place to practice Republican politics than on a college campus. Rove had come to the attention of the hierarchy of the College Republicans, who dispatched him in 1970 to Illinois to organize campuses for Senator Ralph Smith, an old-line conservative who had been appointed to the job upon the death of the venerable Everett Dirksen. His opponent was Adlai Stevenson III.

"It was at the height of the Vietnam War. Ralph was an extremely conservative guy. It was, shall we say, an uphill climb," said Bob Kjellander, then president of the College Republican chapter at the University of Illinois.

Rove had all kinds of ideas, according to Kjellander. Dormitory canvasses. Precinct organizations on campus. Dorm chairmen. Floor chairmen. Rove traveled from school to school, from

Champaign to Bloomington to Springfield. He formed a willing and ready alliance with the Young Americans for Freedom (YAF), the shock troops of the new right on college campuses. The YAFers saw themselves as a counterbalance to the long-haired, drug-using Students for Democratic Society on the left. The YAFers wore ties, revered William F. Buckley, and relished the reaction they got to lapel buttons designed to look like a peace symbol but, upon closer inspection, were actually a B-52 bomber. They were a swaggering, prankster truth squad on the right, up for anything—even dirty tricks.

The Democratic candidate for state treasurer in 1970 was Alan Dixon, a likable Illinois politician who was climbing the political ladder that was eventually to lead him to a seat in the U.S. Senate. The Dixon for Treasurer campaign planned to formally open its Chicago headquarters with a flourish, inviting party officials, the press, and supporters.

Rove had an idea: Disrupt the opening.

He assumed a false name and posed as a supporter to get into campaign headquarters, where he stole some Dixon campaign stationary.

Rove used the stationary to fake an invitation to the opening, giving the correct time and place, but adding, "Free beer, free food, girls, and a good time for nothing." He made 1,000 copies and distributed them at a hippie commune, a rock concert, soup kitchens, and among the drunks on Chicago's bowery. And it worked. On the day of the opening, hundreds of the city's dissolute showed up. Vans arrived with freeloaders attracted by the promise of liquor and food.

"It was funny," Kjellander remembered. "He had all these winos showing up at a fancy party with an open bar."

Dixon had a decidedly different view.

"It was a little upsetting."

Still, Dixon won and he has subsequently dismissed the episode as a minor inconvenience. Although Kjellander recalled that Rove was eventually directed by George Herbert Walker Bush to apologize, Dixon has no memory of receiving an apology.

"I don't recall ever being in Karl Rove's presence. Maybe I was, but I don't recall it," said Dixon, who left the Senate in 1993 and is now an attorney in St. Louis.

He added crisply, "I gather that Karl Rove has become a rather important political operative."

Rove rose swiftly in the hierarchy of College Republicans during the early 1970s, eventually becoming executive director, a staff job with an office at the Republican National Committee and an annual salary of $9,200. He organized 15 regional conferences to instruct young Republicans on the gears and levers of practical politics. Rove and colleague Bernie Robinson traveled the country, to San Diego, West Virginia, Wisconsin, American University in Washington. Mostly the sessions were about organization and message, but Rove could not resist instructing his young audiences on dirty tricks—pranks, he called them.

At a seminar in Lexington, Kentucky, in August 1972, Rove and Robinson recounted the Dixon episode with considerable delight. They talked about campaign espionage, about digging through an opponent's garbage for intelligence—then using it against them. Robinson recounted how that technique had worked well for him in the 1968 governor's race in Illinois when he "struck gold" in a search of an opponent's stolen garbage. He found evidence that a supporter had given checks to both sides in the race, but more to the Democrat, Sam Shapiro.

"So one of our finance guys calls the guy up the next day and told him there was a vicious rumor going around," Robinson said, according to a tape recording of the seminar. "The guy got all embarrassed and flew to Chicago that day with a check for $2,000 to make up the difference," he said.

This was the summer of the Watergate break-in, with the first revelations of a scandal that unraveled the Nixon presidency. The Watergate burglars broke into the Democratic National Committee offices on June 17 and the whole business of political dirty tricks was rapidly becoming a very sensitive subject. Both Rove and Robinson recognized that. They even specifically mentioned the Watergate break-in at the seminars, not as a reason to avoid campaign espionage, but as a caution to keep it secret.

"While this is all well and good as fun and games, you've really got to use your head about who knows about this kind of thing," Robinson warned.

"Again in those things, if it's used surreptitiously in a campaign, it's better off if you don't get caught. You know, those people who were caught by Larry O'Brien's troops in Washington are a serious verification of the fact that you don't get caught."

That was the message: Don't get caught. And there was this swaggering attitude about it, the whole exuberant Young Republican thing: We're young and indestructible and there's nothing so much fun as full-contact politics with a faint menace of danger.

Nobody expressed this better than Lee Atwater, who was about to emerge on the national scene as the bad boy of testosterone politics. Rove had never seen anybody quite like Lee, with his slow-cured manner and take-no-prisoners attitude. Atwater read the *New York Times* and the *National Enquirer*. He quoted Sun-Tzu. ("If your opponent is of choleric temper, seek to irritate him.") He was everything Rove wanted to be: the perfect political warrior.

In 1973, when Rove was recruited to run for chairman of the College Republican National Committee, a group of supporters paired him with Atwater, who at the time was president of the College Republicans in South Carolina. Rove was to be the candidate and Atwater his Southern campaign chairman. In March, Rove took the train from Washington to Columbia, South Carolina, a $25 overnight ticket, where he was met by Atwater and another young hardball Republican, John Carbaugh, later to become advisor to Jesse Helms. With a Gulf credit card, Rove and Atwater rented a mustard-brown Ford Pinto and proceeded to spend the next week campaigning together across the South, visiting state college Republican chairmen, and asking for support.

The deal went like this: Rove was to be chairman and Atwater would take his old job, executive director of the College Republican National Committee. Both of them would be in Washington with an office and a phone and the run of the Republican National Committee (RNC). It was impossible not to like Atwater. He was fun loving and amiable and he was forever scheming about one thing or the other. The two of them had barely taken their new jobs in Washington, Rove said, before Atwater was hustling Republican National Committee Chairman George H. W. Bush for use of his boat.

Rove was awestruck by Atwater's self-confidence.

"I introduced Lee to George Bush. Lee wanted to meet George Bush because he was chairman but also because he'd heard that the chairman had a boat that he kept on the Potomac. Lee had a big date lined up for the weekend and he thought it would be very impressive if he could take this little Strom Thurmond intern named Sally out on the Potomac on George Bush's boat.

"So—classic Atwater—five minutes after he has met the chairman of the Republican National Committee, he was bumming the use of his boat. And the audacious guy he was, he got it."

But to get to Washington, they had to win, and to win, they had to out-politick the other guys. The two of them—Rove and Atwater—crisscrossed the South in the spring of 1973 lining up support in advance of the summer convention where the new chairman of the College Republicans was to be chosen. Atwater knew all the fronts and fissures of campus politics in the region, who was important and who was not. By the time they rolled into Lake of the Ozarks in June for the convention, Atwater and Rove had a battle plan.

In the end, according to his opponent, Rove had to steal the election to win.

The hotel in Lake of the Ozarks was swarming with young Republicans. There were sessions on practical politics in the little meeting rooms and politicking in the hallways, particularly for the election of the new national chairman. Atwater and Rove cruised the rooms and the bar, looking to lock up votes. There were three candidates: Rove; Robert Edgeworth, a Goldwater devotee who had headed up Students for Nixon at the University of Michigan; and Terry Dolan, the future founder of the National Conservative Political Action Committee. Dolan, whose acerbic personality made it difficult to round up support, realized that he didn't have the votes to win and threw in with Edgeworth.

It was a two-man race for a majority of the votes. But which votes? Rove and Atwater's plan, supported by a faction within the College Republicans sometimes called the Chicago Boys, took as a point of pride its influence on the gears and levers of the organization. Atwater and the Chicago Boys decided the best way to win an election was to make sure the votes that counted were their votes. There was suddenly a flurry of challenges at the credentials committee, which went into the night.

"The credentials committee savagely went through and threw out, often on the flimsiest of reasons, most of my supporters," said Edgeworth, who steered his own campaign with a bullhorn and a stack of proxies, which challenged Rove and Atwater.

Tempers flared and there were near-fistfights. Edgeworth supporters shouted at Rove's people, who shouted back. The committee was stymied. The next day, with everybody gathered in a large hall, Rove's name was entered into nomination, and as the roll was called, region-by-region, one voice shouted "Aye" and another voice yelled "No." Then, against a chorus of boos and cheers, Edgeworth was also nominated, just as Rove had been, and the same thing happened. Each side declared victory.

"I gave a nice acceptance speech, thanking everybody for electing me. Then I sat down," said Edgeworth. "Karl got up, gave a nice acceptance speech for everybody who had elected him. Then we both went to Washington, DC."

The issue was to be decided by RNC Chairman George Bush. Both sides made their cases, but Rove seemed to have an advantage, having already met Bush while working as executive director of the College Republicans. Before Bush had announced his decision, Dolan went to the media with some particularly damning material about Rove—tapes and transcripts of the "dirty tricks" seminars.

"I forbade him to but he did it anyway," Edgeworth said.

The *Washington Post* published the story under the headline "GOP Probes Official as Teacher of Tricks":

Republican National Committee Chairman George Bush has reopened an investigation into allegations that a paid official of the GOP taught political espionage and "dirty tricks" during weekend seminars for College Republicans during 1971 and 1972. Some of the 1972 seminars were held after the Watergate break-in.

Bush said he will urge a GOP investigating committee to "get to the bottom" of charges Against Karl C. Rove, 32, who was executive director of the College Republican National Committee.

This was exactly the kind of publicity the Republican party did not need. The storm clouds were building over Watergate. The Senate was investigating. Nixon had announced in April the departure of John Dean, John Haldeman, and John Ehrlichman. And now George Bush, who as chairman of the party had pledged to keep the GOP free of Watergate taint, was having to deal with a published report in the *Washington Post*—adjacent to the day's Watergate investigation story, for god's sake—about tape recordings and "dirty tricks" workshops by a GOP college operative.

In fact, the evidence had been given first to the RNC and quietly reviewed by a committee and dismissed. Only afterward did the tapes and affidavits find their way into the media. Now in the bright light of a newspaper report, Bush promised to reopen the inquiry. Three weeks later, September 6, he sent a letter to both candidates declaring Rove the winner.

Edgeworth wrote back asking on what basis Bush had made the decision—and got a blistering reply.

"He sent me back an absolutely furious letter in which he wrote me out of the party. He said he certainly would not answer such impertinent inquiries from someone who was disloyal to the party and leaked hostile information to the press, which I had never done."

The response was odd, Edgeworth thought. Bush was angry not because a Republican had conducted seminars on campaign espionage, but because someone had gone to the press with the story. Obviously, the priority was containing the scandal, not getting to the bottom of it. This was all about loyalty and the club; no true Republican would violate the party code by going to the media. That was the message that Edgeworth heard.

A few months later, Bush hired Rove as his special assistant at the RNC.

How perfect was this? Assistant to the chairman of the Republican National Committee. Back at Olympus High, Rove had talked with his friend Randy Ludlow about how he was going to Washington, and now he was here, in the big time. Every morning when Chairman Bush arrived at the basement parking garage and stepped into the elevator, rising to the fourth floor, Rove was there eagerly ready for the day. As a member of the personal staff, Rove had all the authority of an assistant to the RNC chairman—which is to say, not much authority at all. Mostly he was a gopher. But the place was the center of the Republican universe, a place to make associations and stay current on the party's latest line.

His most important association, although he didn't know it then, was the boss' son, George W. Bush.

Defining moments of lives are often nothing more than chance encounters. But Karl Rove was leaving nothing to providence, in this case. When it came to George W. Bush, Rove ended up taking chance out of the equation. And in the process, he changed—not just their lives—but also American history.

8

Face Value

Don't be humble. You're not that great.

Golda Meir

K arl Rove's new friend was a lot of things he was not. George W. had graduated from Yale and served a stint as a pilot with the Texas Air National Guard, and now he was a graduate student at Harvard Business School, and from time to time he came to Washington to see his parents and to check out the nightlife with friends. The younger Bush had a kind of easy, almost indifferent, quality. He wore a leather flight jacket, had brown hair and blue eyes and a bronze complexion. He blew gum bubbles while he waited to see his dad. Rove remembered his first impression.

"He was . . . *cool.*"

Rove's task in those days was simple enough.

"I was supposed to give him the car keys whenever he came to town."

The Republican National Committee was a perfect place to make political associations and soak in the influences of Washington, the greatest political city in the world. His strongest influence was Atwater. Both Rove and Lee Atwater had illusions of political stardom, but it was Atwater who first made his name in Washington. He reminded Rove of one of those Southern stock cars exploding with noise and energy and going 150 miles an hour. Lee carried himself with colossal self-confidence, no matter where—greeting a group of blue-chip political donors or drinking with friends at a Georgetown bar.

Rove knew he could never match that.

"We're not alike. He had an incredible gut instinct for how ordinary people would react. I guess I'm more cerebral, he's more gut," Rove said.

The thing that most impressed Rove was the sharp intelligence Atwater brought to the game of politics. That, and what Rove called his friend's "understanding of the thrust and parry of the negative." Atwater looked at politics like war. He liked to say he read "*The Prince*" by Machiavelli every year. He talked with authority on the power and complexity of racial politics in the South, on wedge issues like gun control and the flag, which created rich new coalitions of conservative Republicans and Reagan Democrats.

"Lee had a great knack to visualize," said Richard McBride, a Republican consultant and friend to both Atwater and Rove.

"His whole thing was wedges and magnets. What pulls people apart and what attracts people? You drive wedges and you find magnets. You find ways to bring people to you and ways to divide people who are against you. That was his bottom-line practical theory.

"He had a great knack for hiring a lot of young munchkins and putting them all over Washington—the Commerce Department, whatever department. Every time you turned around, there was somebody that Atwater had put somewhere. And with campaigns, he'd decide which of his good friends ought to be the consultant on this campaign, somebody else to do the polling on that campaign. So he built a hell of a loyalty up."

Atwater rose like a rocket in political Washington, from deputy assistant for political affairs in the Reagan White House to architect of George Bush's 1988 presidential victory to chairman of the Republican National Committee. All by the age of 40. Rove maintained close ties with Atwater even after circumstances led him to Texas, where he watched his old friend's ascension with no small measure of envy.

At dinner one night in Austin, Atwater told Rove, "Karl, you should be up in DC as a strategist like me."

But by then, he'd already set his roots deeply in Texas. While working for Bush in Washington, Rove had met the daughter of a Houston barge broker, Valerie Wainright, and in July 1976 they were married. Valerie's grandmother had been a matriarch of Houston society in the 1940s and 1950s and her family had founded the Houston social register. Valerie was groomed as part of the Republican WASP establishment in Houston, and Rove was a young Republican on the rise, working at that time as finance director for the Virginia state party and a deputy in President Ford's election campaign.

The Virginia Republican party was in debt; the most money it had ever raised was $110,000 in 1972. Rove, who had no particular expertise in raising money, was dispatched to Richmond, where he found himself walking around the Fidelity Building wondering how he—a 26-year-old living from paycheck to paycheck—was going to raise money for a party that didn't even have a fund-raiser on its schedule.

He did have one thing: a magnetic tape with the names of 30,000 past contributors.

And with that, Rove was in the direct-mail business. Within a year, he had raised more than $400,000 and put the party in the black. But his job, like always, consumed much of his time and energy and Valerie was unhappy with Richmond and wanted to return to Houston. So in November, after Jimmy Carter and the Democrats reclaimed the White House, Karl and Valerie moved to Texas, but the threads of their marriage were rapidly unraveling.

As it turned out, Texas was the perfect proving ground for Rove to develop politically. He stayed close to the Bush family, helping the elder Bush with his new political action committee, the Fund for Limited Government, and assisting the son in his 1978 race for Congress.

The Fund for Limited Government was aimed at advancing elder Bush's prospects as a Republican presidential candidate in 1980. Carter was barely in office and already a new crop of Republicans—Bush and Ronald Reagan notably among them—were circling in hopes of winning back the White House for the GOP.

Rove set up shop at 1801 Main Street in Houston, and in the beginning, he *was* the staff—arranging schedules, producing a political newsletter, and cultivating the lists of Republican financial donors who were the mother's milk of any presidential bid. Mostly, the job was traveling. James A. Baker III lent his name as chairman of the committee, but the committee at first was really only three people—Rove, a pilot, and Bush—in pursuit of support from the golden money guys in the glass towers and energy company offices and corn-belt congressional districts in states that elect Republican presidents. Later, Margaret Tutweiler and Jennifer Fitzgerald joined the staff.

Out on the level landscape of West Texas, a kind of referendum on Reagan-Bush was already underway. While the father was pursing the presidency under the colors of his political action committee, the son had decided to run for the nineteenth congressional seat. The district's venerable old Democratic congressman, who had held seat for nearly a half century, had announced his retirement and George W. jumped into the race. At 32 and a newcomer to the oil business in Midland, the younger Bush presented a clear target for political rivals out on this parched stretch of oil and cotton country.

"He's a personable young man from back East," said his Republican primary opponent, Jim Reese.

The operable words hung in the air like an obscenity. *Back East.* As in . . . *Yankee . . . blue-blood . . . New York City . . . effete.*

Reese was a stockbroker and former mayor of Odessa. He was also a vigorous Reagan Republican, and Reagan showed his appreciation by sending along a letter of endorsement, which Reese mass-mailed to every Republican in the district and half the Democrats, too. Reagan's political action committee, Citizens for the Republic, sent money and Reagan surrogates dropped into the district to speak on Reese's behalf. At the Petroleum Club in Midland, everybody was for young George. But the district was more than Midland. It stretched for 17 counties across a largely rural constituency from Friona to Farwell where farmers and roughnecks and small-town shopkeepers were no stranger to hard work and to the red-dust storms that could soil a line of clothes in an instant and turn the windows black.

The elder Bush directed Rove to get involved. Although paid from the father's political action committee, Rove became an informal advisor in the son's congressional bid, offering strategic advice and helping organize fund-raisers hosted by the father in Washington, Dallas, Houston, and Midland. Rove had become a master technician of Republican money, and money flowed into George W.'s campaign treasury. Contributors to the father became contributors to the son: Mrs. Douglas MacArthur, former CBS president Frank Shakespeare, Ambassador Anne Armstrong, former Secretary of Defense Donald Rumsfeld. Auto executives from Detroit, oil tycoons from Houston, the whole blue-chip list was digging into its pockets and dumping money into a West Texas district where the Reagan forces were aligned on one side and the Bush forces on the other.

On the stump, Reese pressed the case that George W. was a carpetbagger, born in New Haven, Connecticut, and educated in the pointy-headed environs of Harvard and Yale.

He even made Rove an issue.

"I am very disappointed that he has Rockefeller-type Republicans such as Karl Rove to help him run his campaign," he said in a letter to voters.

But George W. won the primary and the right to face Democrat Kent Hance, a graduate of Texas Tech who played the good-old-boy card with all the smoothness of a small-town cattle broker. Hance graduated from Dimmitt High School; Bush graduated from a private prep school in Massachusetts.

Case closed.

Two weeks before the general election, the candidates met at the Branding Iron Restaurant in Odessa, where a popular radio broadcaster named Mel Turner acted as moderator for a noon forum. Turner said he was surprised at how thin-skinned Bush was on the outsider issue. At one point during the forum, he asked Bush, "Are you or anyone you know connected to the Trilaterial Commission?"

Bush seemed flummoxed by the question. His father was a member, but he knew that among the hard-shell conservatives of West Texas, the Trilaterial Commission was viewed as the shadowy tool of an oncoming communist, atheist, and one-world government. Afterwards, as he left the Branding Iron, Bush scowled at Turner and said loud enough for several people to hear, "You asshole."

Bush lost the general election by more than 6,000 votes.

Reese offered a prescient coda, "He has a bright future in politics somewhere, but it's not out here."

Two things were to distinguish all future Bush political campaigns: Karl Rove would be totally in charge and Bush would never lose again.

Whatever assistance Rove gave George W. in 1978, his attention was primarily on the father and his pre-presidential effort. The elder Bush's itinerary in 1978 included 135 political events in 41 states, a flurry of plane flights and van rides with Bush out front and Rove scurrying at his side in a gray suit, carrying an over-stuffed valise. A bull roast barbecue in Maryland, Alaska's Republican convention, an Indianapolis fund-raiser for a young, blond Republican congressman named Dan Quayle. And television, lots of local television: Eyewitness News, Action News, Scene 17 News, 21 Alive News. Rove was never home. In 18 months, Rove was back in Houston part of only 16 weekends.

In 1979, Valerie filed for divorce. The climatic moment, Rove recalled, was the counseling session at the Episcopal Church where a trendy young priest in jeans and boots opened the session in a gentle, conciliatory tone.

"Okay, here are the ground rules," he said.

Rove fidgeted in his chair; Valerie sat nervously smoking a ciga- rette. Before the priest could finish the ground rules, Valerie was up.

"Wait a minute," she said. "I don't know why I'm here. I don't love you. I've never loved you. And I'm leaving."

With that, she walked out. It was like a thunderclap, then a long silence. She had *never* loved him. His marriage had failed; he had failed. The priest slowly picked up his notebook and looked over at Rove, who sat shaking, angry, and humiliated.

"Well," the priest said, closing his notebook, "that about says it all."

In the summer in Austin, the sun blazes with a white-hot intensity, making the grass brittle and creating heat waves that rise like liq- uid off the concrete. Along Shoal Creek, on a thin stretch of land, shirtless college students in sandals play Frisbee golf even in the hard heat of September. You can see them playing from the win- dows of Karl Rove's direct-mail office, where he set up shop a cou- ple of years after the divorce and where, in September 1985, he sat down and wrote an important memo.

George W. Bush's road to the White House could not have hap- pened without the resurgence of the Republican party in Texas, which began with a memo by Karl Rove. Texas was rock-solid De- mocrat. For 100 years, from the end of Reconstruction to the pas- sage of the 1965 Voting Rights Act, Democrats owned the South and Texas was part of the South. They had a phrase for it in East Texas, "yellow dog Democrat," meaning you would vote for a yellow dog before you'd ever vote for a Republican in a political race.

At the turn of the century, when O. Henry was a Texas newspaperman, he wrote: "We have only two or three laws, such as against murdering witnesses and being caught stealing horses, and voting the Republican ticket."

Whatever the political tides elsewhere in the country, the South remained committed to a party that pledged allegiance to the common man, delivered the goods of the New Deal, and didn't disrupt the established order under Jim Crow. In 1950, there were no Republican senators from the South. Of 105 southern House members, only two were Republicans.

Earl and Merle Black, the region's premier political analysts, offer the thesis that the national Democratic party made an implicit pact with Southerners that nobody would tamper with segregation if Southerners supported key economic legislation. But by the 1960s, John Kennedy and Lyndon Johnson had broken that pact, triggering a fundamental realignment in the parties. Conservative, blue-collar Democrats, often those with a strong evangelical streak, began moving to the Republican party. White liberals, moderates, and minorities were becoming the dominant expression of the Democratic party.

In Texas, there had been the occasional Republican success— John Tower replacing Lyndon Johnson in the U.S. Senate in 1961 and Dallas oilman Bill Clements in 1978 becoming the first Republican in a century to be governor. But in the 1982 elections, every statewide Republican candidate lost, including Clements, and it appeared the Democratic party had reasserted its long hold on Texas politics.

No way, Karl Rove thought. Something was happening in the shifting demographics of Texas, and he saw it. The Sun Belt had become a magnet for a new economy and a new workforce attracted by factories, high-tech, and corporate relocations. Nationally, Ronald Reagan was the instrument of the political realignment. He was virile and optimistic, the poster boy for "Morning in America," and he was making the Republican party respectable to millions of

Southern whites and a wave of upwardly mobile new arrivals. Reagan represented traditional values and lower taxes, personal responsibility and a strong military—things that struck a responsive chord with conservative Texans and thousands of Yankee émigrés arriving daily who were white, middle-class, settled in the suburbs and voted Republican.

So Rove sat down in his chair on a white-hot September day, under a portrait of his political patron saint Teddy Roosevelt, and he composed a memo.

"It's important to start with a clear understanding of where we are today," he wrote.

The memo outlined a strategy for Bill Clements, who had won and lost the governorship, to win it again. Clements had proved an unpopular governor, strong-willed and difficult. He had made a fortune in the rigorous business of drilling for oil and carried into his first term a tendency to treat other elected officials as paid employees, not political peers. In 1982, he was turned out by Attorney General Mark White in a Democratic tide that also swept Ann Richards into her first statewide office as state treasurer.

Rove outlined Clements' strengths, largely that people knew who he was, and his weaknesses, which were considerable. He said people saw Clements as mean and insensitive and the media would write that the former governor wanted a rematch against White for revenge. It was all dead-on accurate. The key, Rove wrote, was to turn everything upside down by softening Clements' image and defusing the idea that he was a bad loser.

Then he wrote:

The whole art of war consists in a well-reasoned and extremely circumspect defensive, followed by rapid and audacious attack.

—Napoleon.

He went back and highlighted Napoleon's words. *Rapid. Audacious. Attack.* But first, he said, the best defense was for Clements to highlight his record and rehabilitate himself by acknowledging in a humorous, self-effacing way, that he had learned from his mistakes. The new suburbanites would vote for Clements, Rove knew, but only if he seemed sensitive to their interests.

"The purpose of saying you gave teachers a record pay increase is to reassure suburban voters with kids, not to win the votes of teachers," the memo said.

"Similarly, emphasizing your appointments of women and minorities will not win you the support of feminists and the leaders of the minority community; but it will bolster your support among Republican primary voters and urban independents."

Rove understood the potential of the state's changing demographics and he understood Clements. When Rove's marriage was failing in 1979, he moved to Austin and took a job in the new governor's political office, which he pursued with a voracious energy. His job was to manage the campaign-contributor lists and edit new fund-raising appeals for Clements. Rove was teeming with ideas, which he offered in a stream of memos: Convince a supporter with a yacht to host a day cruise from Galveston to Houston at $5,000 a couple; pressure a Houston car dealer who supported Clements' opponent to open his Falfurrias ranch, complete with a mansion and airstrip, to big-dollar donors for a dove hunt.

"Picking up the tab for a hunt might be his way of making amends," he wrote in a memo to his boss.

He arranged the state's political moneymen in a hierarchy of files with colorful names: "Texas Oilmen and Fat Cats," "Cream Republican Donors," "Texans Opposed to Labor Unions." He sought permission to buy more exotic lists—*Free Enterprise* magazine, *Krugerand Buyer*, Dreyfus tax-exempt bond investors—to prospect for new donors.

In short order, he created the gold standard of political lists, a road map of Republican mega-money guys. He worried that GOP rivals might poach the names, especially national direct-mail specialists Richard Viguerie and Brad O'Leary who had made a fortune tapping the anxieties of the party's right wing. Periodically, Texas political candidates were required to file reports with the secretary of state listing their campaign contributors. Campaigns delivered their reports to an office in the west wing of the state capitol. There, on long tables, under chandeliers and rococo trim from the nineteenth century, the general public and—more worrisome to Rove, GOP rivals—had access to the names.

"It can be made more difficult for the bastards," Rove wrote in a memo to his boss, Jim Francis.

"When we file our report, let's put only three or four names on each page of the report—plenty of white space. It costs us little. What's one sheet of legal-sized paper? It will make for a very thick report, which would cost a small fortune to photocopy. At 15 cents a page, three of our master file names would cost Viguerie or O'Leary 11 cents to 13 cents to obtain the keypunch. That's a high cost: one that might deter some raiders."

In the office, Rove rode his own keypunch operators mercilessly. He fired off a succession of memos exhorting his operators to work faster, harder, longer.

"None of these daily totals are impressive. In fact, they are cause for great concern," he wrote in a May 1979 memo. "I am not pleased with the rate of production," he wrote a week later.

Even as letters from regular constituents to the governor's office were left unanswered—a Beaumont doctor wrote in April that he had gotten no response in months on problems with mental retardation centers—political correspondence streamed with glorious efficiency. Rove took enormous pride in his work, so much so that when an Austin Democrat questioned why he'd gotten a Republican fund-raising appeal, Rove could not resist answering personally.

The Democrat had returned the solicitation with a note: "Hell will freeze over, the moon will fall from the sky, and cattle will sing sonnets in the pasture before I would be able to support Bill."

"Enjoyed your letter," came Rove's brisk reply.

"I'm keeping it as a source of good fodder for the letter I write the next time I get one of those DNC appeals from President Jimmy. Sincerely, Karl C. Rove, The Governor Clements Committee."

Rove set up his own direct-mail business in 1981. A year later, his first client was the Bill Clements for Governor reelection campaign. Clements lost but the mailing lists were acquired by Rove and proved invaluable. Nobody had better files than Rove on big dog Republican donors and he used them both to lure political clients and to expand his business into fund-raising for museums like the trendy Phillips Collection in Washington. The museum business provided income independent of the fortunes of the Republican party, which were not particularly good at the moment in Texas.

"Until Karl came along, there was no real Republican consultant of his stature in Texas," said George Christian, former White House press secretary to Lyndon Johnson. "There wasn't anybody with an overall concept. He could pretty much do it all."

His biggest early client was Phil Gramm, who had switched to the Republican party and was running for the U.S. Senate. Both were sticklers for detail and argued, sometimes at length, over the contents and grammar of fund-raising letters and direct-mail brochures. Gramm was a shrewd political veteran on an upward trajectory in national politics. Rove was a young guy with a brand-new consulting business.

"It was hilarious," said Richard McBride, who managed the campaign.

"We'd be hung up on a letter getting out. I was saying, 'This thing's got to go.' Gramm's saying, 'This sentence is not right.' And Karl is saying, 'I'm not going to let it go out, not this way.'"

McBride was at his wits' end.

"Okay, Karl, I'm coming over and picking you up in about 20 minutes and we're going to the airport because Gramm is coming in. And he's going to get into this car and from the airport to the office, ya'll are going to have to resolve this problem. I don't care who wins, who loses. I don't care. It's just got to be resolved."

With McBride at the wheel, Rove and Gramm sat in the back seat, quibbling over a campaign fund-raising letter. Problems with a sentence, then problems with a word. Their voices rose, neither willing to give an inch. Gramm, the former professor, claimed there was a grammatical error. Rove, the college dropout, declared the sentence perfectly correct. Eventually, before reaching campaign headquarters, they rewrote the offending passage in a way that satisfied both.

"I think they both felt they'd won," said McBride. "It was a stalemate."

Gramm's victory in 1984 did not mean the Republicans were back.

Clements' victory two years later did.

The Democrats didn't know it, but Rove had designs on the entire statewide ticket. In little more than a decade, every Democrat in elective statewide office was gone, replaced by Republicans—virtually every one a Rove client.

"It was a cartel," said one Republican colleague.

Rove directed Clements' return to office with characteristic attention to detail: a month-by-month blueprint of how to paint incumbent Mark White as an incompetent, self-serving politico susceptible to defeat on Election Day.

"Anti-White messages are more important than positive Clements messages," Rove wrote in a strategy memo.

"Attack. Attack. Attack."

By happenstance or design, it all worked. The campaign's own polling numbers showed that Rove's strategy had given Clements a slender lead, but White was closing—until the bugging episode, which erupted with a flourish of publicity and fatally stalled White's rise.

The day of Clements' inaugural, the sky was thick with gray clouds and a biting wind. Rove threaded his way through the crowd, a happy man. Limos were double-parked in the street behind the Governor's Mansion, and on the portico, chrome coat racks stretched for yards festooned with mink, fox, and ermine. These were his guys, the golden mega-dollars guys from his computer lists, made manifest in the flesh. These were the CEOs and CFOs who had helped put a Republican in the governor's office and were to become the financial nucleus of the Republican party's rise to power. Rove had the contributors and now he began accumulating candidates: a young ex-legislator named Kay Bailey Hutchison for state treasurer, a Democrat-turned-Republican named Rick Perry for agriculture commissioner.

When Clements appointed a 39-year-old district judge from Houston named Tom Phillips to an opening as chief justice of the Texas Supreme Court, Rove instantly assumed him as a client.

Phillips was tall and gangling, with spectacles and a big, toothy grin. But he knew his stuff: Harvard law, a stint at a bluestocking Houston law firm, eight years as a district judge. Moreover, the appointment of Phillips was a signal.

"It will go a long way toward sending a clear message for these businesses in Texas," said Secretary of State Jack Rains.

What business wanted were curbs on the system for compensating injured workers and caps on jury awards against business. The best way to accomplish that, Rove figured was to change the court by electing a new group of judges, starting with Phillips.

"That sort of led people to feeling they could win something," said Harry Whittington, an Austin lawyer and long-time Republican.

"They went after the Supreme Court. I don't think anybody thought of that being such a political job, but Karl was the man who showed that it could be done."

Through appointment and election, Republicans gradually took over the high court. Like a ritual, the Republican hierarchy cleared all potential candidates through Rove, who then became their paid political consultant and steered money into their campaign accounts. For candidates who were largely unknown, Rove's imprimatur meant all the difference. It was perfect. Business got the judges it wanted, the Republican party was winning elections and Rove got paid.

"Once the Republican leadership in Texas knew that Karl Rove was aboard, it put the mantle of endorsement on it," said Ralph Wayne, the amiable, silver-haired leader of an influential business group involved in vetting potential candidates.

When a Houston judge named Priscilla Owen called one day, asking for an appointment, Wayne asked what was on her mind.

"I'm thinking about running for Supreme Court," she said.

"Have you to talked to Karl Rove?" Wayne asked.

"No," said Owen, taking the hint. "But I plan to."

There was one person Rove did not have under contract, somebody he'd begun to think would make a great candidate for governor: George W. Bush. Over the years, he and George W. had stayed in contact. During the 1988 presidential race, Rove talked with Bush and with his old pal Lee Atwater, who had emerged as an important figure in the elder Bush's campaign.

"The greatest reward in life for Lee was to be Republican National Committee chairman," said Rove, who recalled traveling to Washington a few days after the election to see George W.

Somehow, word had leaked to a Boston newspaper that Atwater was about to be named RNC chairman and Atwater was all nerves, worried the leak might somehow spoil the appointment.

"Lee comes in," Rove recalled. "And he is nervous. His leg is moving and literally all four limbs, as if he has palsy. He's so worried that this leak will screw the deal."

Atwater offered an elaborate explanation, full of themes and subplots, how his enemies were obviously out to get him, how he had been a loyal worker in the political vineyards and a leak like this should not do him in. Rove watched as the younger Bush presented a worried face, nodding solemnly at Atwater's predicament. He had Atwater on the line, flopping like a fish.

Finally, he said, "I talked with Dad and you're okay. Don't worry about it."

Rove wanted to laugh. Bush got Atwater to sweat, but in the end, Atwater also got what he wanted.

"Probably, it was Lee who leaked it," Rove said now in retrospect.

Back home in Texas, and among friends in Washington, Rove began talking up George W. Bush as a possible candidate for governor. During the elder Bush's inauguration, Rove made sure that certain folks knew there was another Bush on the political horizon. At a reception in Washington, a Republican congressman introduced Bush as the "next governor of Texas."

Bush took the lectern and joked, "I don't know what makes people in Texas think I'm considering it, just because we changed the names of our twins to Dallas and Fort Worth."

Bush was interested, buoyed by the picture that Rove painted of the state's political landscape, the favorable demographic shifts and weak Republican field for 1990. Rove arranged meetings for Bush with key Republicans, one of them was Austin lawyer Harry Whittington.

Newspapers increasingly floated Bush's name as a potential candidate. He became the subject of running speculation among political operatives at the Texas Chili Parlor and the Austin Club.

Eventually, Rove's trial balloon went flat.

The White House sent word that it didn't want George W. to run. The fear was that the governor's race would become a referendum on the Bush presidency.

Instead, Republicans in 1990 chose a political novice named Clayton Williams, a jug-earned millionaire rancher from Midland with a penchant for saying the wrong thing at the wrong time. He opened the race with a politically incorrect joke about rape and ended it with an admission that he hadn't paid income taxes the previous year. Democrat Ann Richards, her political star rising fast, beat him easily in November, becoming only the second woman ever elected governor of Texas. But it was no Democrat sweep.

Rove's candidates for treasurer and agriculture commissioner, Kay Bailey Hutchison and Rick Perry, both won.

The Perry race was particularly noteworthy. The dark-haired, handsome son of a West Texas rancher, Perry had grown up a Democrat and served in the Legislature, but Rove convinced him to switch political parties and run for higher office.

"He got Lee Atwater to send me a note. You know, 'Come over, the water's fine,'" said Perry, now governor of Texas.

Rove decided Perry should run for agriculture commissioner. His opponent was the incumbent, Jim Hightower, a formidable figure in populist circles.

"I think Karl saw it as great sport that he was trying to beat Hightower with this young, three-term House member."

The contest had all the signature marks of an Atwater campaign, including the wedge issues of patriotism and race. Hightower said he saw no need to outlaw flag burning in the Constitution, so Rove recruited Senator Orrin Hatch of Utah, sponsor of a constitutional amendment against flag burning, to visit Texas on Perry's behalf. Hightower had supported the Rev. Jesse Jackson for president, so Rove flooded East Texas with mass mailings and a television commercial featuring Hightower and Jackson, their fists aloft in an image that seemed designed to coax a recollection of the Olympic black-power salute.

But the thing that truly caused Democrats to take note was the federal investigation. The last time the FBI got involved in a state political race was 1986, the bugging of the Clements' campaign office . . . *Rove's office.* This was beginning to look like a pattern to Democrats, first the bugging episode that stalled Mark White's campaign and now a federal investigation that could derail Hightower.

In both cases, Rove's clients were the beneficiaries.

A few weeks after word first appeared in the newspapers that a federal grand jury was investigating the agriculture department, Rove breezed into Perry headquarters and plopped down in a chair next to campaign manager Ken Luce. He outlined his plan for beating

Hightower in typical Rove fashion—an avalanche of words, statistics, constituencies, demographic groups. A careful time line, month-by-month, issue-by-issue. Deploy the Farm Bureau. Peel off some voters here in East Texas, some votes there in West Texas. Flag burning. Jesse Jackson. *Attack. Attack. Attack.*

Luce remembered sitting at the table, marveling at the sweep and detail of the plan and thinking, "You want Karl on your side. I don't ever want to be against Karl Rove, ever."

In a business where the politics of the day is paramount, Luce recalled that Rove was playing a very long game, planning not months, but years ahead. And as they sat there talking, Luce thought it odd that the candidate who most occupied Rove's thinking was not even a candidate at all, but George W. Bush, the new managing general partner of the Texas Rangers baseball team. Even then, in the spring of 1990, Rove had plans for George W. beyond the Governor's Mansion.

Luce remembered exactly what Rove said.

"If George wants to, George can be governor. George can be president."

"This is how it would work: If George were governor, he would have the state of Texas, a base. You have the electoral votes. You have the money. That's how you can launch a presidential bid."

And that's exactly what Rove and Bush intended to do.

9

Perchance to Dream

I have only a second rate brain. But I think I have a capacity for action.

Theodore Roosevelt

A covey of Senate sergeants arranged the walnut tables carefully in the center of the chamber, making a long rectangle, like a scaffold. The room had the brittle energy of a hanging. Karl Rove stood in the back of the chamber between paintings of the fall of the Alamo and the bloody victory at San Jacinto, looking across the floor sloping in the direction of the lieutenant governor's platform. In the high leather chairs where the state senators usually sat, there were lobbyists, reporters, and some members of the newly installed Ann Richards administration, drawn by the promise of a spectacle.

When the Texas Senate is not in session, its chamber is used for committee meetings, and on this day in March 1991 the Senate Nominations Committee met to consider the appointment of Karl Rove to the East Texas State University board of regents. Rove had been appointed by Governor Bill Clements before leaving office, but needed confirmation by the Democrat-controlled Senate. Traditionally, the committee approved the nominees of governors, even governors of the other party. But Rove had found his way onto the radar screen of Texas Democrats, who had questions. There was the bugging episode and the investigation of Hightower and the other election-year inquiries into Democrats that had the faint, acrid smell of political dirty tricks. At least, it looked that way to Democrats, so the chance to get Rove to sit down, under oath, was an opportunity to be taken.

"Mr. Rove," said Senator Bob Glasgow, "I have a few questions for you."

Glasgow was from Stephenville, dairy country. He had the thin look of a Calvinist, with a razor-straight jaw line and the glint of spectacles perched on the bridge of his nose. Glasgow was a lawyer, skilled in the art of questioning witnesses, so he led the assault on Rove.

"Mr. Rove, would you now tell us publicly who bugged your office that you blamed upon Mark White publicly and in the press statewide?"

"First of all," said Rove, "I did not blame it on Mark White. If you'll recall, I specifically said at the time that we disclosed the bugging that we did not know who did it, but we knew who might benefit from it. And no, I do not know."

They went back and forth, the senator and the conferee, their voices beginning to rise.

Glasgow asked about FBI agent Greg Rampton, Rove parsed his answer, and they began loudly talking over each other until the chairman picked up his gavel and pounded on the table for order.

"In campaigns that you've been involved in," Glasgow pressed on, "do you know why agent Rampton conducted a criminal investigation of Garry Mauro at a time you were involved in the campaign, pulled the finance records of Bob Bullock at the time you were involved in that campaign, pulled the campaign records of Jim Hightower at the time you were involved in that campaign?"

Rove professed his innocence, said he didn't know much about the first two campaigns, barely knew Rampton. As for the FBI investigation of Hightower, he said it was prompted by newspaper stories, not by him. But it was all really beside the point. This Senate was going to reject his appointment. He looked down the long length of the table at the serious faces, all Democrats but one. Behind him on the wall were the images of victory and defeat: the Alamo at dawn, where Texans had fallen to the forces of Santa Anna, and the battle at San Jacinto, where Texas won its independence. The two canvasses filled much of the wall around the chamber's ornate entrance. They were sweeping landscapes with dark swirls of smoke, broken warriors, and the tattered flags of battle. One was a portrayal of an army being attacked. Another was of the attackers being done in by their own assault.

"God, it was horrible," said David Weeks, a Republican consultant who watched from the gallery. "You could tell it bothered him because he really wanted to do it. He didn't get his degree, so he wanted this."

Glasgow quizzed Rove about education funding and the state budget.

"Senator, I'm a nominee for the board of East Texas State University, not for the comptroller or the Legislative Budget Board," Rove fired back.

Other senators jumped in, raising questions about his brief partnership in a dog-racing track, his lack of a college degree.

"I was told that you made the statement that you do not expect to be confirmed by the Texas Senate, but that you welcomed the opportunity to 'confront' this democratic body," said Senator Judith Zaffirini of Laredo.

Rove shook his head. "I did say that I don't think I've got a particularly good chance of getting confirmed in the Senate, but in that I'm simply following you, senator, and all your declarations that you've got 20 votes in your back pocket to bust me."

"I don't even have a back pocket, sir," said Zaffirini. "My pocket's up front."

The Senate did reject the appointment, as Rove predicted. And the memory of it stayed with him. Years later, long after his political success had taken him from Texas into the White House, Rove still remembered how his enemies had come after him.

"I was going to make them do it," Rove said in Austin one day after visiting the president at his ranch in Crawford. "It was unfair and it was political and they wanted a pound of flesh. But I didn't want to give up and step aside. Let them do it for their reasons and put it out on the record."

The university appointment was important to Rove, in no small part because he had never graduated from college himself. He had gone to college, lots of colleges: a couple of years at the University of Utah, 25 hours at George Mason in Virginia, some classes at the University of Maryland, the University of Houston, the University of Texas at Austin. When someone asked why he'd never finished, Rove said, "Couldn't afford it." But that wasn't the reason. The real reason was that he found himself forever pulled into the exhilaration of practical politics from College Republicans to the Republican National Committee to the roller coaster of political campaigns.

In his study at home, Rove had built a wall of bookshelves with a ladder to accommodate a prodigious library. When Max Sherman, dean of the Lyndon B. Johnson (LBJ) School of Public Affairs in Austin asked Rove to teach a graduate class in American politics and political campaigns, he jumped at the chance. Rove was forever compensating for his lack of a formal degree, and teaching college students offered a kind of compensation. If others had graduate degrees and professional experience in education or criminal justice, Rove devoured books on his off-time with a manic passion that allowed him to debate on equal terms with the experts, first in Austin and later at the White House. There simply was no time to get a degree, much less earn a string of graduate degrees that were the solid-gold credentials of public policy. But he could learn on his own terms and he could teach.

So he snapped at the offer to teach at the LBJ school. And after Paul Begala was called back to Washington to help the beleaguered Clinton White House, Rove took his place teaching an undergraduate class on politics and press at the University of Texas. His teaching partner, *Austin American-Statesman* political columnist Dave McNeely, remembered Rove arriving from campaign flights and sitting down with a pile of memos, polling results, phone callback messages. Head down, writing, Rove seemed absorbed in his paperwork as students expounded on the historic lessons of the 1800 presidential race or McKinley's use of the mail in 1898.

"That's 1896." Rove's head was suddenly up; he'd been following every word. "There were 14 pieces of mail and publications for every voter who voted in the 1896 election—a Croatian-American list, the first mass-produced political publication in Yiddish. It was a pretty amazing campaign underneath the surface . . ."

And Rove was off and running, connecting the threads of past scholarship with the details of this week's campaign, drowning the class in statistical data, painting the big picture. When asked in a lawsuit how it was that he could teach college without a degree, Rove said, "I'm very good at what I do." Without a doubt, he did value education and his appointment to the board of regents of a state university really meant something—and his rejection was an injury he likely would not forget.

George W. Bush went to all the best schools, Phillips Academy, Yale, Harvard Business School. His style—the Bush style—was not to master a broad range of subjects, but instead to confront issues as needed. If he needed to know something, he would learn it. Friends knew that he was smart, but no intellectual. He was, in fact, rigorously anti-intellectual, deeply suspicious of gratuitous intellectualism, which opponents sometimes misread as a lack of intelligence.

"He'd always wait until the last minute to write his paper," said college roommate Clay Johnson. "But he held his own academically both at Andover and Yale."

His college transcripts from Yale—published in the *New Yorker* during the presidential campaign—revealed that he never earned an A as an undergraduate, but never flunked a course, either. His grades most often reflected a "gentleman's C." He scored a 73 in Introduction to the American Political System, a 71 in Introduction to International Relations. In Spanish, which was to serve him well in his bid to touch every willing voter, he averaged 77.

"I wasn't exactly an Ivy League scholar," Bush told a reporter for *Texas Monthly.* "What I was good at was getting to know people."

Few jobs offered a better avenue for getting to know people—and getting people to know you—than managing general partner of the Texas Rangers baseball team. After his father won the White House in 1988, Bush moved his family back to Dallas, where a friend tipped him the team was for sale. Using family influence and affiliations, Bush helped organize the purchase of the Rangers, sold his Harken Energy stock to buy a piece of the deal, and emerged the team's most visible figure. He had a seat in the stands with the fans where he sat with his boots up on the railing, greeting kids, and signing autographs.

He'd always loved baseball. He was a catcher in West Texas Little League and a junk pitcher in prep school and in his freshman year at Yale. In the attic of his Dallas home, he had a collection of autographs and boxes of baseball cards. His first day on the job with the Rangers, Bush ordered copies of all 26 major league media guides, as well as the *Baseball Register,* which carries the statistics of every major league player. If he did not know the date of the battle of Hastings, what the hell—he could identify the entire lineup of the 1959 New York Yankees, complete with jersey number and batting average.

The business of baseball was good. He and his partners decided to build a new stadium, which enhanced the value of the team.

Having a father as president, he told a reporter, has "dovetailed very nicely for me with selling tickets." But from his eleventh floor office, Bush saw something that disturbed him.

Just below, among the cluster of storefronts and office buildings, Ross Perot had opened his headquarters to run for president. Looking down, Bush saw a growing hive of activity. Cars filled the parking lot—new Cadillacs, Porsches, Mercedes-Benzes.

"These were our guys," Bush said, alarmed.

He repeatedly called Washington to warn that something was happening, that the Perot challenge to his father's re-election was real. But he said the campaign team didn't take Perot's third-party challenge seriously, not until it was too late.

"The irony is that his father's defeat in 1992 opens the door for 43 [younger Bush]," said Rove, as if it were an equation.

Rove had encouraged Bush to run for governor in 1990, but to no avail. He had squired George W. around Austin, meeting privately with Republicans who had money and ideas. Rove had visited the eleventh floor office in Dallas, where the two of them talked politics and Rove laid out his assessment of the changing political landscape of Texas. But there were too many obstacles: concerns at the White House, the new job with the Rangers. Bush himself had doubts about whether he had the portfolio to make the race.

Roland Betts, a friend from Yale and partner in the Rangers deal, told a *Houston Chronicle* reporter that Bush made it clear one day the time just wasn't right.

"You know," Betts recalls Bush saying, "I could run for governor and all this but I'm basically a media creation. I've never really done anything. I've worked for my dad. I worked in the oil industry. But that's not the kind of profile you have to have to get elected to public office."

The Rangers job changed all that. He had successfully guided the team, raised his public profile, and helped direct construction of the Rangers' new stadium, the Ballpark at Arlington. His father's defeat, as Rove said, now opened the door for George W. to enter the 1994 race for governor.

First thing, Bush had to learn about Texas government. He was well grounded in the gilded assumptions of country club Republicanism: taxes are bad, free enterprise is good, government that governs least, governs best. He was an attractive candidate, with his father's handsome features, piercing blue eyes, a thin, athletic build, and a bright smile. He had a shrewd instinct for politics, which wasn't surprising for someone who had been steeped in political life as the son of a president and grandson of a U.S. senator. Moreover, he was a quick study—something Rove understood when many others did not—the kind of student who preferred all-night cram sessions to deep preparation.

Bush knew almost nothing, however, about state government. The machinery of Texas government was huge and sprawling, like the state itself. It regulated oil and eggs and the number of grade school students permitted in a classroom. Texas government oversaw fisheries on the Gulf Coast and seed corn programs in the Panhandle, administered the largest prison system in the free world, and limited how much sales tax big cities like Dallas and Houston could charge to operate mass transit. The state budget was $70 billion and growing, and the biggest portion went to public education. Much of state government was invisible to the average Texan, but voters knew their public schools and cared a great deal about education. They cared about crime, too. Those were two major issues in any governor's race, crime and education, and a key to beating Governor Ann Richards, was to prove she had done a bad job on both. To do that, Bush had to understand both issues as well as Richards did.

In early 1993, a few months after the elder Bush's loss, Rove called an Austin lobbyist named Mike Toomey and asked if he would go to Dallas and begin briefing Bush on state government and the budget. Toomey was the perfect pick for the role of tutor. He was knowledgeable and discreet, a former Republican member of the Texas House who had earned the nickname "Mike the Knife" for his conservative pursuit of budget cuts. Toomey was cowboy thin, with dark hair and dark eyes and a serious expression. There was no campaign at this point, only Rove and Toomey and a bundle of papers in a briefcase that Toomey carried as he flew to Dallas to meet Bush at the Texas Rangers' office along the expressway.

"I remember standing up there with charts on the budget," said Toomey. "It was early 1993. No one else was hired. This guy was just starting to call for money and it was the very beginning. Then they asked me, as the campaign was heating up, to put the policy together. Karl didn't know who was the expert on criminal justice, tort, whatever. No one knows about me, but I'm contacting the experts in state government on public education and everything, putting together these teams."

Bush was reluctant at first. Toomey recalled watching Bush, bored as a schoolboy, as he discussed the intricacies of the state's $70 billion budget. But as Bush began absorbing details, he warmed to the task.

"He was a very ambitious guy," Toomey thought.

When Bush flirted briefly with the idea of running for governor in 1990, he and Rove had made the rounds of a few experts to discuss state government. They had visited Austin lawyer Harry Whittington, a former member of the state prison board, to talk about crime. Rove arranged meetings with some judges about the increasing number of juveniles committing serious crimes, a policy issue that particularly interested Bush. But it was not until early 1993 that Rove formalized Bush's education with the tutorials.

The tutoring sessions lasted for months. Teams flew to Dallas, and met with Bush in a small conference room, where they delivered a crash course on Texas civics. Bill Ratliff, a Republican state senator from East Texas and expert on school finance, flew up on two separate occasions for daylong sessions with Bush.

"He didn't know much," said Ratliff, who was chairman of the Senate Education Committee. "He knew that public schools were hidebound in too many regulations and needed to go to a more market-based approach. He didn't take notes that I remember. It was me very much trying to pour out all this stream of everything I knew about public education and he was trying to absorb it."

At one meeting on welfare and the state's network of social services programs, Bush had trouble distinguishing between Medicaid, the federal government's medical program for the poor, and Medicare.

"Now, I hear these two. They're different. What's the difference between the two?" Bush asked, according to an aide.

Business issues came easier to him. At Harvard Business School, Bush had negotiated a rigorous course of learning that emphasized case studies, not so much business theory as the workings of real companies and their problems in meeting production, paying taxes, and dealing with government regulations. Every week, he wrote a 1,500-word paper and every night he was up past midnight—except on weekends when he put on his leather bomber jacket and headed with a couple of buddies to the Hillbilly Ranch nightclub in Boston for an evening of cold beers and country music.

Classmates remember Bush as serious, and scrupulously apolitical. If Bush felt alienated from the campus' intellectual elitism with its revolving series of protests in the Harvard Yard, the environment inside the business school was more to his liking. The curriculum was about business, about entrepreneurship. The MBA program was designed to prepare a generation of business leaders, future CEOs, not only with its challenging course load but also through its growing network of contacts and associations that inevitably proved valuable in the future.

At Harvard, Bush roomed with Ron Spogli, who went on to become a partner in a spectacularly successful investment firm in Los Angeles, Freeman Spogli & Co. Through Spogli, Bush met Brad Freeman, a convivial North Dakota transplant in the heart of Hollywood. In Bush's race for governor and later in his bid for president, Freeman and Spogli were to become his financial anchors among West Coast business types in raising campaign cash.

Bush knew business, the oil business, the marketing of the Texas Rangers baseball team. He didn't have to be told that the state's franchise tax treated partnerships differently than corporations. He had a business-friendly aversion to government regulation and was instinctively suspicious of the claims of environmentalists. When his friend Ralph Wayne dispatched a team of three people from Austin to brief him on the effort to protect business from the growing number of injury lawsuits, they found in Bush a natural ally. Bush called Wayne to reassure him that he was preaching to the converted, although he couldn't resist a good-natured jibe over the makeup of the team. It included a lobbyist with close ties to Democrats, a top aide to the last Democratic governor, and the son of a former advisor to Lyndon Johnson.

"You sent me three Democrats to brief me on tort reform," Bush said. "If I run, you do know I'm going to run as a Republican?"

It wouldn't have bothered Rove that they were Democrats, because they weren't really Democrats at all—not in a way that would hamper Bush's chances. Texas had long ago divided itself into two parties, the conservative Democrats and the liberal Democrats. Business sided with the former to advance its agenda. Railroads, cattle, then oil and energy and construction—the business lobby in Texas had long cultivated conservative Democrats in positions of power. With the emergence of the Republican party, business began gravitating to the GOP. For the first time since the Civil War, they needed to build ties with politicians who called themselves Republican.

Philip Morris and other companies began paying Karl Rove to give them advice on how the political scene was changing and his counsel typically was to support his candidates, who would be more likely to advance their agenda. One thing that business had in common was the desire to limit the size of jury awards in accident and injury cases. A faulty tire blows out or a lawn mower explodes or somebody is scalded with hot coffee and the resulting jury award could put a crimp in profits or drive a company out of business.

Under the typical contingency fee arrangement in accident and injury cases, the lawyers took a third of a jury's award as compensation. Over time, that created a fairly wealthy class of attorneys with a stake in assuring that politicians and the courts did not curb their lawsuits and limit their fees. On the other side was business, especially tobacco and construction companies, which sought ways to limit the awards.

The politics was simple enough: Since trial lawyers supported Democrats, business should support Republicans. Rove's work in the late 1980s helping to elect Republican judges to the Texas Supreme Court, starting with Tom Phillips, was only the beginning. Now, Rove worked fiendishly to steer business money to candidates—his candidates—all the way up the ballot. Trial lawyers were among the biggest source of campaign contributions to Democrats, including Ann Richards. Rove's task was to systematically direct business contributions to Republicans, especially George W. Bush.

One day in the office of the Texas Association of Business, a group of influential business executives gathered for a private meeting to talk about prospects of a race between Governor Ann Richards and George W. Bush. By almost any measure, Richards seemed unassailable. She was smart and funny, one of the most popular governors in Texas history. She had remade the boards and commissions that govern state agencies by appointing a record number of women and minorities. She had emerged as a national celebrity, the wisecracking governor who derided George W.'s father from the stage of the Democratic National Convention and thereby earned the enmity of the Bush family, especially George W., who relished the prospect of unseating Richards. The conventional wisdom was that beating the governor would be hard, maybe even impossible.

Not so, said Ralph Wayne, looking around the table at his colleagues. Wayne represented a confederation of tort-reform business interests called the Civil Justice League.

"Governor Richards can't win," he said. He explained that while Richards would have the backing of minority voters and organized labor, business would line up behind Bush. Wayne's assessment quickly reached the Richards camp. Not long afterwards, Richards had an announcement: She was establishing the Governor's Business Council, made up of some of the biggest corporate names in Texas and headed by Ken Lay, chief operating officer of Enron.

Wayne called Rove to apologize, saying his remarks likely prompted the governor to act. Rove wasn't upset at all.

"Naah. She's not going to get any votes there."

What Rove knew, and Richards did not, was that Ken Lay and most of his business colleagues were firmly in the Bush camp. Rove knew Lay through the father. Ken Lay had been one of the elder Bush's biggest campaign contributors, co-host of the 1992 Republican National Convention in Houston, a long-time family friend. His was a name that bubbled to the top in every Rove campaign money list. Rove knew that Lay and Enron would have to give some money to Richards as the incumbent, but that their true interest was with Bush.

He was right. In the final accounting, state records show that Lay and Enron executives gave $146,500 to Bush, nearly seven times more than they did to Richards. Enron's political action committee and executives went on to become the largest donors to Bush's re-election and to his presidential campaign. And the rest of business would do the same. Bush was simply the better candidate for business interests, and Rove knew that whatever support Richards attracted as the incumbent, the blue-chip donors whose names festooned his computer lists would see in Bush a very good thing.

Eventually, the tutorials ended and Rove created formal policy teams, which began meeting at campaign headquarters in Austin: one on education, headed by school-administration lobbyist Margaret LaMontagne; one on welfare with Christian-magazine editor Marvin Olasky, an eventual architect of "compassionate conservatism"; a team on business issues; a group on crime.

By the time Bush announced his candidacy for governor in late 1993, the policy teams were meeting regularly at campaign head-quarters in Austin, culling the best ideas, and advancing them as possible campaign issues. Rove recruited a bright young lawyer named Vance McMahon, as policy director. Veteran Oklahoma politico Joe Allbaugh came on board as campaign manager.

"We put ideas together and Karl put the political spin on it," Toomey said.

Karen Hughes, the third member of what was to become the "Iron Triangle" of Bush advisors, was still with the Texas Republican party, where she had spent three years aggressively attacking almost every policy, appointment, and peccadillo of the Ann Richards ad-ministration with advice and ammunition from Rove.

"The sense was that she was popular but had no real great achievements," Rove said, recalling the Bush campaign years later. "The state faced a problem of leadership in that the people wanted somebody to do something, whether it was education, which was the No. 1 issue, or whether it was crime, particularly where we faced this generation of juvenile criminals."

Welfare reform as an issue, the idea of nudging welfare recipi-ents toward work but in a program that had a softer, more compas-sionate look, was something that Bush wanted. Tort reform didn't have the same public appeal as education or crime, but it was an issue most important to Rove's business clients and potential contributors.

In short order, they had an agenda: improve education, get tough on crime, reform welfare, and limit lawsuits against business. Moreover, they had a detailed battle plan, which an aide recalled that Rove developed "like an artist in a burst of creativity."

"He would go into his office at 8 in the morning, shut the door, get on his Apple computer and work for 12 hours straight, then go get something to eat and come back. And it was like Karl would just download the plan into his head, tracking the whole campaign: In February, this is what you're going to do and where you're going to go, what you're going to say, the groups that are going to endorse you. Here's what you're going to do to the other guy.

"It was all laid out from January to October: Go back to East Texas eight times during this time period—not seven times, not 10 times—eight times. Karl is a big, big believer in having a scripted plan."

Toomey was struck by the effectiveness of their collaboration.

"My first impression was that Bush had very good political judgment. For a businessman jumping into the race, he obviously had learned something from his background. What he didn't know, what percentage of the budget went for education, he picked up."

Rove was a kind of organizing principle, Toomey thought, directing Bush's considerable potential and charmed life to a higher level. He was creating in Bush a candidate of immense potential.

"Some people think they're going to do great things, but they're crazy. Some people think they are destined to do great things and they know it," said Toomey. "Bush knew it. I think he knew he could win this race and he'd be a great governor and would kick butt. If he knows he's not bright—grades and all—he has to know that he was good looking and had excellent judgment and knew the contacts. And whether Karl snowed him or not, he was confident."

At campaign headquarters one day, Toomey noticed a set of books lining the wall. There was a large dictionary and a dense collection of volumes that Rove had given Bush over time. Myron Magnet's *The Dream and the Nightmare,* Marvin Olasky's *The Tragedy of American Compassion,* Gertrude Himmelfarb's *The Demoralization of Society,* James Q. Wilson's *The Moral Sense* and *On Character.*

Bush had always bristled at the pretensions of intellectualism. In 1988, he told author Doug Wead that he had always read more for entertainment than knowledge.

"I was never a great intellectual. I like books and pick them up and read them for the fun of it."

Rove was the reader; he was forever carrying around a heavy volume on history or political theory. Once, when a friend invited

Rove to join him at a National Football League playoff game between the Dallas Cowboys and the San Francisco 49ers, Rove brought along a book about the Civil War, which he read between plays, during time outs and at half time.

Rove brought intellectual ballast to the collaboration, but was sensitive to the perception that Bush wasn't smart and he worked hard to promote his boss' image. Six months before Bush formally launched his campaign for the presidency, a story appeared in the *National Review* about Bush and his prodigious reading habits. The source of the article was Rove.

"In addition to Magnet's book," the article said, "Bush has read and admired Wilson's *The Moral Sense* and *On Character*, Himmelfarb's *The Demoralization of Society*, and Olasky's *The Tragedy of American Compassion*."

This was Karl Rove's reading list. Not Bush's.

Not only that, according to the magazine, Bush had recently read Paul Johnson's mammoth *History of the American People* and that he "with Rove kept a running list of Johnson's minor mistakes."

The tutorials were the beginning of Rove's efforts to assure that Bush appeared knowledgeable and in command of the issues as a fledgling candidate for governor. The article was part of the campaign to promote Bush's intellect as a nominee for president. During the 2000 race, Bush himself would carry a book through the cabin of the campaign plane, a thick volume about the Civil War or a biography of Winston Churchill. Bush was always a willing student, but in the beginning as Bush launched his first campaign for governor, Rove knew it would take more than a few months of grooming and preparation to ready him for the press.

In November 1993, Bush took his fledgling gubernatorial campaign to San Antonio, where he addressed a small group of school administrators. He delivered the message he and his policy team had developed: the state's education system under Ann Richards had suffered, teachers had too much paperwork and Texas' method of funding public schools needed to be changed.

After his speech, Bush wandered out into the richly ornate courtyard of the Menger Hotel adjacent to the Alamo. He moved with a kind of breezy confidence, smiling, shaking hands, and introducing himself to people getting their first look at the man who had chosen to challenge the vaunted Ann Richards.

A reporter from Austin approached and asked about his education plan. Bush resurrected some sentences from his speech, asserting that education was his top priority. When the reporter asked him a question about the workings of the state's education agency, apparently not in his briefing book, Bush stood for a moment, blinking.

He did not know the answer.

Exactly how would his plan change the school-finance formula? He didn't know.

How much would it cost?

Again, he demurred.

"Will voters know how much money would be involved before election?"

Bush shifted from foot to foot, his brain swimming.

"Probably not."

It was not an auspicious start. An early news conference with the Austin Capitol press corps proved nearly as bad with Bush stumbling over some of his answers.

"He was shaky and you guys sensed it," a Bush associate recalled. "Everything is confidence. And Bush is really transparent. He does not play act; he's a real direct guy who wears his emotions on his sleeve."

Heading for the campaign plane, Bush looked deflated. An aide offered some advice.

"Look, you are the son of a president. You've got an MBA from Harvard. You want to be governor. You can stand in front of these Capitol reporters for 20 minutes and take their questions, because if you can't, what are we doing?"

At campaign headquarters, Rove mapped a travel schedule that gave Bush more seasoning on the small-town Rotary circuit. For several months, Bush traveled to little communities where he introduced himself to business and community groups, did radio interviews and learned to answer questions largely outside the glare of the media in Austin, Dallas, and Houston. His campaign travels took him to a mobile home lot in Navasota, Sadler's Bar-B-Que Sales in Henderson, the leather company in Yoakum, the wire works in Shiner. He shook hands at a community reception in the Hawkeye Hunting Club near Center; he walked down the main street of Stamford in the Cowboy Reunion Parade.

It was a brilliant piece of political engineering. By summer, Bush was a better candidate, well-prepared and well-positioned to face Ann Richards in the fall. The race for governor was to be the showroom where Karl Rove displayed his product; the man he was grooming to be the next president of the United States.

10

Gain with Pain

It isn't important who is ahead at one time or another in either
an election or horse race. It's the horse that comes in first at the
finish line that counts."

Harry Truman

The landscape of West Texas lies as flat as a billiard table,
unadorned but for a tangle of desert scrub and the bob-
bing heads of tireless pump jacks pulling oil from the
ground. Oil has been the business of Midland since 1923,
when a rig called Santa Rita #1 hit the first big strike 60 miles
southeast of town in what is known as the Permian Basin. Midland
had been a farm town before that, just a brief stopping point along
the Texas & Pacific Railway that crossed the unceasing distances
of the American West. When the Santa Rita blew, everything
changed. As it turned out, Midland and its sister city Odessa were
on top of the largest concentration of oil ever found in the continental United States.

Oil made millionaires of a whole group of rugged West Texas
gamblers, including John Cox, who had made a fortune and lost a

fortune and made it back again in the roller-coaster economies of black gold. He was one of the Midland Eight. When *Forbes* magazine ran its first list of the wealthiest people in America in 1982, eight were from Midland, with its modest population of 80,000, and Cox was one of them.

In early December 1990, Ann Richards traveled to Midland to see John Cox, and she brought with her Lena Guerrero. The day before, Richards had named Guerrero to the Texas Railroad Commission, the first major appointment of her new administration. Guerrero was a 33-year-old state representative from Austin, dark-haired, attractive, and politically shrewd. She represented everything Ann Richards wanted to say about opening the doors of opportunity—a young Hispanic woman, a former migrant farm worker in the Rio Grande Valley, a rising political star in a New Texas where "men and woman, and white, black and brown alike are going to be in positions of power and responsibility in this state."

"I want the appointment of Lena to send a message to the people of Texas," Richards told the crowd in the Senate chamber.

The Texas Railroad Commission regulates oil and gas production, and Guerrero seemed an unlikely choice for the job. She had no experience in the energy business. She was an unabashed political liberal whose district included Austin's barrio and modest working-class neighborhoods on the city's East Side. On announcement day, Guerrero said she hoped to use the post to improve environmental protection and to strengthen the state's ties with Mexico.

The next morning, Richards and Guerrero flew to Midland to see John Cox, who had read about the appointment in the local newspaper. Cox was 65, a plainspoken petroleum engineer with a lifetime of experience drilling dry holes and gushers in the fickle moonscape of the Permian Basin. The first thing that struck him was how young Guerrero was and how inexperienced. And that she was a woman. Guerrero was the first female member of the Texas Railroad Commission in its 100 years of existence.

He looked at the front page of the Midland paper, then at the young Hispanic woman with jet-black hair, standing before him in a neat business suit.

"Forget about environmental issues and trying to get jobs in Mexico. Your job is going to be railroad commissioner."

Guerrero nodded. "Give me a chance," she said, "and take me to an oil field."

The appointment of Guerrero was more than a message. It was a very public act that signaled Ann Richards' successor on the political stage in Texas, the next political superstar, and a 1000-watt candidate of the future. She *was* the future—a future governor, a future U.S. senator. Even a future president. That's how sky high the expectations were for Lena Guerrero among Democrats in Texas. She was smart and articulate and she was funny—like Ann Richards was funny. Two weeks into her job, she spoke at a luncheon for about 80 men in the trucking industry and during the question-and-answer period, someone asked, "What is your bra size?"

There was hurried apology by someone else, but Guerrero shrugged and instantly won the room over.

"Someone finally asked a question I know something about."

Governor Richards landed Guerrero a nationally televised speaking spot during the 1992 Democratic National Convention. She spoke Tuesday night, dubbed "girls night" because a half-dozen women were on the agenda that evening opposite the All-Star baseball game on national television. Guerrero opened her speech by giving the score.

Lena Guerrero was the next big thing in Texas, a young, bright, Ann Richards-in-waiting. Even the Texas governor agreed.

"I have very high hopes for her future."

Because her appointment was to an unexpired term, Guerrero had to stand for election in 1992. She was the prohibitive favorite. Although Republicans had begun to win a few offices, the state remained largely Democrat. Guerrero was the incumbent and she had the exuberant backing of Ann Richards, a national celebrity whose popularity back home was among the highest ever for a governor in the state's long-standing survey, the Texas Poll.

Karl Rove, and almost Rove alone, was confident that Richards could be beaten in 1994 and that George W. Bush was the candidate to do it. But in developing a plan to make Bush governor, his actions demonstrated a belief that he needed to go beyond simply unseating Richards after one term. He would have to stop future Democratic stars. And more—he would take great pains to discredit, eliminate, and damage those associated with Richards.

The evidence of subsequent events makes it clear that Rove took steps to eliminate the Richards network of political friends and allies, undercutting their performance in state jobs and damaging their careers in the private sector. Every vestige of Richards had to be eliminated and every shining prospect of the party's future destroyed if Bush was to become governor and the Republican party was to triumph.

First, he had to stop Lena Guerrero.

Rove's client in the race against Guerrero was Barry Williamson, an affable energy lawyer from Midland with soft features and a tousle of brown hair who had served in Energy Department posts in the Reagan and Bush administrations. Nobody had ever heard of Barry Williamson, at least nobody outside a small circle of oil industry types and members of the Bush family. Williamson's father-in-law was a millionaire oilman and had been chief fund-raiser for the elder Bush, which offered certain credibility in Republican circles and assured a ready source of campaign money. Williamson, however, had none of Guerrero's political sparkle.

In July, Rove produced a mass mailing for voters that described Guerrero as soft on crime, pro-gay rights, antigun, and an enemy of traditional family values. But as Election Day approached, Guerrero was still leading in the polls and, with Richards' help, was raising more in campaign contributions than her Republican opponent.

"We needed to do something to cut off her money," Rove later told a reporter.

One piece of information in Rove's possession just might do the trick. From a fellow Republican with ties to the University of Texas, Rove learned that although Guerrero claimed on her campaign resume to be a graduate of the University of Texas, school records indicated she had never graduated. Rove picked up the phone and called a newspaper reporter with the information.

Even Rove hadn't anticipated how badly she would botch the response.

Guerrero initially denied it, but a day later issued a statement acknowledging that she had only recently learned that she was four hours short of a college degree. The story hit Saturday's newspapers. Guerrero's campaign hurriedly called a news conference for Sunday.

On Sunday morning, the day of the news conference, plans went ahead as scheduled to film a campaign commercial originally designed to burnish Guerrero's star status. A few miles outside Austin, Mark McKinnon, the campaign's media consultant, sat on top of boom crane filming long, sweeping shots of Guerrero walking through a mock oil field.

"Lena had $2 million in the bank so we're going to run this unbelievable bioepic—the poor, humble girl who is now running Texas," said Chuck McDonald, the communications chief. "McKinnon's got this crane. Lena's walking; she's got on a dress, the wind blowing. Then we go to the Governor's Mansion for shots on the porch and patio. We're just out there shooting this while the world's falling apart."

The press turned out in force for the news conference that afternoon at the downtown Marriott. Television crews erected a battery of cameras pointed, like guns, at Guerrero, her husband, her 4-year-old son, and her mother. She told reporters that she mistakenly thought she had graduated from college and that she had never noticed that her news releases over the years erroneously claimed she was a member of Phi Beta Kappa.

"Nobody's going to believe this story," McDonald told Ann Richards.

And nobody did, certainly not Rove, who began circulating every press release Guerrero had ever issued, every biography, as if to cast doubt on everything she had ever said. He urged reporters to demand her college transcripts, which she released out of fear that Rove would somehow get them anyway—and that spawned a new round of stories because Guerrero actually was far more than four hours short of graduation. Every new revelation produced a new story. Every story reinforced the theme that Rove advanced like a drum beat with reporters—Lena Guerrero can't be trusted to tell the truth.

Shortly after the initial story broke, Republican Barry Williamson was on a campaign swing in East Texas. He dropped by a small diner in Navasota and moved from table to table, shaking hands and introducing himself as a candidate for the Railroad Commission and asking people for their vote. A man looked up from his chicken fried steak.

"I have one question for you," he said. "Did you graduate from college?"

Williamson smiled. "I knew we had won. If that man in that town had figured this out, I knew this race was ours."

The swooping aerial shots of Guerrero never aired. A vanity photo of the candidate sitting smartly on an oil well valve did make the cover of *Texas Monthly* magazine just before the election, but with a screaming two-word headline: "Lena's Lies." Guerrero lost in a landslide by 845,000 votes.

"I think that was the beginning of the end for Ann Richards when they blew up Lena Guerrero," McDonald said.

The effort to damage two political confidants of Ann Richards was something else entirely. Jane Hickie directed the state's office in Washington; assisting the Texas congressional delegation and representing the interests of state officials back home. Cathy Bonner headed the Texas Department of Commerce for three years before returning to her public relations business. Both were long-time Richards' friends, instrumental in her election in 1990, and both returned to help direct the re-election. The assault on Guerrero was on the party's future. The attack on them was an attack on the party's present star, Ann Richards; even before her re-election campaign was fully underway.

Hickie was scrupulous in her operations of the Office of State-Federal Relations in Washington. She kept detailed records, a strict schedule, and she always made certain to clear everything with both Democrats and Republicans in the state's congressional delegation. If Republican Representative Dick Armey didn't want something included on the state office's agenda of things to do, it was scratched. If Republican Senator Kay Bailey Hutchison wanted something added to the list, it was added. Hickie worked to make the office as nonpartisan as possible, even retaining some young Republicans on staff from the previous administration. Her predecessor in Washington was a gifted political operator whose convivial style led to lavish entertainment of lawmakers and lobbyists well into the night with alcohol and good cigars. Hickie's approach was decidedly more businesslike.

Rove still had Bush on the small-town circuit when stories began appearing in the *Houston Post* questioning the finances of the state's Washington office. First there were stories about expenditures at the state office, then about whether political fund-raising was happening on state time. Some phone records back in Austin had been destroyed, prompting a new round of stories. Outraged over the "ethical lapses," the Bush for Governor campaign issued a statement recalling the Guerrero debacle and then denouncing Hickie and operations of the state's office in Washington.

"First, there was political work being done in that government office. Then, public documents were destroyed to cover it up. Now, we have evidence of further misuse of taxpayer dollars by Ms. Hickie."

At the State-Federal office in Washington, Hickie gathered telephone records, press releases, and receipts, and called a news conference. She showed that the office finances had actually saved the state money and that there was no political fund-raising in the office. In the end, the flurry of news stories had led to little evidence of wrongdoing, but the damage had been done. Questions had been raised publicly about a Richards operative in Washington mixing government and politics.

The issue of doing political business on state time was fresh in Rove's mind. A year earlier, Rove had defended one of his own clients against exactly the same charge. Kay Bailey Hutchison, newly elected to the U.S. Senate, was indicted by a Travis County grand jury in September 1993 on charges she misused her office as state treasurer. Specifically, prosecutors said workers on her payroll made campaign fund-raising calls on state time and used a state computer to keep track of contributions.

Republicans launched an assault on District Attorney Ronnie Earle's credibility, orchestrated by Rove. As Hutchison rode in the back of a van to the courthouse where the grand jury was meeting, Rove was on the cell phone reassuring her.

"He was constantly with the candidate and had people around her stay on the attack—either an attack on Ronnie Earle or a total denial of the charges," said an associate.

Attorneys for Hutchison were desperate to advance the idea that the district attorney was a publicity-hungry politico looking to higher office. Their best evidence was their insistence that reporters had been tipped in advance—assuring maximum publicity—of a raid on Hutchison's treasury office to rescue records. It was not true, but Rove took the stand in court and said it was.

"Do you have information about whether reporters were notified in advance about the June 10th Treasury raid?" defense lawyer Dick Deguerin asked Rove at a pretrial hearing.

"Yes."

Rove testified that he got a call from the *Dallas Morning News*. It was not true. In fact, The *News* did not get advance word, but learned about the raid from one of Hutchison's employees after it was well underway. Rove testified that an Austin newspaper reporter, David Elliott, had been tipped in advance.

Not true, Elliott said years later. Elliott, like other reporters, got word of the raid long after it had begun.

"I specifically remember them telling me that the treasurer's office was being raided. It was not anything like advance knowledge. That, I'm absolutely certain."

Rove's testimony, however, reinforced the thesis: the district attorney was a publicity-hungry politico. The case never went to trial. The judge dismissed evidence important to prosecutors, the district attorney dropped the case, and Hutchison took her place in the U.S. Senate.

"They mounted a political defense," said Earle. "they wanted to portray the entire effort as a political prosecution. They played that defense both in the courtroom and outside. Their courtroom tactics and their public relations tactics were the same."

In a political endnote, the state Republican party issued a news release saying the district attorney's time would better be spent investigating Ann Richards. Whatever else Rove was doing, he never lost sight of his primary goal: putting George W. Bush in office. Richards was the obstacle; Richards was the enemy. The news release came two months before Bush formally announced his candidacy and was written by Karen Hughes, who eventually was to join Rove on the Bush political team.

Like Jane Hickie, Cathy Bonner found herself the subject of unfavorable publicity generated by Rove as part of the campaign against Ann Richards. Bonner resigned from the Texas Department of Commerce and returned to private business in order to join the Richards' 1994 re-election effort. Rove targeted her for years. His political investigators sought out information about her business, which Rove tried to get reporters to write. When her old firm got a state contract from the Texas Education Agency, stories questioning the deal popped up in Texas newspapers. Even after George W. Bush became governor and Bonner was no longer a political threat, Rove continued an unrelenting campaign against her in calls to reporters complaining about her business dealings.

"The fact that he comes after you and tries to ruin you professionally is kind of bizarre," said Bonner.

One political nemesis frequently on Rove's radar was George Shipley, a Democratic consultant who had represented Richards in her campaigns. Shipley's business clients included the Texas Medical Association. Rove called an influential member of the group's board of directors, convincing him to drop Shipley as an advisor to the group's political action committee. Fearing that Rove might damage health-care legislation it supported, the association moved Shipley to its regular payroll to advise on professional issues, but not political matters.

"They got what they wanted," said medical association lobbyist Kim Ross. "It was in Karl's nature to engulf and devour and control and to rule."

Rove did not limit his aim exclusively to Democrats. He targeted Republicans as well, those who might challenge him professionally. Democrats were political opponents; Republicans could be professional rivals. There's a political cliché that each side wants a level playing field. In Rove's case, it appeared as if he wanted to level everything on the playing field.

Bill Miller, a veteran consultant who represented business and political clients, said Rove is one of the most compelling and accomplished allies—and enemies—he's ever met. Miller teamed with Rove in a Texas Senate race in the early 1990s. Miller handled the phone banks and Rove was directing the mass mail operation. The candidate called one day and wanted a status report.

"I do my deal, pretty straight forward," said Miller, who then watched in awe as Rove offered a presentation so elaborate and thorough he was mesmerized.

"Karl had the entire history of the campaign, the history of the earth from day one. It is a huge, wonderful presentation—way beyond the scope of what was asked for, but it's a tour de force. And I sat there and thought, if there ever was a doubt, if there ever was a question about who really is always going to get the upper hand in everything, he won the game today."

Years later, Miller found himself in Rove's cross hairs in a legislative fight. Miller had done nothing but grow and prosper, adding business clients that did not always support everything on the Bush agenda. One day, some of Miller's business clients were summoned to Rove's private office on Shoal Creek. When they arrived, they found not only Rove but also Bush's chief of staff, Joe Allbaugh. Allbaugh's presence left no doubt that anything they had hoped to accomplish in the legislature that session was in jeopardy.

"Karl proceeds to tell them how much Bush doesn't like me," Miller said.

"He's telling them, you couldn't have hired a worse guy; he's not going to help your deal."

The clients kept Miller. But the episode underscored Rove's deep suspicion of any Republican competitor.

"You can't challenge him. If you challenge him, you're going to lose," said David Weeks, a Republican media consultant and frequent Rove partner on political campaigns.

"When I first hooked up with Karl, I did direct mail. But I gave it all up, every bit of it, because he did direct mail. Karl was comfortable with me because I never challenged him as being the king. I gladly gave him credit for being the general consultant and for being the architect."

Less deferential colleagues sometimes had problems. Years after a disagreement with a Republican consultant from Houston named Elizabeth Blakemore, Rove contacted a state senate candidate who was considering hiring her.

"You don't need her," Rove advised Republican Steve Ogden.

Rove never offered any criticism of Blakemore. He didn't need to. Ogden accepted the counsel as strategic advice. Rove was able to damage Blakemore's chances without her even knowing it.

John Weaver was one of Rove's best friends and became his most bitter rival. Weaver was a tall, laconic figure, deeply introspective.

Rove was a careening burst of energy. But they both shared a brilliant instinct for politics and considered forming a single company until small frictions began to develop and it became clear that Rove did not want competition. Rove worked harder, longer, and undercut Weaver in Texas, then discouraged other candidates nationally from hiring him.

In the 2000 presidential race, they met in the biggest showdown of all—Rove directing Bush's effort and Weaver advising maverick Republican John McCain. Again, Rove won and he pursued Weaver even from the White House, where word reached potential business clients not to hire his old political enemy.

Eventually, Weaver left the party entirely and took a job advising Democrats.

Rove simply worked harder than anyone else, harder and longer, driven by some internal need to tackle 100 things at once in pursuit of the single goal: making George W. Bush the most powerful political figure on earth, and lifting himself in the process. As the architect of Bush's political fortunes, Rove was obsessive about protecting their relationship; a collaboration he was convinced would lead to the White House. He jealously guarded his proximity to Bush and was forever blocking others from getting too close. When Bush contacted a fellow Republican and expressed some interest in his help, Rove called to warn the operative to keep a distance and clear every contact through him. When Bush turned to a Democrat seated near him during an event and engaged in conversation, suddenly Rove appeared as if to guard his role as gatekeeper. Bush was the game—the prize—and Rove never forgot it.

As he traveled the Rotary circuit according to Rove's script, Bush privately had doubts whether he could beat Ann Richards. The showy confidence he reflected during his tutorials early on had dimmed. Richards seemed too strong, too popular. But Rove never stopped reassuring him that he would win. Rove hauled out charts and graphs and repeated his elaborate thesis that Richards could not withstand the right challenge from the right candidate, and Bush was that candidate.

"For a while, he was just afraid. He didn't want to get beat so badly he would embarrass the legacy of his father," said a campaign aide. "But by September, he began to think he could win."

Bush was watching television one day when he saw a Richards' commercial in which her white hair was lost in the white background.

"There's something wrong with that campaign," Bush said. "Somebody's not paying attention."

As he climbed aboard the campaign plane with a couple of aides in the heat of late summer, Bush was having trouble reconciling his opponent's powerful persona and the fact that she was running a lackluster campaign. He had always feared that Richards would simply switch on the jets and win, but it wasn't happening.

"Is this all there is?" he asked no one in particular, buckling his seat belt. "I thought she was this great politician. But she's not doing a damn thing."

Bush looked out the window at the familiar stretch of tarmac and the line of live oaks on the horizon. Maybe Rove was right.

"I'm going to win this goddamn thing."

11

Born to Run

Leadership is a combination of strategy and character. If you
must be without one, be without the strategy."

General H. Norman Schwarzkopf

Karl Rove got stiffed.

Even with the collapse of Dick Thornburgh's embarrass-
ingly inept campaign for the U.S. Senate in Pennsylvania,
Rove figured he'd get paid. Thornburgh was a lousy candidate, but Rove never thought he'd be a deadbeat, not the nation's former attorney general, the top cop, a pillar of rectitude and personal
responsibility, and all the other shining Republican values the party
wore like so much jewelry.

It's not as if political candidates always pay their bills on time or
even pay their bills at all, especially candidates who lose and find
themselves facing a mountain of debt. Political campaigns are spectacularly erratic operations, giant machines created suddenly and
launched at high speeds, careening along, spewing money wildly on
phone banks and TV commercials, rented planes and office space.
Usually, there's enough money at the end to pay off everything—the

consultants, the phone bills, a final burst of television spots . . . but not always. Sometimes, candidates don't pay their bills or can't pay their bills, especially candidates whose hopes of victory evaporate on Election Day. Candidates like Dick Thornburgh, a two-term governor of Pennsylvania and U.S. attorney general whose Senate bid held such promise in the summer of 1991, but ended badly.

Thornburgh looked like a sure thing when he jumped into the special election for the Senate in Pennsylvania. The seat had been held by John Heinz, a Republican killed in a plane crash in April 1991. The special election to fill the vacancy lasted little more than three months. The Democrat candidate was former Bryn Mawr College president Harris Wofford, who was making his first run for high office and was largely unknown outside the party. By contrast, Thornburgh had impressive credentials: governor of Pennsylvania, director of the Kennedy Institute of Politics at Harvard, attorney general of the United States in the Bush administration. He was a recognizable presence on television, an *eminence grise* with a high forehead, round horn rims, and a confident, no-nonsense demeanor. He was the clear favorite, up 45 points in an early poll. Thornburgh's campaign manager dismissed Wofford with a whiff of condescension. "A well-meaning, behind-the-times college professor," she said.

Rove knew a top Thornburgh aide, Murray Dickman, from his college Republican days and made a pitch to handle the campaign's mass mail account. Dickman hired him immediately.

From the beginning, Thornburgh's campaign seemed to have a tin ear for the mood of the country. Thornburgh was a Washington insider promising stability at a time when voters wanted change. Every time Thornburgh said experience, voters heard status quo. Wofford steered a perfect populist course, exploiting the resentment of Washington and anxiety over the national recession. By Election Day, Wofford had painted his Republican opponent as a habitué of the corridors of power, all pin stripes and indifference, and himself as champion of an economically battered middle class.

Thornburgh went down to defeat in a final burst of television commercials. The campaign ended with $377,000 in debts and $32,000 in the bank. Rove's bill for $169,732 reached a campaign that said it had no money and no intention of paying. The fact that Thornburgh actually wouldn't pay didn't occur to Rove until some time later, long after the election was over and the campaign had disbursed and all the promises about checks in the mail had faded. Typically, a political consultant stiffed by a candidate has a problem: Pursue the claim in court and be labeled a troublemaker, which could hurt chances of future political work in other campaigns, or quietly absorb the loss and move on. Rove could have moved on, but the idea of getting stiffed by the nation's top cop made him angry.

He decided somebody was going to pay.

"The guy owes me a bundle of money," said Rove. "It was money I paid out to the post office and paid out to the printers and mail shops and computer houses and list owners. He had raised a bundle of money off what we had spent on his behalf with his knowledge and concurrence. They told us the check was in the mail, and then they said they decided to spend the money on a few extra television ads."

In March 1992, Rove filed suit in Austin. The trial opened a year later, on April Fool's Day, in the cool light and austere environs of a federal courtroom, Rove and his lawyers at one table, Thornburgh and his legal team at the other. The issue seemed simple enough: Rove had done the work and Thornburgh owed the money.

But Thornburgh claimed he didn't owe the money, his campaign committee did. He said he personally never negotiated with Rove and another company seeking payment, and knew precious little about the mechanics of the campaign.

"I had no dealings with either of these people. The liability they're asserting is the committee's," Thornburgh told a reporter on the eve of the trial.

Rove had negotiated with his old friend, Murray Dickman, manager of the failed campaign. Thornburgh's lawyers warned that making the candidate personally liable for the debt would be bad for democracy because it would discourage people from running for public office. Rove's team saw the issue a different way, as a simple debt collection case. The campaign was a business, Rove's lawyer told Federal Judge Sam Sparks, "in most respects identical to any other kind of business enterprise, whether it was Thornburgh's Hardware Store or Thornburgh's Development Co. or whatever."

A debt's a debt, a deal's a deal. Pay what you owe.

Thornburgh could have shielded himself by incorporating the campaign or by entering into a contract explicitly saying he wasn't personally liable, an idea that seemed to intrigue the federal judge. Thornburgh testified that none of his past political campaigns had been incorporated.

"Not a bad idea, though, is it?" Sparks asked Thornburgh.

"Well, I don't know," the former attorney general said, squirming on the witness stand.

It was not going well, everybody could see it, Thornburgh most of all. Rove had lured him into a Texas courthouse and now the noose was tightening around his neck. Rove was no lawyer but he carried a kind of preternatural confidence in court cases. Like in his high school debates, he always felt like he was better than anybody in the room. He could beat anybody with the strength of his argument or the weight of his will. When a team of blue-chip lawyers in a tobacco case grilled Rove for a deposition some years later, he was not just confident, but arrogant, fending off their questions with playful insults. On the stand in the Kay Bailey Hutchison trial, he was masterful in frustrating the prosecution. Now he had a former U.S. attorney general in his cross hairs, and as Rove sat at the table in the federal courthouse, he turned his head slowly and looked over at the defense side with the thin sliver of a smile. It was a dark smile, determined, and there was no mistaking the message: You are my enemy and you will pay.

Rove won the case, big time. The judge ruled that Thornburgh's testimony was not "particularly credible" and awarded Rove $294,000—the amount of the original bill plus 18 percent interest and attorneys' fees. Rove's original bill was $170,000. The judgment was nearly twice that amount.

"Outrageous," Thornburgh said, emerging through the courthouse doors. "If the law held that candidates be made personally liable for their campaign debt, I think a lot of people will be extremely wary about subjecting themselves or their families to that."

Thornburgh immediately called Senate Minority Leader Bob Dole, the man he felt had gotten him into this mess in the first place. Dole had urged him to jump into the special election after the death of Senator Heinz, and now Thornburgh was left with a big debt. He told Dole he didn't want to pay the judgment and complained the whole episode would have a chilling effect on the party's efforts to recruit future political candidates. Dole promised to help. When Thornburgh appealed to the Fifth Circuit court, the Republican National Committee produced an ally—former U.S. Solicitor General Ken Starr, who wrote an amicus brief that warned in grave tones that to make candidates liable for their campaign debts could jeopardize democracy itself.

"A reasonable candidate is willing to devote some portion of his life to public service, not to becoming a litigant—and a litigant who potentially might be (hauled) into court in any state and under any state's substantive law," Starr wrote in his brief.

It was an odd argument for a man who, as the Whitewater prosecutor, demanded on principle that President Clinton take personal responsibility for his actions. In the Thornburgh case, he argued just the opposite. As an advocate for the Republican National Committee, Starr said he feared the specter of having public servants hauled into court; as special counsel against the president, he led the legal charge. Starr warned in the Thornburgh case of "nighmarish" liability problems for political figures in the event of a runaway legal system that scrupulously followed the law rather than the national interest. It was only days after Rove's case was heard on appeal that Starr was named special counsel for the Whitewater investigation and Bill Clinton's biggest nightmare.

Clearly, the big guns were lined up against Rove: a former U.S. attorney general, a former solicitor general, the minority leader in the U.S. Senate, the apparatus of the Republican National Committee. Thornburgh's side approached Rove about a settlement, 15 cents on the dollar. Rove said no. He wanted 100 cents on the dollar, nothing less. And, in a manner that was surely aimed at humiliating Thornburgh, the young Texas political consultant suggested ways he might raise the money—a joint fund-raiser with the Pennsylvania Republican party, perhaps, or Thornburgh could rent his contributor list to other candidates. By now, the egos of both sides were inflamed. Neither side would back down.

The case went before the federal appeals court in New Orleans in August 1994. Both sides argued the case and waited for a verdict. It was a full season for Rove. In November, Rove's candidates won big in Texas. George W. Bush was elected governor, Kay Bailey Hutchison was re-elected to the Senate, former legislator Rick Perry became the agriculture commissioner, and novice politico Priscilla Owen won her first political office, a seat on the Texas Supreme Court.

The appeals court also ruled in November—for Rove. Thornburgh now owed $310,000 and the meter was running. Rove was jubilant at the news. Thornburgh, humbled and defeated, decided to quit.

"As it turned out, (litigating) was not a prudent matter," Thornburgh told reporter Robert Elder of the *Texas Lawyer.*

Word spread, first through the network of local political consultants in Texas, then among Rove's clients around the country, and then to the hallways and cocktail parties of Washington, where the politicos inside the Beltway trade the latest news and gossip like currency. The opinion by the Fifth Circuit said many candidates are saddled with debt and it identified by name a dozen widely known politicians in the same situation. Sometimes vendors don't get paid. It happens, but people generally don't make a federal case about it—and almost never do they go so far as *Karl Rove and Co. v. Richard Thornburgh,* case No. 93-8451. So when a young Texas political consultant decided to drag the nation's top lawyer into the courtroom and delivered the whipping of his political life, word spread.

The message, said Republican campaign consultant Brian Berry, was immediate and unmistakable.

"Don't mess with Karl Rove."

O utside the Loews Anatole Hotel, a glittering line of Mercedes and Cadillacs and steel-grey Lincoln Town Cars reflected the glory that is Dallas. Inside the ballroom, the television lights blazed. And in the halo of television lights, accepting the applause of the crowd, newly elected U.S. Senator Kay Bailey Hutchison positively beamed as she stood on stage.

"I will be a senator for all of Texas. All of us want our country to get back on track," she said into the cheers of the Republican throng.

In winning the special election for the Senate in June 1993, Hutchison toppled Governor Ann Richards' hand-picked Democratic candidate, giving the Republican party both seats in the U.S. Senate for the first time since 1875. Her colleague, Senator Phil Gramm, stood with her on stage, as did a retinue of Republicans of importance and semi-importance, among them the managing general partner of the Texas Rangers baseball team, George W. Bush, who on this night was just another face in the crowd.

This night belonged to Hutchison. She had followed the blueprint of her consultant, Karl Rove, and crushed her opponent by a margin of 2–1. She was the newest, brightest star in a Rove constellation that was overtaking politics in the Lone Star State. In the newspapers, the pundits and party apologists were to say that her opponent, a former college dean named Robert Krueger who quoted Cicero on the campaign trail, had been a bad choice and that Democrats must do a better job fielding candidates in the future. But the truth was that Krueger was the canary in the coal mine, an early signal that the Democratic party's days were numbered. At the Anatole, the Republicans were giddy with victory. Music boomed over the loudspeaker and Hutchison's campaign manager, Brian Berry, worked his way around the ballroom in a burst of adrenaline that masks fatigue on election nights. Bush came bounding down from the stage and, spotting Berry, poked him on the shoulder.

"Hey, buddy. Are you ready for another one?"

Berry seemed confused.

"We might have some plans here," Bush said.

Even in the hoopla of this election night, Rove was already at work on the next campaign—the big one this time, the campaign to put George W. Bush in the Governor's Mansion. And he wanted Berry on the team. Berry was a veteran campaign operative, bright and impulsive, with long, skinny limbs, red hair, and a commitment to the Young Republican school of smash-mouth politics. Rove had cleared the way for Berry to head the Southwest region for President Bush's reelection race in 1992, had picked him to direct Hutchison's Senate campaign. Berry was part of a growing Rove team, an ensemble cast of political players inserted into the various roles in various campaigns—but there was never any doubt who the director was, who was serving as the production's impresario.

"This is the way Karl works. He always is into personnel. Personnel is power," said Berry.

"He knows whether you can go into a role and be part of the team and be helpful. So he automatically has an incredible resume line of talent, early. And Rove is master control. If you have a list, you have power. And he has all the voter lists, he has all the organization lists, the operative lists. He's literally a one-stop shop operation set up in seconds."

Rove knew that since Bush was running against a woman, the campaign needed a female face as its messenger. He called conservative activist Terry Eastland, who recommended Deborah Burston-Wade, a young Black woman he'd known from the Justice Department in the Reagan years. Rove wanted Fred Steeper as the pollster. And to produce the campaign's television commercials, Rove's choice was Don

Sipple, a California media whiz and master of the 30-second sound bite. Sipple and Rove worked together on campaigns for John Ashcroft of Missouri, first for governor, then senator. Typically, there is a competition among media firms for campaign jobs. Consultants from both coasts flew in to Dallas and trooped to Bush's office near Preston Road, where they showed off their commercials and made their pitches, touting their win-loss record in past campaigns. In the end, it was Bush's decision to make. But it was Rove who guided the choice.

One day, a consultant from the Washington Beltway arrived for his appointment and popped in a reel of his best commercials, featuring an impressive series of spots for a governor's race that had proved successful.

"That ad right there elected that man governor," the consultant said proudly.

Bush pushed away from the table, a pained look on his face.

"So did the candidate have anything to do with it?"

Sipple didn't make that mistake. Sipple's presentation was dazzling, impressive; exactly what Bush was looking for, exactly what Rove wanted. Bush and Sipple met for three hours, one-on-one, just the two of them, and in the end Sipple came away with the job and with a deep impression about Bush the candidate. First, were Bush's eyes, which had a kind of brittle blue intensity that were perfect for a commercial.

"He looked at me with those steely blue eyes and I said, 'Holy shit.'"

Second, Sipple was struck by Bush's pledge not to go negative against Ann Richards. Bush said Richards' record was fair game, but he would not go after her personally. He declared that he would run a high-minded campaign without attacks that could be construed as personal. He would win on the high road or not win at all.

In fact, the campaign against Richards was to be negative, harsh, and very personal. There actually were two campaigns against Richards, one in which Bush floated above the fray and another in which Rove targeted the Democrat's politics and gender. It was an arrangement that allowed Bush plausible deniability, no matter what. And it was a model of future Bush races: Bush traveling the high road, Rove pursuing the low. Rove's strategy in the Richards' race was simple enough: Bush the candidate engages his Democratic opponent by respectfully challenging her record on improving public schools and fighting crime. Meanwhile, Bush surrogates, operating at arm's length, undermine Richards on the issues of guns and gays, including a vicious whisper campaign about lesbianism that ran with an evangelical fervor through the coffee shops and church parlors of East Texas.

If Bush needed an object lesson in how not to run against Ann Richards, it was the 1990 governor's race in Texas. The Republican nominee, a Midland oilman and would-be cowboy named Clayton Williams, drove away moderate suburban Republicans—especially women—by appearing boorish and insensitive. He told a crude campfire joke comparing inclement weather to rape: "If it's inevitable, just relax and enjoy it." He refused at one point to shake Richards' hand in full view of television cameras. Whatever Richards insistence that gender not be a factor in the race, Texas voters retained a quaintly Southern view of any man who would refuse the extended hand of a woman. When Williams popped off around the time of her 10-year anniversary of sobriety—"I hope she didn't go back to drinkin' again"—voters lost all patience. Richards won and became an iconic figure in Texas politics, a kind of solar myth as the feminist with the hot white hairdo and a reputation for leveling opponents with her considerable gift of language. She was funny and acerbic and politically wily.

She made a national splash at the 1988 Democratic Convention when she took aim at Bush's father and delivered the line heard around the political world: "Poor George, he can't help it . . . he was born with a silver foot in his mouth." The remark struck a deep nerve with the family. Barbara Bush, watching on television while on retreat at Kennebunkport, let it be known the comment made her physically sick. In a single phrase, Richards had highlighted the twin weaknesses of the Bush clan politically, attacking it as both ardently patrician and vaguely ineffective.

The image of Ann Richards in her luminescent blue dress and white hair, standing on the podium in Atlanta, cheerfully delivering that attack on his father, left Bush . . . *steaming*, and he could not forget it, would not forget, as he made clear in the private confines of his office where he spoke of Richards with contempt. Bush listed her among the cabal that contributed to his father's defeat, Ann Richards and Bill Clinton and all the GOP traitors who he felt were more interested in protecting themselves than serving his father in the final days, men like Jim Baker III and other lower-level Republican toadies—these were who Bush blamed for his father's humiliating loss.

Bush harbored his father's loss like a wound. Nobody understood Bush's visceral desire to redeem the family name better than Rove, who acted as a kind of political Bundini, constantly assuring that for all her popularity, Richards was vulnerable politically and could be beaten.

"They like her hair, but they're not strongly anchored to her," he said.

Rove was the picture of confidence, but in the beginning Bush believed the news clippings about the glib and gifted Ann Richards, political superstar.

Self-doubt was not a suit that Rove wore.

As always, he found substantiation in the numbers. He studied immigration patterns and voter rolls, the bursting growth in the suburbs north of Dallas and around Houston, the blooming high-tech industry, the shifting election trends in which the voters of Texas— once stalwart Southern Democrats in the Roosevelt tradition—were increasingly identifying themselves as independents and Republicans. Private polls intimated at the positive prospects of a candidate like Bush, but the first public head-to-head survey, the Texas Poll published in state newspapers in October 1993, was a revelation. It had Richards at 47 percent and Bush at 39 percent. Richards had been governor for three years, Bush had never served a day in office, and in their first poll, Bush was only trailing by eight points. Eight points! And Bush hadn't even announced yet.

In the early planning sessions with the skeleton crew that would advance to a swelling campaign team by year's end, Rove set out his blueprint for victory. Berry marveled at its precision with 30-day, 60-day, and 90-day plans. It was like some giant chemical equation: the qualities Bush brings to the race, the broad themes to be enunciated, separating the son's accomplishments from the father, building the careful architecture of a campaign against an iconic figure by casting her as the defender of the status quo and Bush as an agent of change.

"If you have the Bush name, you have instant things, name identification, the ability to raise money," said Brian Berry. "Dad Bush was from Texas and Karl always liked existing advantages. Clearly, he knew the guy was capable. He'd been on the campaign trail with his father, so Karl knew he had talent and skills. And these were interesting times when you didn't want a professional politician type."

If the father and the father's name was a strength, Rove knew also it was a weakness, especially in Texas where the notion of dynasty carried with it the nasty connotation of the Kennedys. Bush would have to answer the question: What have you done?

"He knew what the Democrats would do, that they would tag George W. as the son of George Bush, as somebody trying to trade on your father's name. And from that, Karl developed a policy to trump Richards by not engaging on that turf. We had a standard line: I love my father. That was George W.'s line. Every time they said, 'Aren't you trading on your father's name?' he said, 'I love my father.'"

Though father and son talked frequently, the decision was made to keep George Bush largely out of sight, except for a pair of fundraisers in Dallas and Houston where the ex-president joined his son but did not speak. His first campaign finance report was top-heavy with contributions from his father's biggest donors. The strategy—Rove's strategy—was to reap the advantages of being a president's son while minimizing the problems.

"Here you have a businessman, manager of the Texas Rangers, a popular sport," said Berry. "You can show your charismatic side, but you also show your business side, that you're not a pol. You can have the separation from your father just on the basis of that, that you're running your own gig."

This was hardly a newfound thought for Bush.

His foray into business had largely been a flop, characterized mostly by a series of takeover deals in which outside investors with ties to his father periodically swooped in to save one foundering oil company after another. Arbusto Energy became Bush Exploration, which merged with Spectrum 7, which merged with Harken Energy. And while the companies were losing money because of depressed oil prices, Bush's equity increased in value until 1990 when he sold 212,000 shares of Harken stock for $848,560 to pay off his investment in the Texas Ranger baseball team. By 1993, when Bush was preparing his race for governor, the major league ball team had become a smashing success with a bright new stadium and a devoted fan base in the community.

Construction of the new ballpark in Arlington was subsidized by an increase in the sales tax in the team's home city of Arlington. In the public campaign to promote the sales tax hike, Bush remained prudently out of sight. Otherwise, in operations at the team's old ballpark, Arlington Stadium, and association with the new field with its red-brick retro design, Bush was very much the front man, the president's son as pitch man. "I like selling tickets," he told a reporter for *Time* magazine.

On game nights, Bush typically left the office by 5:30 P.M., drove his four-year-old black Pontiac to Arlington Stadium and wandered among the concession stands, ticket windows, and the first base dugout. He distributed baseball cards he had printed with his picture of them. He took a seat, not up in the air-conditioned owner's box but in the stands, in full view of everybody, where he enjoyed signing autographs and rubbing shoulders with the crowd and "eating the same popcorn, peeing in the same urinal" as the fans.

The political potential of the baseball deal was not lost on Bush. A month after closing the deal to buy the team in 1989 in which Bush helped assemble the consortium of investors, a reporter asked whether purchase of the Rangers might portend some future political plans.

He didn't even blink. "This job has a very high visibility, which cures the political problem I'd have: 'What has the boy done?'"

In promoting Bush as a potential candidate for governor, Rove told a newspaper reporter: "Ownership of the Texas Rangers anchors him clearly as a Texas businessman and entrepreneur and gives him name identification, exposure and gives him something that will be easily recallable by people."

Curiously, in a detailed discussion of Ranger business, Bush was quickly out of his depth. The half-cent increase in the city sales tax that helped finance the new ballpark in Arlington was only the tip of a complicated financial transaction that involved a network of loans, development of an adjacent 274-acre site, revenue streams not only from ticket sales but luxury boxes, concessions, and a bond issue to finance the sale of seat options.

As managing general partner, Bush had an office in the new stadium with a glorious view of the field. He had a large desk with a spacious area for a couch and comfortable chairs and one wall fully glass that looked out onto the pristine green expanse of the ball field as if it were some giant LeRoy Neiman mural, shimmering under the lights in a vivid splash of color. The adjacent office, with an identical view of the field, belonged to Tom Schieffer, a former state legislator from Fort Worth and partner in the Ranger deal. Schieffer was the detail guy on the financing. He went to Austin in 1991 to help steer the lobbying effort necessary to make the deal work.

But it was Bush's role in running the club, his business acumen, that Rove pushed in the campaign's early months. Bush was a businessman; Richards was not. He was the linchpin that made the transaction happen. So when a reporter asked about details of the Ranger deal, Bush appeared ready with answers.

"Am I going to benefit off it financially? I hope so," he said. "But I also hope that the $100 million that comes into Arlington will help Arlington schools and helps Arlington streets and police. And I hope Arlington becomes the finest city in the metroplex."

Bush and Schieffer fielded the questions together, questions about the annual rent, land condemnation, future ownership of the property. Then the phone rang in Schieffer's office and he left to take the call. Bush sat alone now and the reporter asked about the seat bond program. Why was it that fans were being asked to front the club money—ranging in price from $500 to $5,000, with discounts for longtime season ticket holders—to purchase season tickets in the new park?

Bush turned and looked in the direction of Schieffer's office, but his partner was still on the phone. Bush hazarded an answer, but it was incomplete. Clearly, he did not fully understand the deal even though his campaign was trumpeting his management of the Rangers as evidence of his business skills. Bush turned again, looking anxiously for Schieffer.

"Let's wait until Tom gets back," he said.

Schieffer did know the answer.

The bonds were an "interest-free loan" from the fans to the Rangers. The fans would be repaid over time from a $1 surcharge levied on each Ranger ticket, but the team would pocket the interest. In lieu of interest, Schieffer said, fans got the right to buy preferential seating. But if Bush appeared lost in the financial minutiae of his company's tax breaks and interest-free loans, Rove knew it didn't matter. What did matter was that Bush was a businessman with a name and political pedigree that guaranteed money and attention. Moreover, the very public campaign against Richards was turning on issues the people of Texas cared about, especially education and crime.

"The sense was that she was popular but had no real achievements," Rove said years later in an interview recalling the campaign's early days. "The state faced a problem of leadership in that the people wanted somebody to do something, whether it was education, which was the No. 1 issue, or whether it was crime, particularly where we faced this generation of juvenile criminals.

"The idea was to pick things that Bush cared about deeply and put them out there."

Rove understood what many of the early campaign staffers did not, that Bush was not only a country-club Republican—lower taxes, less regulation—but also a social conservative in a way his father was not. Bush disliked the openness and lassitude of the 1960s. He felt a generation had been damaged by a counterculture philosophy of "if it feels good, do it"—a line he was to use repeatedly in his race for governor and, later, in his campaign for the presidency. Rove suggested he talk to Marvin Olasky, a University of Texas professor who had just written a book skewering the liberal approach of the welfare state, *The Tragedy of American Compassion*. In Olasky's view, nineteenth-century America's religious-based charity was a better model for dealing with the poor, not the hoary apparatus of the War on Poverty in which public assistance had become a matter of entitlement, squeezing out personal responsibility—just goo-goo social policy that delivered a state-sanctioned subsistence and asked nothing in return. Bush called Olasky and suggested they meet.

Olasky was a small man with a thin face, a close-cropped beard, and large eyes that never seemed to blink. He had a bird-like quality, as if forever looking sideways at an object. He was a communist turned atheist turned evangelical Christian who burned with the conviction of a convert. Unlike some professional moralists, Olasky lived his faith; he and his wife adopted a Black child who needed a home, worked in soup kitchens, assisted ex-cons in need of a second chance. He believed deeply in helping the poor and Bush came away from their discussion won over by Olasky's view that the missing element in the current welfare state was spiritual rather than material. The program's problem was that it didn't promote values.

"The two issues, education and juvenile justice, were on his agenda list. And they were on the people's agenda list," said Rove. "Now, welfare was not, the idea of the compassionate conservative, faith-based institutions—that was not on their radar scope in a public way, but it was on Bush's. This idea of culture change was really the dominant driving influence here, the idea that we had to change the culture from one that said: 'If it feels good, do it. If you have a problem, blame it on somebody else.' So he chose welfare reform because he said we're not just about educating every child and locking up the bad actors. There's a caring side of this that is aimed at changing the culture.

"Later, we added tort reform. I sort of talked him into that one."

Tort reform, the effort to shield businesses from rising jury awards in personal-injury lawsuits, was standard Republican boilerplate, but Rove wanted that issue elevated. Although he would never admit it, he had to know that its most ardent advocates in Texas could provide millions of dollars in campaign contributions needed to unseat Richards. Rove was a paid consultant to Philip Morris, which faced enormous liability problems, and over the years he had depended on the deep pockets of business—*uber*-givers like Houston builder Bob Perry, Enron's Ken Lay, East Texas chicken processor Lonnie "Bo" Pilgrim—to elect candidates who would be good for business.

Rove had the golden money lists. He had organized the early tutoring sessions, assembled the issue-development teams. He had put Bush early on the small-town circuit. ("Limit GWB's public appearance" in Austin "to reduce the attention of the Capitol press corps," he wrote in an October 1993 memo.) But when the campaign's senior staff gathered, Bush wanted it known that he—not Rove—framed the agenda of his campaign. At the meetings, Bush was clearly in command.

"When you're developing things," Bush said one day, looking around the table, "I'm going to tell you what I believe. You guys are the wordsmiths. You can smith it out. But it's going to start with what I think."

Everyone nodded, Rove included. There was a curious dance between the candidate and the consultant in which Rove clearly sought to steer Bush in a particular direction and Bush periodically would jerk the reins and reassert his authority. Early on, Bush was sensitive of being perceived a lightweight and Rove his Svengali.

"Bush puts down a marker and says don't get too much into my world, don't try to over-manage me," said Berry. "Rove is trying to work out the best avenue to take so he's not blamed for being the puppeteer. Bush repelled from that. So there was this beautiful, interesting relationship. They absolutely had a silent language about each other, about how far you would go to the line. And sometimes one would get their back up or the other would get their back up. Sometimes you had disagreements about who's running the show."

When Bush fumbled criticism of Richards over the destruction of state phone records, Rove sought to instruct his charge on doing a better job in the future—only to be cut short by a stern rebuke on the other end of the phone.

"I got confused," said Rove, suddenly back pedaling. "You did great."

Their odd rivalry, prickly and contentious at times, continued after Bush became governor. After a news conference one day on the lawn of the Governor's Mansion, Bush began walking back inside when he noticed reporters were clustered around Rove, continuing to ask questions. Bush stopped.

"Is the Rove news conference about over?" he asked in an irritated voice.

Rove blanched, turned abruptly, fled the circle of reporters, and followed the governor back into the mansion.

Whatever the impression of some Democrats outside the campaign—that Bush was a lightweight and Rove was at master control—those inside the campaign knew that something more complicated was going on. Bush was very much the chief executive, distilling information, evaluating proposals, pushing and prodding advisors to defend their positions. When Bush learned that school districts that couldn't meet state standards governing overcrowding or paperwork simply had the state waive the rules year after year, he turned to his education advisor, Margaret LaMontagne.

"Now let me get this right," he said. "Ann Richards is the governor of the state of Texas. And we've got a screwed up education system. And the issue is hundreds, maybe thousands of waivers every year. Don't you think that's broken?"

Public school waivers became an issue in the campaign. Berry watched the give and take with interest. "It was Rove letting Bush be Bush, not jamming things down his throat, but letting George W. go back and forth with people. It's like Bush is saying, 'If I'm going to run for state office, I've got to learn about the issues.'"

Crime was a perfect issue.

Houston television stations, locked in a ratings war, were broadcasting hysterical reports nightly on every rape, every shooting as if the city were under siege. Even in Austin and Dallas, where news reports were more tempered, people were worried about crime.

Rove knew Texans were worried; polls showed it. Polls also showed that voters had more confidence in men than women when it came to fighting crime and protecting the rights of gun-owners. The fact that Richards had a good record on crime during her tenure as governor—violent crime was falling and she was responsible for the largest prison-building program in state history—seemed unimportant. In fact, it was irrelevant.

Rove's thesis was this: In designing a media message, you must build on what the public already believes. The public believes that women are softer on crime than men, especially women who are Democrats. And most especially, liberal women Democrats. So a media strategy was born to present Richards as soft on crime. She immediately would be on the defensive and respond with arguments and statistics showing otherwise, but it didn't matter.

Explaining is losing.

The true course of a winning campaign is just as Rove set out in his 1985 memo: *Attack, Attack, Attack.*

Sipple's clients in the 1994 race included Bush and two incumbent Republican governors, Pete Wilson in California and Jim Edgar in Illinois. All three were facing female opponents and in all three contests. Sipple produced virtually identical ads on crime. He even used the same black-and-white footage of a staged abduction and asserted the same promise to get tough on "rapists and child molesters." In a solemn voice, an announcer says: "Crime—more random, more violent. Incredibly, Ann Richards says she's reduced crime and violence in Texas."

Official state crime statistics showed the rate of violent crime in almost every category had topped out the year Richards took office and had fallen every year since, except for juvenile crime, which was up 52 percent. If the law-abiding burghers in the suburbs were concerned about crime in general, they were terrified at the prospect of violent young thugs with guns, stealing cars, committing murder.

"Crime is crime is crime," said Sipple. "But the campaign found one piece of the crime issue that was new, which I thought was genius. Juvenile crime was a way to open up a new front on the crime issue and it worked very well."

With the issues set—education, crime, welfare, and limiting lawsuits against business—the campaign focused on the crucial matter of tone. A Richards' consultant, George Shipley, was telling reporters Bush was a hothead who eventually would snap under the pressure of the campaign. As evidence, Shipley recalled how the younger Bush earned a reputation among Washington reporters as arrogant and ill-tempered while spending time around the White House as his father's protector. Shipley predicted that, eventually, Bush would show a flash of anger and impatience at Richards. But he never did, not publicly.

Rove had studied the voter trends in 1990, how the moderate suburban women flocked to Richards. Bush needed to win those voters back, and Rove was convinced the best way to do that was to maintain a respectful tone—criticize Richards' stewardship of state government, but never Richards personally. It was the perfect confluence of interests: Bush embraced the idea because it appealed to his instinct of fair play; Rove promoted the strategy because it was good politics.

"Here's what I'll do and here's what I won't do," Bush said, outlining the policy at an early campaign staff meeting. "On the attacking thing, I'm not doing this bit where we're tearing down. I'm not doing this same old kind of stuff. If that causes me to go in the ringer, that's fine. But I'm not going that route."

The campaign even institutionalized the notion with a 30-second television spot called "Personal." In the spring 1994, Bush and Sipple were filming a set of positive television commercials at a school. The night before, Sipple had scribbled an idea on a yellow pad about how Bush could protect himself from anticipated attacks by the Richards camp. The idea was for Bush to film a commercial in advance expressing disappointment that his Democratic opponent had decided to abandon the usual political discourse and launch personal attacks.

"We can put it in the can so we have it in case we need it," Sipple said.

Sipple sat Bush in a chair with a soft, golden light across his face. Bush looked directly into the camera and spoke in slow, measured tones.

"I have said all along I'm going to treat Governor Richards with respect, that my campaign would focus on the issues, the facts and the record," Bush said. "For whatever reasons, the governor has chosen to attack me personally."

Sipple was delighted. "We hit the seams just right with that one. I don't think I've ever seen anybody deliver something as well as he did. I remember he was quite enamored with it."

As the campaign moved into the summer, Bush traveled the state in accordance with Rove's methodical blueprint, complaining that schoolteachers were burdened by too much paperwork and that the state's accountability system of testing students needed to be strengthened. He said crime was up and promised to halt the early release of felons from prison. He challenged Richards' handling of welfare, questioned whether she'd done enough to promote jobs. Internal polling, which Rove pored over as if it were sacred script, indicated Bush was gaining ground. Richards found herself increasingly irritated by her opponent's assaults on her record.

"You just work like a dog, do well and all of a sudden, you've got some jerk who's running for public office telling everybody it's all a sham and it isn't real," she told a crowd in the sweltering August heat of Texarkana.

Bingo! The Bush campaign rushed its prepared spot onto the air. On televisions all across Texas, people saw the Republican candidate sitting solemnly, looking directly into the camera with the sad knowledge that his opponent had crossed the line.

"For whatever reason, the governor has chosen to attack me personally . . ."

A nn Richards sat in the confines of her campaign plane, cruising just above the clouds. Below was the tawny patchwork of East Texas, once the rugged heart of yellow-dog Democrat country, now a region very much in play. She knew the place: the small town squares, the deep thickets of loblolly pine, the huge neon sign above the Swinnytown Baptist Church that declared in a blazing blue light: "A Going Church for a Coming Lord." Richards had won East Texas four years ago, wooing the region's conservative Democrats. But her appeal was very much in jeopardy this time because a dark whisper campaign was underway, maddeningly decentralized but marvelously effective.

"You have been hearing a very skillfully crafted Republican message," Richards said. "We confronted it first in East Texas in the spring."

"What message?" the single reporter on the plane asked.

She hesitated, "I know what it is, but I don't want to say."

It was virtually impossible in the summer of 1994 to get a haircut in East Texas or visit a coffee shop or go to church Wednesday nights without hearing about Ann Richards and the lesbians. It was a mean and virulent whisper campaign, born, as such things are, by a small fragment of fact. One of the main powers of a governor is to appoint thousands of people to the boards and commissions that operate government, and Richards had opened that process to record numbers of women, Blacks, and Hispanics. With Richards naming so many women and with her liberal social politics anathema in some quarters of East Texas, word spread that the governor was filling state government with lesbians. The truth was that some of her appointees were gay, including a high-profile appointment to the agency regulating utilities that created a buzz when the Lesbian/Gay Rights Lobby of Texas said the selection of "an 'out' lesbian to such a powerful commission gives our community something to celebrate."

Rove knew that Richards' appointees were a ripe target for attack. He enlisted business groups and conservative religious organizations to raise questions about their professional experience and qualifications. Bush set the issue in motion a full year before the election, cautioning that his opponent's appointees "have been people who have had agendas that may have been personal in nature." The code word was "personal." Nobody mentioned sexual orientation; they didn't need to.

"There was clearly an organized Republican movement to keep out there a couple of issues, gays and guns, in the forefront," said Chuck McDonald, who was Richards' press secretary. "And I don't think it's any secret that the person who really set the Republican agenda was Karl Rove. He drove it."

Rove's direct-mail firm produced a campaign brochure for distribution across East Texas attacking Richards for vetoing a bill to allow people to carry concealed handguns. But if Rove was driving the debate on Richards and homosexuality, he left few fingerprints. He professed no involvement whatsoever. Bush, he was quick to remind everyone, was committed to a positive campaign with no personal attacks.

But the matter was moving just the same, from courthouse to coffee shop, with a quiet efficiency along an informal network of Bush surrogates. So as Richards traveled in her campaign plane high above East Texas in August, she faced a dilemma. Ignoring the whisper campaign, which by now had metastasized into lurid gossip, didn't protect her from its damage. But talking about it legitimized the subject. She decided that if the Bush campaign wanted to put gays in her administration on the front page, it would have to do so itself.

A few days later, it did.

Bush's East Texas campaign chairman, state Senator Bill Ratliff, told reporters for the *Houston Post* that Richards' appointment of homosexuals could cost her support in the region. "It is simply part of their culture, and frankly part of mine, that (homosexuality) is not something we encourage, reward, or acknowledge as an acceptable situation."

Richards' press secretary, Chuck McDonald, woke up to a storm of headlines. "The whisper campaign had come to life," he said.

The Bush campaign issued a news release praising the senator as a man "of great integrity and strong convictions," but said the Republican candidate was running a positive campaign about the issues of education, juvenile crime, and welfare reform. "This is not an issue in this campaign." But the issue had been catapulted onto the front page of every newspaper in the state and the damage done. In November, Bush swept East Texas and crushed Richards' re-election effort.

The Sunday before the election, Bush sat in the backyard of his home in Dallas, lobbing tennis balls into the pool for his dog, Spot, to retrieve. He had been reading Bob Woodward's new book about the workings of the Clinton White House, *The Agenda*. "This guy is mighty fucked up," he told an aide.

His father's loss still gnawed at him, both because he felt Clinton was not worthy of the White House and because his father had failed. Bush took solace in the knowledge that he was going to win; Rove had assured him. He had run his campaign as if it were a war. He had stayed focused and disciplined, never departed from the blueprint.

Bush and Rove, the underestimated candidate and the man with the plan.

They were heading off to make history.

PART
III

History Makes Men

12

Voices in the Room

The race may not go to the strong and swift, but that's the way
to bet."

Damon Runyon

When the end came, when his most important policy initiative failed, his legacy as governor, the achievement
that would burnish his credentials and stamp him
ready for higher office—when everything went to hell
for George W. Bush in an instant of collapse and betrayal, Karl Rove
was not in the room.

Rove stayed away from negotiations between Bush and members
of the Texas Legislature. He was not wanted, was not trusted, at
least not by the Democrats. The Legislature had a long history of
bipartisan compromise; Rove was the supreme partisan. So when
Bush introduced his bold initiative in 1997 to reconfigure the way
Texas finances public schools and dramatically cut property taxes,
Rove was relegated to the basement and the back rooms of the capitol, out of sight.

"If Rove had been seen," said former Democratic Representative Mark Stiles, "it would have poisoned the water so badly that every-body would have died within 100 yards."

Bush was on his own. The governor felt strongly about changing the way schools were funded in Texas, a system that had been in and out of the courts for years. For one thing, property taxpayers in his own Dallas neighborhood of Highland Park complained their money was being rerouted to subsidize dirt-poor districts in the Rio Grande Valley. Poor districts, meanwhile, insisted they still weren't getting enough money to adequately educate their kids. It was a monumental policy dilemma, one that a long line of governors had failed to solve.

Bush decided to solve it.

He developed a plan, pressed the issue in the legislature, built al-liances, lobbied lawmakers, and pledged to spend his political capi-tal on what became the premier issue of his governorship. Bush cajoled legislators over dinner at the Mansion. He invited them fish-ing at Rainbo Lake in East Texas. He invested himself more com-pletely in this issue than he had anything before. For nearly six months of legislative maneuvering, and a year of preparation before that, he and a band of political allies in the governor's office steered the plan to simultaneously lower property taxes and invigorate state spending on public schools. The idea attracted some powerful op-ponents, mainly commercial interests that faced higher business taxes in the overall scheme. The bill passed the House, but was now stuck in the Senate, and time was running short in the session.

Friday night, 10 days before adjournment, and the mood was sour in a small conference room adjacent to Bush's main office in the capitol.

"We've got to move something," Bush said.

The governor was at one end of the table, House Speaker Pete Laney at the other. Around the table sat Lieutenant Governor Bob Bullock, the presiding officer in the Senate, and several members of the Senate and House. They had trooped through Bush's spacious capitol office, past the glass case with the baseball collection, past the oil portrait of the Methodist circuit rider on horseback, and arranged themselves in this small back room, which, after an hour of bickering, had taken on a nasty, claustrophobic feel.

Stiles, representing the House, blamed the Senate.

"If people had just read the bill over there."

"I ain't listening to that shit," said Bullock.

Tension grew around the room. Bush said something, apparently ill considered, and Bullock, wiry and unpredictable, lunged across the table at him, reaching for his throat.

"Don't talk to me like that!" Bullock screamed, his face flaring.

Bush recoiled. Stiles grabbed Bullock and pulled him back across the table.

"The only way this will pass," Bullock growled, "is you're going to have to lay your credibility on the line with these senators."

Bullock was right.

The governor's problem was a group of conservative Republicans, wary of the new business taxes in the package despite its enormous appeal of cutting property taxes in half. Bullock could move some Democrats in the Senate, but Bush would have to use every ounce of personal diplomacy to convince his Republicans.

Bush leaned defiantly toward Bullock. "I'll do it if you'll do it."

"By god," said Bullock, "I can do it if you can."

In the exhaustion and elation and testosterone of the moment, Bush tied himself to the single issue he hoped would highlight his legacy and demonstrate his standing as a leader. Months earlier, Bullock had pulled Karl Rove aside outside the capitol and warned against it.

"This will kill his chances to be something bigger. This will ruin his chances for great things!"

Rove didn't disagree. He cautioned Bush against the political downsides to his thinking on taxes. But Bush decided, in this one case, to depart from Rove's advice. It was the only time he'd ever strayed from Rove on an issue of such importance. The governor was committed to the idea of accomplishing something big, some-thing he felt was good public policy, and so he laid himself open by saying a vote on the tax bill was a vote on George Bush himself.

"In the history of this state that I've been a part of, I've never seen a governor make it that personal, make the whole tax vote a personal issue on George Bush's personality," said veteran Represen-tative Paul Sadler, a crucial Bush ally. "That's what Bullock was con-veying to him: 'You're going to have to make it personal. This is a vote against George Bush.'"

For hours, the group called in senators, one by one, offering en-ticements, appealing to their patriotism—whatever it took to win support for the bill. By 10 P.M., a deal appeared to be in the offing.

The next morning, however, everything had changed. There had been late-night calls, early morning calls, and now in the clear light of day the agreement was in danger of unraveling.

Senator Florence Shapiro of Dallas, leader of the Republican caucus, was the key to saving the bill. She arrived at the Capitol by 9 A.M. Bush greeted her warmly and came around his desk to sit in a chair beside her, took her hand, and in what Stiles described as "the whole LBJ forearm-your governor needs you" appeal, explained how crucial it was that he have her vote.

Shapiro shook her head.

"Governor, I'm not drinking that Kool-Aid."

Bush was stunned. He had lost the Republicans . . . *his Republi-cans* . . . and failed spectacularly in the one major policy initiative of his tenure.

After almost everybody was gone, Bush turned to two legislators who had stayed behind, both Democrats.

"I can't get us there. They won't do it."

Then he put his head in his hands and he began to cry.

Karl Rove never liked the tax idea. He always feared that what-ever the political benefits of cutting property taxes—and the benefits would be enormous in places like Iowa and New

Hampshire—rewriting the state school finance system carried considerable risks. School finance and property taxes are intrinsically tied in Texas. Public schools are funded largely by local property taxes. If the state were to cut property taxes in half, the financial shortfall had to be made up somehow; either with budget cuts or tax increases elsewhere.

"The politics of it was butt-ugly," said Rove.

He talked to Bush about the politics of his tax cutting, but the governor decided to move forward anyway.

"His point was, I'm here for big things. He has this sense that leadership matters, that a president or a governor can shape public opinion. So his question is, is this the right thing to do?"

During the campaign for governor, there was a running commentary among some Democrats comparing Bush to the Robert Redford character in *The Candidate*, a well-meaning but ultimately corrupted young politician. The better comparison was another Redford movie, *The Way We Were*, in which Redford played a golden boy for whom everything seemed to come so easily.

That was Bush, the golden boy.

He arrived as governor filled with easy confidence. He seemed not so much to walk through the capitol as to glide through it, popping unexpectedly into the offices of legislators, greeting tourists on the steps out front. Bush brought to office an engaging personality and a gift for winning people over, even the mercurial Bullock. During an early meeting at the Governor's Mansion, Bullock suddenly got angry over some disagreement with the new governor and declared their honeymoon over.

"Okay," Bush said, walking over and throwing his arms around the aging Democrat. "But if you're going to fuck me, I want a kiss first." It was enough to break the ice.

He was open, sometimes goofy and self-effacing, forever pursuing favor with an unpretentiousness that became his signature style in Austin. Entering a room one day for a ceremony, Bush spotted a reporter along the back wall, made a wildly silly face, then turned back to the crowd and strode solemnly to the podium to swear in Alberto Gonzalez, a future White House general counsel, as Texas secretary of state.

In his capitol office, he and Rove took turns mimicking people. Rove would drop to his knees and imitate Heinz Prechter, a diminutive Detroit industrialist and big-money Republican beloved by the Bush family, throwing out his arms and adopting a thick, booming German accent. Bush, a gifted mimic, did a dead-on Dana Carvey doing his father.

"He didn't take himself too seriously. He enjoyed it," said George Christian, who served as White House press secretary for Lyndon Johnson and advisor to a generation of Texas governors.

On the wall in his office, Bush hung an oil painting he had resurrected from capitol storage. It was a strange and florid portrait of Sam Houston dressed in a Roman toga and surrounded by the scattered wreckage of an ancient city. During a low point in Houston's life, he commissioned the portrait of himself as the Roman conqueror Gaius Marius.

"Evidently, he must have been in a drunken stupor to have done this, to go to Nashville and have himself painted as Marius in the ruins of Carthage," said Bush. He put the painting in his office as a daily reminder to stay grounded.

In Bush's first legislative session in 1995, most of his big campaign ideas were enacted into law, largely because the legislature was already considering them.

"He aligned himself with the train that was already moving and got some credit for that," said University of Texas political science professor Bruce Buchanan.

The staff Bush assembled was close-knit and loyal—loyalty was the primary virtue. At the top were Joe Allbaugh, Karen Hughes, and Karl Rove. The three—later dubbed "The Iron Triangle"—were to be the nucleus of Bush's presidential campaign and his White House staff.

"He had roles assigned to different people and they did them pretty well," said Christian, the former LBJ aide. "Joe Allbaugh was his hammer. Karen was his thinker, communicator, and wordsmith. And Karl was his political guru."

All three had made their way to the governor's office from the campaign, Rove from the inception and Allbaugh and Hughes after the campaign was well underway.

Allbaugh, a big-boned Oklahoman with a blond crew cut, replaced Brian Berry as campaign manager following the primary. Berry had grown increasingly irritated over meddling from an influential Bush pal in Dallas and found himself in the middle of a personality spat between the hyperkinetic Rove and press secretary Deborah Burston-Wade.

"Brian made the mistake of thinking he was really the campaign manager, which means that he should have some say in what they did. Wrong. He's supposed to sit there and Karl calls with 20 things to do that day, get those done, then call back the next morning and get the next list," said a Bush associate. "What set him off was Karl telling Deborah Burston-Wade what to do, and she would go and complain to Brian and Brian made the mistake of whining about it to people in general. One day he picked up the phone and screamed at Karl. I just knew instinctively, that's the end of this guy."

A couple of weeks later, Berry was out and Allbaugh was in.

Hughes, a former TV reporter from Dallas, had made a reputation at the Texas Republican party, where she spent four years softening up Ann Richards with crisp, rapid-response attacks on the Democrat governor's every move. Hughes became a close confidante—smart, direct, exceedingly loyal, and instinctively gifted at managing his image. She was Rove's biggest rival for Bush's ear inside the administration.

In the governor's office, Hughes imposed a strict discipline aimed at controlling the message—a precursor of the White House press office. Calls to the governor's division directors and even some state agency heads were redirected to the press office. Leaks were rare. It was not uncommon for Hughes, whenever the governor found himself straining for a point, to step in and begin fielding the questions herself.

Once, when a reporter began quizzing the governor about campaign contributions at a news conference concerning faith-based organizations, Hughes stepped forward from the side of the room and, her voice booming, took over. All heads turned to Hughes. The governor, long accustomed to this, stopped talking. Hughes simply took command. Standing next to Bush was former national ethics czar William Bennett, whose face reflected a bemused fascination not only with Hughes, who handled the prickly questions and steered the conversation back on message, but also the fact that everyone in the room seemed to consider this so ordinary.

Unlike the others, Rove didn't go on the public payroll. He continued to operate his direct-mail business, but he collected a $7,000 monthly retainer from Bush's political account (the real money was in producing campaign material for his stable of political clients) and was an ever-present figure in the Capitol and the Governor's Mansion. Although he was a private consultant, Rove attended virtually every senior staff meeting and had a special phone line installed at his Shoal Creek office exclusively for Bush. He cleared every appointee the governor named, measuring nominations against financial contribution lists, political campaign work, and other tests of Republican orthodoxy.

"Our job is to say is there a significant political problem that would be created by appointing this individual or one by not appointing this individual," he said dryly in a deposition about his informal role as gatekeeper. Every appointment of a judge or member to an agency board went through him, every important policy decision. He pored over the polls, evaluated the political implications.

A common refrain in the governor's office was: "Where's Karl on this?" or "Has Karl signed off on this?"

Rove wasn't even on the governor's staff, but nothing important happened without his imprimatur. He had achieved a political trifecta, advising appointments to the judiciary, counseling some Republican legislative candidates and serving the chief executive—all three branches of government. He had carried the campaign into the office and turned the office inside out.

Rove had turned it into a permanent campaign.

In his 1980 book *The Permanent Campaign*, Sidney Blumenthal chronicles the rise of the political operative in modern American politics, from the godfather of early twentieth-century image making, Edward Bernays, through the more current crop of campaign consultants. Bernays' fundamental contribution was to apply a scientific method to the practice of marketing and public relations—attaching numbers to the hunches. His term for manipulating opinion was "engineering consent."

Much of the development of campaign message making owes a debt to Bernays. By the end of the century, the consultant had largely supplanted the party bosses. With the rise of the consultant, Blumenthal noted, came the diminishing influence of the political parties, which served the needs of organization and patronage. Now it was the consultant who steered the machine. The consultant had a place inside the campaign, advising candidates on message, shaping the look and tone of a campaign through the media. Typically, the consultant was a hired gun who directed the political wars of the campaign and moved on, leaving the task of governing to those they elected. It was only a matter of time before one would subsume the other in what Blumenthal calls the permanent campaign.

"Under the permanent campaign," he wrote, "governing is turned into a perpetual campaign. It remakes government into an instrument designed to sustain an elected official's public popularity. It is the engineering of consent with a vengeance."

Rove became the apotheosis of the permanent campaign. He ran every discussion of policy through the alembic of politics, evaluating the implications on various groups with a voracious energy, factoring the latest poll results and statistical voter trends. But just as Hughes was sensitive to a precise tone Bush preferred to express an idea, Rove was careful not to present his conclusions as the product of raw politics. That's what Clinton did. Bush was fixated on the idea that Clinton made decisions exclusively on the basis of polls and focus groups. He viewed the administration as so devoid of principle that every action was the product of a shrewd political calculation.

Bush understood Rove's genius in analyzing the politics of a situation—he needed it—but he insisted that arguments be made on the basis of merit and not the grubby, Clintonian business of sticking a finger into the wind to measure public opinion. Everybody around the table understood that in discussing, say, student testing or allocating lottery money, any mention of polls or focus groups was not only unseemly but also verboten. The Bush doctrine was clear: Decisions were to be made on substance.

And who better to marshal the armies of substance—*demographic data . . . historic models . . . moral constructs . . . legal arguments*—to make a policy-based argument than Karl Rove? At senior staff meetings, there was a general understanding that as long as politics wasn't specifically mentioned, politics was not part of the equation, even though everybody knew that Rove had probably already considered the political implications. For six years, Rove moved Bush toward more politically expedient positions on school vouchers, ending the practice of social promotion and shaping property tax cuts in a round number to sell better in Republican primary states—but always by framing the case with facts and moral suasion.

"There's nothing scattergun about him," said George Christian. "When he talks to you about something, you have the very definite impression that it's not off the top of his head, that he's thought it through and it makes sense. He just knows more about it than anybody else knows. And when you go into a situation where you have more information and use that information wisely, you're going to be hard to argue with.

"I have the impression that he and Bush will argue back and forth. If he doesn't like what Rove is saying, he'll tell him. I would guess deep down, Bush resents Rove's alleged power. He needs it, but resents it a little."

Periodically, Bush would swat down his political consultant just to remind everyone who was boss. When the *Boston Globe* published a story in June 1995 comparing Bush to his father, it quoted Rove: "George W. has a worldview that is significantly different than his father. His father has a sense of *noblesse oblige* that drives him. George is driven by his desire to make a difference."

Bush was livid. He arrived for a staff meeting and glowered at Rove.

"No one will promote me at the expense of my father. Karl, I expect you to write a handwritten apology."

Rove did write an apology, immediately.

Sometimes, when Rove was particularly puffed up about a particular point, Bush deflated the moment by offering the briefest acknowledgment.

"Thank you, Mr. Big Shot."

Bush was Rove's premier candidate, the keys to the kingdom, but even as he counseled the governor, he maintained a list of private business clients who paid for his political advice. Among them was the tobacco giant Philip Morris. Rove signed on with Philip Morris in the spring 1991 after getting a call from his old friend from the Young Republican days, Bernie Robinson. It had been 20 years since Rove and Robinson traveled the Young Republican circuit, teaching campaign strategy and dirty tricks, and now Robinson was a lobbyist in New York for Philip Morris.

Rove was hired by Philip Morris to periodically provide what he called "political intelligence," such as how future candidates were likely to fare and, as a result, the prospects of legislation that could affect Philip Morris. The company used Rove's information to target its support for legislative and statewide candidates. Presumably, Philip Morris also hoped that Rove's proximity to Bush would pay dividends in advancing the company's agenda. In a deposition, Rove said he told Bush in 1993 about his tobacco client and claimed Bush had no problem, but that he didn't want to hear about it.

Philip Morris had an ample agenda in Texas. Every biennial session, state legislators tried to boost taxes on cigarettes, curb smoking in restaurants and limit access to minors of tobacco products. But the big-dollar issue was tort reform, the campaign by business to curb its liability from lawsuits involving injury, illness or death. Big Tobacco was a big supporter of tort reform.

When lawyers who filed suit against tobacco companies deposed Rove as part of the litigation, they asked about his role advising Bush on tort reform. And for once, Rove's grasp of the complex and detailed, his photographic memory, his mastery of names and dates and minutiae failed him.

"Did you ever discuss with Governor Bush during the year 1995 and during the year 1996 tort reform legislation?" a lawyer asked.

"I'm sure I did, but I don't recall specifically. That was not in my area."

"But you do recall that generally that was an area that you did discuss with him?" the lawyer pressed.

"The governor had a very specific tort reform package that he laid out in the 1994 campaign that he largely enacted in 1995."

"And you were involved and participated in discussions with him regarding tort reform?"

"I can't say that I did. But I can't say that I didn't. I do not recall. I know that tort reform was a significant part of his legislative agenda but it was not my area."

Rove's effort to distance himself from the issue appears at odds with his recollection, years later, of setting the agenda for Bush's gubernatorial campaign.

"We added tort reform. I sort of talked him into that one."

At one point in the deposition, the lawyer asked Rove about the measure of his influence.

"Is it fair to say, Mr. Rove, that you are an influential man in Texas politics?"

"It's a subjective judgment."

"Do you believe you have influence, political influence?"

"Again, that is a subjective judgment. I can help candidates and do."

The lawyer tried again.

"You are close to the governor, aren't you?"

"Yes."

"You have his trust and his confidence I assume. Correct?"

"I hope so."

"And you have access to him, do you not?"

"Yes, I do."

"And is it fair to say that you have influence with the governor?"

"I can."

When the tobacco lobbyists met in February 1996 to review the draft of their push poll, there was still hope of dissuading Democrat Attorney General Dan Morales from filing suit against the industry. Texas was among the first states to consider taking tobacco companies to court to recover Medicaid costs for treatment of tobacco-related illnesses.

To head off the suit, the tobacco industry commissioned a Republican polling firm in Virginia to test what issues would be most successful in a campaign to politically damage Morales, who planned to seek re-election. Rove reviewed a draft of the poll and made recommendations for tweaking the design of some of the questions.Unlike traditional political polls, the survey, known as a *push poll*, measures the impact of negative information the pollster provides. The results would give enemies of Morales a model for a campaign against him. Maybe the results would scare Morales from filing suit.

As a state legislator and then attorney general, Morales had always cut a fairly independent line. He was a Harvard-educated lawyer in thin horn-rims and pressed jeans, serious-minded, articulate, and not easily bullied. Rove saw in Morales a rising star in the Democratic party, an attractive young politico, and, most certainly, a potential threat to GOP candidates down the road.

The push poll presented a clear method for damaging Morales. Respondents were asked if they'd be less likely to vote for Morales if he believed "young gang members don't need harsh treatment and prison" or if he "regularly flies for free in private planes provided by some of the country's richest personal injury lawyers." Questions measured the drop of public support if Morales were linked to affirmative action, gun control, and Nation of Islam leader Louis Farrakhan.

The survey concluded that Morales could be vulnerable "if a strong, well-funded candidate ran against him."

That was a message the industry wanted delivered.

Late one morning, Rove arrived at the eighth-floor office of Jack Dillard, the Philip Morris lobbyist in Texas. The building was across the street from the Texas capitol and out the window was a spectacular view of the pink granite dome glowing in the sun. A half-dozen lobbyists sat around a table with a representative of the polling company, reviewing the results. One of the lobbyists, Mark Harkrider, was assigned to show the poll to Morales. The rest were to distribute it to other key elected officials. Rove delivered his copy to the governor's office, dropping it off with Bush's executive assistant, Joe Allbaugh.

Morales filed suit anyway.

He hired five prominent Texas trial lawyers, who ultimately won the state $15.3 billion in a settlement with the tobacco industry.

When word of the poll leaked to the media, Rove sought to reconcile his dual roles as advisor to the tobacco industry and counselor to the governor. He had gone to the meeting as a representative of Philip Morris, he said, but delivered the survey to the governor in his role as political consultant. Karl Rove was good with such murky distinctions.

"My job advising Philip Morris has nothing to do with my job working for the governor," he said.

In fact, Rove's job with Philip Morris had everything to do with Bush, but not in the way the press and the lawyers for Morales and

Democratic critics believed. The conventional thinking is that special interest groups hire lobbyists and others to influence elected public officials. Big Tobacco wants to prevent cities from regulating cigarette machines or restricting sales to minors, and it hires Rove to help win Bush over to its side. But Bush vetoed the cigarette-machine bill sought by the industry in 1995 and signed tough legislation restricting sales to minors.

Rove was never about helping Big Tobacco at the expense of George Bush. Just the opposite. Where their interests ran parallel— say, curbing jury awards against business and limiting money to trial lawyers who bankroll Democrats—the governor and tobacco were simpatico. But when the industry's agenda didn't help Bush politically, they parted ways. Politics was policy in Rove's world; issues were simply instruments to advance the political cause of electing Bush to ever-higher office.

Although he delivered the push poll to the governor's office, Rove never intended that Bush see it. The poll was about damaging a young Democrat's political future and keeping money out of the pockets of trial lawyers. It was about Rove's relationship with the to-bacco industry, whose support and soft-money contributions to the Republican party were crucial to electing future presidents. Bush advanced the cause of tort reform, not because tobacco wanted it, but because it was good for business and that was good for Bush. In everything Rove did, in every business group he cultivated and every political alliance he drew, the essential question was always what they could do for Bush, not the other way around.

Tom Pauken was doing nothing for Bush, so far as Rove could see.

Pauken, chairman of the Texas Republican party, had long had a frosty relationship with the Bush family and its allies. He was a Goldwater Republican and former head of the nation's volunteerism agency in the Reagan administration. When he sided with Bob Dole over George Bush in the 1988 presidential race, the younger Bush searched him out at barbecue during the state GOP convention in Houston.

"You son of a bitch, how dare you do this? I'll never forget. You've crossed the line out there," Pauken recalls Bush saying.

Pauken said the message was clear.

"Loyalty is the number one virtue as far as George W. Bush is concerned, but it's loyalty to the Bush family. Everybody is expected to serve the purposes of the Bush family, and if you don't, you have broken the trust and you are no longer in the club."

No one was a stronger adherent to the Bush loyalty code than Rove. Much as Lee Atwater had served the father, Karl Rove was serving the son. But in the two counselors, Pauken saw a difference.

"Lee was the kind of guy who'd say, hey, you were against us here, but you can be for us the next time. Karl is very different. If you cross him, you're on the list. And the more you cross him over a period time, the higher you go on the list. I've risen high on Karl's enemies list."

Rove opposed Pauken's election to head the state Republican party and was outraged two years later when social conservative delegates snubbed Bush, the sitting governor, and made Pauken chairman of the delegation to the GOP national convention in San Diego. Rove convinced the party's blue chip givers to shut off contributions to the state party, effectively rerouting the money to another fund that Rove controlled.

"It was Karl turning the spigot off. He could turn it on, he could turn it off. If you don't play ball, then he's going to make life difficult."

As Bush prepared to introduce his school tax plan to the 1997 legislative session, he feared Pauken would be a problem. His plan to cut property taxes by $3 billion would require raising the sales tax and creating a new business tax—both anathemas to staunch conservatives like Pauken. Even if the average Texan ended up paying less in taxes overall, he knew Pauken wouldn't like it. Bush summoned the party chief to the capitol.

"You have to support this," Bush said.

"I don't know enough about it, but I have some concerns."

"No. You've got to support this."

Pauken was resolute.

"Can't do it. It's not personal, governor. It's just something I'm philosophically opposed to."

The day Bush introduced his plan with a grand flourish in a speech to a combined session of the Texas legislature—"Discontent over property taxes runs deep and wide in Texas"—Pauken issued a press release panning the idea.

"Once you put new taxes on the books, they never go away. And the new taxes, along with the old ones, just keep going up," the release said.

The Bush plan was in trouble from the beginning. The right didn't like the tax hikes. The left was suspicious big beneficiaries were likely to be companies like Enron and the petrochemical giants. Representative Paul Sadler, a brilliant East Texas trial lawyer who was to become Bush's most important ally in the House, wondered as he listened to the governor deliver his speech in the immense House chamber what had happened to his friend, George Bush, whose passion two years earlier seemed to be education, not tax cuts.

"Somewhere between '95 and '97 he got off message and it bothered me," said Sadler. "He was talking about how we've got to do something about property taxes, property taxes, property taxes. He wanted to separate property taxes from school finance, which is an impossible thing to do in Texas. He got strictly on property tax relief and I couldn't figure out why."

As a candidate for governor, Bush focused on how to improve education by reducing paperwork, giving local school districts more authority and changing the antiquated system for funding schools. He wanted to change the system in which rich districts were penalized and poor districts were under-funded and students in the classroom suffered as a result.

Shortly after he was elected governor, Bush invited Sadler to lunch.

"We've never met," Bush said. "I've followed you around the state and heard you speak on education and I appreciate the fact that you never made it partisan. I want you to know that I understand that in order to fix school finance, we have to change the tax structure in Texas."

Sadler was heartened. Bush's priority clearly was to improve education, and he understood that changing the state's tax structure was a tool to achieve that end.

"You're light years ahead of everybody who's been here before," Sadler told him.

But by 1997, as Bush's name began popping up among future presidential candidates, tax cuts had become the end. Bush appointed a committee to conduct statewide hearings, dubbed "the tax road show." Rossanna Salazar, a respected former aide to Governor Bill Clements, was tapped at Rove's behest to help promote the committee and generated bundles of fresh press clippings, which a staff assembled amid the thrum of photocopiers in the basement of the Capitol.

"I'd go down there to get the clips and Rove would always be down there. It was like he had an office down there in the basement," said Cindy Rugeley, who worked on the promotion effort.

Rove dispatched Perry, the lieutenant governor, to sell the idea to Republican-friendly business groups. But when Perry arrived at the Woodlands, an upscale community north of Houston, he met a storm of protest.

"I made the pitch and they hated it," said Perry. "They raped me. They were in my face, all over me. There was a car dealer and a beer distributor who got in my face over this. I was the demon child."

Former Governor Clements called, concerned that the politics of shifting business taxes would undo Bush's future. Sipple, the campaign's ad man, sent a note warning that the downside risks seemed to outweigh any upside advantages. But Bush had now staked too much on the idea and moved forward.

Before the legislature convened, Bush held a news conference next to the gazebo on the grounds of the Governor's Mansion and publicly laid claim to $1 billion of surplus in the state budget to cut taxes. "I started getting worried," said Sadler. "You've got a Republican governor who's talking about property tax relief, not school finance, which is what the issue should be."

Sadler had his staff pull old newspapers and documents from the state archives and he began reading them. As he read, he came to a startling conclusion: Bush's tax plan was the mirror image of one advanced by conservative Washington lobbyist Charls Walker, the architect of Ronald Reagan's sweeping tax proposals in the 1980s. Walker ran a think-tank and an anti-tax policy group whose members were Shell Oil Co., Exxon, Browning-Ferris Industries, and Enron—the same industries that would benefit under the Bush plan. The Bush tax committee that "made recommendations" to the governor actually included an Enron executive recommended by Ken Lay. It turned out that Walker had visited Bush at the capitol in August 1995 and provided a model on how to construct a new tax system. These were Karl Rove's guys, the big-money guys, and the financial foundation of the national GOP. Whether Rove was a reluctant traveler or the engineer, one thing seemed clear: once Bush decided to move forward on a plan to cut taxes, the voices shaping it sounded remarkably as if they all belonged to Rove.

"You're not doing this for school finance," Sadler told the governor. "You're doing this for capital-intensive companies."

Sadler shelved the Bush proposal and his House committee began working on a plan of its own. What surprised Sadler was how quickly Bush came around to the committee's view. He and Bush struck up a strong friendship. And as they talked—long, deep conversations about education and taxes, about family and the future—it was clear to Sadler that Bush was very much committed to improving public education in Texas. He was remarkably open to other ideas for financing schools and altering the tax system—ideas he apparently never considered or were never presented.

As they met in Bush's office at the capitol or talked into the evening over coffee and cigars at the mansion, Sadler grew to understand in a vivid way exactly how Bush thinks and makes decisions.

The Bush method was to delegate responsibility to top aides, directing them to study an issue and report back. Bush's strength was making decisions, not thinking through specific issues on his own. He wasn't afraid to have strong people around him, and he gave them wide latitude to evaluate problems and recommend a solution. Bush delegated authority to his advisors and trusted their advice. He had a limited attention span and no stomach for philosophizing endlessly over an issue.

Clay Johnson, Bush's long-time friend from prep school and his appointments secretary as governor, recalls staff meetings as brisk and short.

"It's sit down. What's the subject today? Boom! Boom! Boom! Here are some alternatives here's a recommended course of action, here's why, here's the likely results and implications. Good, let's do it. Next!"

Bush's gift, Sadler came to believe, was his ability to sift through the various recommendations and come to a crisp, final decision.

"I have absolutely no question in his ability to make the right decision if he's presented the facts from all sides. I have watched him do it. Where I found he gets off track is if he only has once voice in the room. There's what's always bothered me," said Sadler.

"It's not that he's not smart, not that he's not intelligent, not that he's not a quick study, not that he's not capable of making a decision. It's about the need to have different viewpoints in the room. Part of my training as a lawyer is trying to understand what the other side thinks. He comes from an MBA background. He doesn't have that training. I want to know why I think the way I do, but I always want to know why the other side thinks the way they do. He doesn't go through that thought process as often. To me, it makes it more important to make sure the counselors around him come from different viewpoints."

One Monday, Sadler was in his capitol office and Bush popped his head in the door. The conversation drifted to the subject of hate crimes.

"You know I can't sign that," Bush said.

"You can't sign that because it mentions gender," said Sadler. "And you're afraid—you're not but your party is—so afraid that if it ever gets in a statute somewhere it will somehow embrace the lifestyle. That's just such an idiotic argument, I can't believe you would even make it."

They went back and forth, Sadler arguing that enhanced penalties for hate crimes was the law-and-order position, and Bush defending his opposition to a law he felt was flawed.

"Paul," Bush said. "How do you know if they're gay or not?"

Sadler was startled by the question. Bush thought he had found a soft spot in the administration of a hate crimes law.

"The issue is not whether or not they are gay, governor. The issue is whether or not you believe them to be gay, and because of your hatred, you kill them."

It was clear that Bush had not thought through the issue in any systematic way. He had not turned the idea over in his head and come to a conclusion on his own.

In so many of their conversations, Bush seemed to have come to conclusions based on the summaries of his advisors.

The school tax bill was an example.

For months, the Sadler committee worked on its version of the school tax bill, inviting hundreds of people to testify with ideas. Lawmakers poured through the Byzantine filigree of school finance, its formulas, and its assumptions. The result was a plan that gave property tax relief to homeowners and boosted state spending on schools. The bill was guaranteed to attract opposition from some business groups— it shifted some taxes around—but Bush adopted it as his own. This was the premier issue of his governorship, and he laid his credibility on the line by urging passage by the Senate.

Bush worked the bill, lobbied, and cajoled. On the Saturday it all fell apart, Bush was exhausted from long hours, frayed tempers.

"We had been to hell and back," said Sadler.

But in the end, the coterie of Republican senators refused to go along. Florence Shapiro said no and now the room was nearly empty and Bush slumped in the chair.

He turned to the two Democratic legislators, Mark Stiles and Paul Sadler.

"What do you think I should do?" he asked.

"What do you want to do? Who are you trying to help, governor?" Stiles asked.

Bush paused.

"I want to help the poorest Texas homeowner."

There would be no massive property tax relief, no long-term fix for the state's school finance problems. But there was still $1 billion in surplus available for a modest tax cut for homeowners.

"Take the billion dollars," Sadler said.

Bush put his head in his hands and his eyes welled up with tears.

"I did not know how to read his emotion," said Sadler. "I didn't know if it was disappointment that something good was going down. I didn't know if it was, 'My political future is over.' I didn't know what it meant and I didn't want to ask. I really didn't want to know."

The next day, Sadler got word that Bush wanted to see him in his office. This time, his staff surrounded Bush, including education chief Margaret LaMontagne and press secretary Karen Hughes. Bush said they had decided to apply the $1 billion outside the school-finance formula. This meant teachers wouldn't get a pay raise.

"They've never been with us," Hughes said of the teacher unions.

This did not sound like Hughes. It didn't sound like Bush or La-Montague. This had a hard, political edge. This sounded like Rove.

Sadler protested and after some argument, Bush relented and teachers got a raise. Once Bush was presented with a wider range of voices in the room, once he went outside his small circle of advisors, he made a better judgment. But the sour impression of that moment stayed with Sadler into the next legislative session in 1999, when Bush rolled out his last legislative agenda as governor.

It was an agenda befitting a presidential campaign.

This time, there were no complex school-tax proposals that might alienate business. Instead, there was a strong ideological bent guaranteed to find favor among Republican primary voters. Bush advocated stricter limits on abortion. He pledged to end the practice of automatically passing students, a theme consistent with the conservative message of personal responsibility. His legislative lobby team kept a hate-crimes bill bottled up and away from his desk. School vouchers, something Bush hadn't pushed in years, were back on his agenda. As a new governor, Bush had privately assured Sadler, "Don't worry about vouchers." But now school vouchers were suddenly important again.

"Where did this voucher stuff come from?" Sadler asked. "He just grinned at me."

Most important, tax cuts were back, this time a neat $2 billion in tax relief from budget surplus—and the governor fought every effort to whittle down the amount. When lawmakers tried to put money into a prekindergarten program, Bush resisted. When the legislature needed money to fund a teacher health program, Bush fought it.

"What's so magic about the number $2 billion?" Sadler asked. "Why isn't $1.9 billion enough? Why isn't $1.8 billion enough?"

"I just have to have $2 billion," Bush said.

"You want $2 billion because you have to beat Christie Todd Whitman," Sadler said.

Sadler saved the kindergarten funding, but only after the Bush team rummaged through the budget to find money elsewhere for a full $2 billion. Everything was about the presidential race now. Whitman, who had cut taxes in New Jersey, was on the long horizon of Republicans Bush would have to beat to win his party's presidential nomination—Whitman and Steve Forbes and John McCain and Elizabeth Dole. Now, politics was everything. Whatever Bush did was determined by the dominant voice in the room, and Sadler knew to whom that voice belonged.

Bush's agenda was Rove's agenda.

"When I'm asked about his management style, I say look to the dominant personality. Look to the person he trusts the most, and that's the person he'll ultimately go to," said Sadler.

"This is a personal friend of mine and I will do anything in the world for him. My concern about him has always been that if he only has one voice in the room, or one strategy in the room, he gets off message and is not true to his nature.

"I will tell you, I have been concerned many times since September 11 because of that. Because I know how he makes decisions. I know how he does it. And I've watched as they have drawn that circle up there, closer and closer and tighter. And I know who's in the middle of it, and it bothers me a lot."

When the plane touched down in Cedar Rapids, Iowa, under a crystal-bright sky in June 1999, the crowd corralled in a huge metal airplane hanger began waving signs and cheering for the governor of Texas, who was making his first campaign stop of the 2000 presidential race.

The 727 arrived bursting with a full Bush entourage and the squeaking, beeping mob of the national news media, which streamed down the stairway to capture every sight and sound. There was NBC. There was CNN. There, at the top of the stairway, were Bush and his wife, Laura, waving to the jubilant crowd.

"I'm ready," Bush declared. "There's no turning back. I intend to be president of the United States."

The crowd and the cameras all followed Bush, the candidate. Rove blinked as he stepped out into the bright Iowa sun and descended the stairway of the plane dubbed Great Expectations. They were now in Iowa, the first test of the 2000 presidential race, the land of cornfields and political caucuses. A candidate had arrived with the credentials to be president of the United States—a compassionate conservative, an advocate of personal responsibility and a champion of tax cuts with the nice, round $2 billion to show for it.

Brian Berry, watching television, marveled at how Bush and Rove had made it, how they were finally in Iowa.

"They were long friends and this was a long dream."

13

He Shoots, He Scores

The blood-dimmed tide is loosed.

William Butler Yeats

As it turned out, Rove was wrong about New Hampshire. He was depending on intelligence from Senator Judd Gregg's organization and from his own political contacts. Mostly, he was depending on poll numbers, his Cartesian tellers of truth, which never failed him, not if properly analyzed. And nobody could analyze the numbers like Karl Rove.

"Look here!" he said, hunched over a small square table at the Days Inn in Merrimack.

On the table was a napkin with a series of lines drawn like jagged horizons, rising and falling, sometimes crossing. The lines represented different poll results. There were recent network polls and Republican party polls and the Bush campaign's own polling. One of the lines represented something called PortraitofAmerica.com, a Web site that Rove pored over daily in his voracious search for every tic and shift in American opinion.

"Look at the trends. We're going to win New Hampshire," Rove declared. He pointed to the napkin and explained that the momentum, which initially seemed to favor Bush and then McCain, now favored Bush again. Bush's numbers were on the ascendancy and, given time, he would overcome McCain. By Rove's calculation, there was time before the February 1 New Hampshire primary, the first in the nation. So now he was bouncing around in the plastic chair in the snack bar of the motel, confident, exultant.

Outside, the snow had stopped falling. Inside, in the bright reflected light, Rove was in full-turbo mode, offering up a lavishly dense explanation about cross-tabs and voter trends and New England historical precedents as evidence of an impending Bush victory.

Why not? The ghosts were all good for George W. Bush in New Hampshire, starting in June 1999. Two weeks after the legislative session ended, Bush launched his maiden campaign trip, first to Iowa and then on to New Castle, New Hampshire, where a news conference was arranged under a white tent against a backdrop of New England coastline.

Every national newspaper, magazine, and network had sent reporters. Maureen Dowd of the *New York Times* sat on the front row, wearing sunglasses. Chris Matthews of MSNBC stood among the cluster of camera crews. Thick fog had settled over the coast, obscuring the lighthouse that was to have provided a picturesque backdrop.

"This was his debut on the national stage, the big moment. And you could smell fear in the air," said Mark McKinnon, Bush's television media consultant. "You could sense the press just ready to put him through his paces and see if he was ready. He was up there on the high wire for the first time without a net and some of us in the campaign were very nervous and I think he was, too."

Rove and Hughes and McKinnon all knew this was a moment of no small import. "It was a new jungle and new animals," said McKinnon.

The team watched their man step onto the platform. Bush assumed a veneer of confidence, but his body language telegraphed apprehension. He offered stiff answers to the first volley of questions.

"It was almost like one of those Arnold Schwarzenegger movies where all the dials in his brain were surveying the room and downloading information. Danger! Danger! Heat-seeking here! Friendly fire over there!" said McKinnon.

Then, about five minutes into the news conference, Bush's shoulders started to relax and his arms fell easily at his side. He rolled slightly on his hips, like a quarterback throwing an easy spiral.

"Matthews," Bush said, singling him out in the crowd. "It's good to see the larger personalities are starting to show up."

The fear in the Bush camp began to dissipate.

"I remember literally seeing the moment when he physically changed and was saying, 'I can do this,'" McKinnon said.

In the months that followed, Bush sought to cultivate the national press in much the way he had done in Austin—with attention and flattery and a talent for suggesting they were seeing in his informality a glimpse of the inner man. This was not so much Rove's doing as Hughes'. She recognized the value of Bush's engaging personality and arranged that he wander up and down the center aisle, making small talk with every reporter. Although Bush privately was wary of reporters, he had confidence in his ability to make friends and influence antagonists.

Rove typically stayed up front in the first-class section. It was Hughes' job to accompany the candidate back to the "zoo" section where the media rode. Bush wandered through the plane, giving reporters nicknames and asking about their families. He would emerge nuzzling a Mini Me doll from the Austin Powers movies and do an impression of Dr. Evil.

"Zip it!" he'd say, moving around the cabin.

So with Bush making inroads among the media and Rove advancing the battle plan, the campaign appeared to be very much on course.

Iowa, the first test of the campaign, was a success. Touring the courthouse square in Glenwood with a media mob in tow, Bush poked his head into a bank and offered greetings. A couple of women came out to shake his hand, one carrying a rubber Clinton mask. Bush grasped the mask and briefly held it aloft, as if he were a conquering warrior with the severed head of an enemy. At campaign headquarters in West Des Moines, a former furniture warehouse next to Stacey's Bra and Lingerie shop, Bush circulated among an enthusiastic corps of volunteers. Outside was a red pickup truck with Iowa plates and two bumper stickers: one for Bush and the other about Willie Nelson. Everything seemed right on course.

But there were disconcerting signs in New Hampshire, which Rove and the rest of the Austin crew did not take seriously enough. Bush skipped two early debates in New Hampshire, which rankled some supporters. When Hughes visited the state in late 1999, she went to Bush campaign headquarters and noticed that almost all the volunteers were from somewhere else.

"I thought, that doesn't seem right," Hughes said, but then disregarded it like so many other signals that the Bush effort wasn't going well.

Rove did not see the McCain challenge until it was too late. He was immersed in the master plan—Bush campaign organizations in all 50 states, the hierarchy of the Republican party falling in line: Certain victory by March.

"If you are the establishment choice on the Republican side, you are the inevitable nominee. No ifs, ands, or buts," Rove told a group of Austin business lobbyists at a private luncheon 10 weeks before the New Hampshire primary.

"At the end of the day, there will be 30 members of the 55 Republicans in the U.S. Senate for George W. Bush, despite the fact that one of their own is running. More important, a majority of Republicans in 32 state legislatures have endorsed George W. Bush."

The Republican leadership had, indeed, fallen in with Bush, seduced by his front-runner status and a carefully orchestrated succession of visits to Austin conceived by Rove in the manner of William McKinley's "front-porch campaign" a century earlier. Mark Hanna was the key architect in 1896, bringing a procession of prominent visitors to McKinley's modest home in Canton and effectively locking up the Republican nomination. Now it was Rove engineering the flow of Republicans to Austin in early 1999. Governors and state legislators came.

Even the territories sent delegates to the Governor's Mansion.

At lunch one day, Don Luis Ferre, the 95-year-old patriarch of the Republican party in Puerto Rico, stood and declared allegiance to the governor of Texas. "We are all for George. It's best for America." The delegation from Puerto Rico all applauded.

Cesar Cabrera, executive director of the Republican party in the territory, turned to Rove and extended an invitation to visit and go swordfishing in the warm Caribbean waters.

"You have a very important decision to make," he said, attributing to Rove a remarkable influence.

"Who will come in second in the Puerto Rico primary?"

"Cesar, that's up to the voters," said Rove.

"Oh no. That's up to you. The voters will decide whether or not they get 10 percent."

Rove must have reveled in this role . . . *kingmaker* . . . even if he knew that Cabrera's assessment was comically overblown and the Bush campaign faced considerable obstacles in the road ahead. In his speech to the business lobbyists in mid-November, Rove emphasized how Bush, the front-runner, was entering every primary while his opponents could pick and choose.

"We're going to face a series of sequential battles," Rove said. "In Iowa, there'll be Forbes. In New Hampshire, it's going to be McCain."

He suggested New Hampshire was well in hand, although he was oddly critical of the voters there.

"They're crazy. They like being obstreperous and they want you to spend a lot of time there. As of the 18th of October, McCain had spent more on media in New Hampshire than we did. He had used one-third of the money he can spend. There will not be a single day from here to the end of the campaign where he will outspend us on TV and message."

But it was already too late. The vaunted Rove sonar had failed to pick up the seriousness of the McCain threat.

In December, Richard Berke of the *New York Times* wrote that some Bush allies were complaining lapses by the campaign had left the Texas governor unnecessarily vulnerable to McCain. There were frustrations that Austin—that is, Rove—had scheduled so few Bush trips to the state, and that the visits he did make were too often large events, not the personal campaigning favored by New Hampshire voters. Bush's lead in the polls was evaporating and John McCain was on the rise:

> . . . New Hampshire may no longer be the make-or-break state it once was for presidential aspirants. Still, no matter what happens, many Bush supporters in New Hampshire said the campaign should never have put itself in jeopardy. Their recrimination underscores a tension—one that many strategists say was inevitable—between the campaign's tightly run high command in Austin and its supporters on the ground in this tiny state.
>
> Former Governor Stephen E. Merrill of New Hampshire, who ran Bob Dole's campaign here in 1996 and backs Mr. Bush, spoke out for the first time in an interview about his qualms about the governor's organization.
>
> "The Bush campaign believed it was the front-runner in New Hampshire," said Mr. Merrill, who did not seek re-election in 1996. "There's no such thing as the front-runner in New Hampshire. You simply become the biggest target."

Still, Rove remained confident of his national strategy to compete everywhere, and ride as the front-runner above the rabble. Bush's first appearance on a Sunday morning show was with Tim Russert on NBC's "Meet the Press." Russert had been aggressive about courting Bush, flying to Austin months earlier to meet informally with the governor, staying at a hotel near the Governor's Mansion, stopping by the Texas Chili Parlor to soak up some Austin atmosphere with the regulars. More importantly, "Meet the Press" had the highest ratings among the Sunday shows and Russert had a reputation as a tenacious but fair interviewer. Bush could introduce himself to a national audience and, Rove was confident, help dispel the idea that he was dumb. As a measure of preparation for the show, Rove presented Bush a list of every question Russert had ever asked about Bush on "Meet the Press." Bush, true to form, gave the list scant attention.

"He looked over it briefly," said Hughes.

Bush did well on the show, in part because Rove and Hughes had worked to lower expectations, but also because Bush appeared to have a grasp of the issues. Now came his first debate in December in Manchester. Six candidates dividing an hour and half, which amounted to less than 15 minutes apiece of actual Q&A.

Rove had long been concerned about Steve Forbes and his anti-tax message. That was red meat for the Republican crowd. Through much of 1999, Rove was convinced that Forbes, not McCain, was the serious challenge in the GOP field. The pressure to get a full $2 billion in tax cuts during the last legislative session was a preemptive effort to blunt an anticipated Forbes attack.

Campaign workers for Forbes were on hand at a manufacturing plant in Nashua, New Hampshire, where Bush made a campaign stop. When the press bus arrived, the workers began handing printed flyers to reporters traveling with the Texas governor that listed scores of business taxes Bush had considered increasing in his effort to lower property taxes. Many of the reporters on the campaign were from Washington, New York, and Los Angeles, and had not had time to go deeply into the Bush record. The journalists wandered into the building, curiously scanning the long list of increases—solar energy, vending machine sales, magazine subscriptions, sludge recycling—75 proposed tax hikes in all.

Company employees were arranged in a semicircle in front of a lectern. As Bush entered the room, there was warm applause, even cheers. Karen Hughes leaned against a back wall, silently mouthing the text she knew by heart.

Frank Bruni, a reporter for the *New York Times*, read over the Forbes attack piece with a furrowed brow. He approached a Texas reporter and asked for more detail.

"Is this whole thing true?" Bruni wondered.

The Texan read the sheet carefully. "Yeah, that's pretty much the way I remember it."

Bruni approached Hughes with the Texas reporter following close enough to catch the conversation.

"Karen, is this Forbes' piece true?" Bruni asked.

Hughes scanned the paper quickly, and then leveled her gaze at Bruni.

"Frank, Governor Bush is responsible for the largest single tax cut in Texas history," she said. "It was $2 billion."

"Yeah, I know that. I hear it every day. But is this true? Did he really try to raise all of these taxes before backing off?"

"As I said, Governor Bush's $2 billion tax cut is the largest ever passed in the history of Texas."

"Karen, how about a simple answer? Just so you understand, let me clarify my question: Before cutting taxes $2 billion, did Governor Bush attempt to raise taxes on numerous businesses so that he could, in turn, lower property taxes?"

Hughes was unmoved. "The $2 billion dollar tax cut by Governor Bush was the largest in our state's history, Frank."

Bruni tilted his head, shrugged, and gave up. As he passed the Texas reporter, Bruni rolled his eyes and lifted his hands, in a gesture of helpless resignation.

Team Bush had its ready response on the tax issue and the matter sputtered in the press. So Forbes launched a new attack in advance of the December debate, warning that Bush might raise the retirement age for Social Security. In fact, Bush had refused to rule out such an option. Forbes responded with a withering television attack that seemed to run around the clock on WMUR-TV, the mother ship of New Hampshire media.

Sitting in the Governor's Mansion at midmorning, three days before the December debate, Rove and the rest of the campaign senior staff ran over the issues with Bush. Josh Bolton, the policy chief, pointed to something in the briefing book. It was an editorial Forbes wrote in 1977 advocating raising the retirement age.

"Steve wrote this?" Bush asked, smiling.

When Forbes launched his attack on Social Security during the debate, Bush had a ready response. Finding the editorial was good work by the policy team. Using it effectively was pure politics. Stuart Stevens, a Bush media advisor and long-time political consultant, said he's seen few people who bridge the two camps better than Rove.

"In most campaigns, there is a gulf between strategy/tactics/ media and policy, with each side viewing the other as a necessary evil," Stevens wrote in a book about the 2000 campaign, *The Big Enchilada*. "Media guys like me tended to look on policy as that stuff you had to have a little of to be credible but too much was either distracting, consuming valuable time and resources without attracting votes or highly dangerous, exposing the candidate needlessly to positions that might alienate potential voters. Policy wonks see media consultants and campaign operatives as nasty and brutish tools regrettably required to get through that awkward stage of actually getting elected so that the world can embrace their brilliant ideas.

"In the Bush campaign world, Karl bridged the gap. He was actually interested in the details of policy, a trait which I might have found suspect if I didn't know that he was also completely committed to the messy business of getting elected. Karl even read the briefing books prepared by the propeller heads, which is a bit like finding a 15-year-old who actually read the articles in *Playboy*."

By the time he arrived in New Hampshire, fresh off his win in the Iowa caucuses, Bush was trailing the runaway McCain campaign in the polls. Forbes was a distant third. But Rove took heart in tracking polls that showed Bush gaining and he assured the governor victory was possible.

In fact, Bush was doomed.

McCain had struck a deep and receptive nerve in the cranky voters of New Hampshire, a yearning for a hero, a maverick, a leader who would crash the party of politics as usual. Bush talked about restoring the dignity of the office, but McCain seemed to embody the idea. Bush arrived in a private jet with his entourage following in the 737. McCain had been on the ground for weeks, preaching the message of reform in the back of a bus called the *Straight Talk Express* that bumped along the snowy highways from Milford to Portsmouth to Merrimack.

Rove held firm to the idea that the strategy—stay positive, stay presidential—could work. He saw it in the numbers on the napkin as he sat in the snack bar area of the motel in Merrimack. He saw in the tangle of polling numbers the potential for Bush to overtake McCain in the final days of the primary and to emerge with what he called "a nomination that is worth having." In the final days, Bush went snowmobiling. And sledding. And candlepin bowling.

While Bush toured the Department of Safety headquarters in Concord with a press pool, Rove and reporters in the parking lot began lobbing snowballs at each other. Rove quickly escalated the pace.

He stood in the lot lined with mounds of snow and threw snowballs with a manic energy. He threw and threw, bashing a reporter in the head a few yards away, taking a splattering shot to the back of his overcoat. He scooped up snow and threw with such force that he seemed like a machine, throwing again and again, sweating in the bright chill of the day, flailing wildly against his enemies, beyond fatigue, beyond any reasonable limit of play.

This was no casual snowball fight, but a war. He didn't simply want to win; he wanted to crush his opponents. He wanted his enemies to flee. Standing in the snow-covered parking lot, battered and triumphant, Rove began jeering at the opposition. He strutted back and forth along a line, offering himself like a target in a shooting gallery. Snowballs came in on a long arc, but he dodged them.

"Missed me!" he taunted.

His face was ruddy with exhilaration and fatigue, his hair matted against his head. Many in the press had retreated to the bus.

"Losers!" Rove yelled, the darkest insult he could dredge up, the most denigrating label he could imagine.

"LOSERS!"

The night Bush lost New Hampshire, Rove made the telephone call to McCain's hotel suite. An aide answered, but the voice in the background belonged to John Weaver, McCain's political director.

"Consultants don't concede to candidates," Weaver instructed the aide to say.

This was McCain's night, and the protocols of such a night required that the losing candidate make the concession call and wait on the line for the winner, not the other way around. As it turned out, the Bush campaign didn't have a phone number for McCain, so Rove asked Alexandra Pelosi, an NBC producer who was shooting footage for her documentary, *Journeys With George*. Pelosi did have the number on her cell phone and did give it to Rove, but in exchange she wanted to film Bush making his concession speech. Rove agreed and took the phone, but later reneged on his deal with Pelosi. There would be no pictures of Bush conceding defeat.

When a McCain aide answered, Rove asked if this were the right number for Bush to call. But Weaver was insulted that Rove . . . *his arch-enemy Karl Rove* . . . was calling with any expectation that McCain would come to the phone. Weaver's message was clear: You lost, we won, tell Bush to make the call.

Bush did make the call. It lasted 90 seconds.

"John, you ran a great race, congratulations."

"Thanks for calling," said McCain. "We've run a campaign that you and I and our families can be proud of."

Weaver was exuberant with the results in New Hampshire, not that you could tell by looking at him. He was a tall, thin ex-Texan who wore on his face a perpetual look of worry. McCain nicknamed him "Sunny" as a joke because he clearly was not. He was dour, forever suspicious of the tactics of political opponents, and he carried in his head brilliant political instincts that associates back in Texas said made him every bit the equal of Rove.

They had been good friends 15 years earlier, had planned to go into business together—the two best young political minds in Texas in one shop. When Bill Clements won the Republican nomination for governor in 1986, Rove got Weaver the job as deputy campaign manager. They worked well together, Rove the outside consultant and Weaver the inside manager. Clements won and was so impressed he asked Weaver what he wanted. What Weaver wanted was to be executive director of the Texas Republican party.

It was then that the friction started between Rove and Weaver, according to political associates. In the 1988 presidential race, Weaver met with George Herbert Walker Bush in a hotel suite in Houston and, with Clements' backing, the future president handpicked him to head the Bush campaign in Texas, Victory '88.

The Republican party had a finite budget for the 1988 race and established a plan allocating sums for television and radio commercials, direct-mail advertising, salaries, phone banks, the light bill—everything required to operate a successful campaign. Rove's firm had the direct-mail account.

"Karl was really permissive in the way he did the mail. And he started doing some mail that didn't necessarily get approved or disapproved. When he was doing mail early on, he was trying to generate revenue, so Karl was pushing mail," said a Republican colleague.

Weaver, sitting at party headquarters, saw Rove's invoices roll in for work never formally approved. Weaver decided to pull rank and warned Rove that no work should be done without his okay. When he felt the order had been violated, Weaver refused to pay.

"He made Karl eat the cost. It was a lot of money," said the Republican.

"Weaver and Karl were very much alike—two bulls in a china shop."

Weaver decided to start his own consulting firm and hired Rove's ace copywriter, John Colyandro. Stole him, the way Rove saw it.

Colyandro called it a personal decision, something he wanted to do to develop professionally. "But Karl was not pleased with that," he said. "My team, your team—that's the way he's always conducted himself."

In the Manichaean universe of Karl Rove, there were only friends and enemies, his side and the other side, black and white, good and evil. The Democrats were clearly the enemy. But now Rove was dividing the field within the Republican party, those who were loyal and those who were not. During the 1980s and into the 1990s, Rove built a network of successful candidates who admired his skill and a coterie of loyal operatives who needed him for work in campaigns. Those who were with him won, more often than not. And those who crossed him, like Weaver, would pay for it.

The acrimony between Rove and Weaver grew. Rove lost some national clients and blamed Weaver. When Rob Mosbacher Jr., the son of President Bush's commerce secretary, took over the 1992 Bush re-election committee in Texas, he gave Weaver the big direct-mail account. Rove had a small contract for fund-raising, but Weaver had the important business of mass-mailing campaign appeals directly to voters. In September, a syndicated column by Evans and Novak appeared in newspapers suggesting the Texas re-election committee was in disarray and that President Bush was in danger of losing his home state.

The column said a secret meeting of worried Republican power brokers was held in Dallas in mid-September and that Mosbacher had been stripped of his authority and replaced by a Rove ally, Jim Francis. The column said Mosbacher "has been attacked for running the Victory '92 Committee out of Houston as a personal 1994 launching pad for governor." Several Republicans active in party affairs at the time said there was, indeed, criticism of Mosbacher's handling of the committee—from Rove.

After the column appeared, Phil Gramm issued a news release defending Mosbacher and making it clear he remained very much at the helm of Victory '92. Rove's contract was terminated. But the damage had been done to Mosbacher and, by extension, to Weaver. Rove had his own candidate in mind for governor in 1994 and it wasn't going to be Team Mosbacher.

"The thing that separates Karl from other people is his determination," said Colyandro. "Despite setbacks, whether on a business level or a personal level, he remains dogged. Look at the bodies on the political battlefield and they refused to remain dogged and determined. That determination, that's what separates Karl from the rest of the crowd."

In the special election for U.S. Senate in 1993, Rove's candidate was State Treasurer Kay Bailey Hutchison. Weaver signed up with Republican Representative Jack Fields. Hutchison won. When Phil Gramm launched his presidential bid, he took Weaver—but the campaign sputtered and collapsed.

Along the way, Rove built a shiny roster of winners: Hutchison in the Senate, George W. Bush as governor, John Cornyn as attorney general, Rick Perry as agriculture commissioner. And with every win, Rove pushed Weaver out until Rove controlled the political apparatus of virtually every Republican officeholder and Weaver eventually couldn't get work in Texas. It was like one of those flickering, black-and-white Western movies where the two fastest guns face off in the dust against the antique admonition that the town's not big enough for both of them.

"John decided that he didn't want to see Karl getting all the credit and he made his move. He made it with Gramm, he made it with others," said Austin political consultant David Weeks. "He didn't want Karl to own the mantle of being the consultant. He basically challenged Karl to king of the hill. And that was a big mistake."

In everything Rove did, he played to win. He simply worked harder and longer and with an intensity that burned the edges of the field of play. His second wife, Darby, told a reporter for the *New York Times* that Karl had learned to "lay back a little bit" when playing chess with their young son, Andrew. "But even in croquet he'd be hitting my ball so far I was crying on vacation."

"I told Karl the other day," she said, "You see things in black and white. I see lots of gray."

No one was immune to his manic energy and competitive zeal. No candidate, no operative, no journalist.

When Harvey Kronberg, the editor of an online political newsletter, *The Quorum Report*, made a remark at a restaurant one day in Austin, word got back to Rove that the journalist planned to peel the Teflon off Governor George W. Bush on the issue of taxes. Kronberg was just having a conversation at a table—*he hadn't even written anything yet*—but the next morning came an angry call from Rove.

"He tried to flay me, calling me an enemy and saying what's my agenda?" said Kronberg. "Our relationship was chilly from that point on."

When an article appeared in the *Dallas Morning News* about a state prison inmate getting a fund-raising solicitation letter from the Bush campaign, an embarrassed Rove was forced to deal publicly with a flaw in his mailing operation. The story died, but Rove refused to let the matter drop. He began flooding the reporter with periodic packages of solicitations he'd receive at the office—appeals from the Clinton campaign, from Democrat senators, from antigun groups, and the ACLU. His point apparently was to show that he wasn't the only one sending direct mail to the wrong people. But the intensity of his response, relaying letters for months with brief scribbled notes across them, seemed all out of proportion.

Jack Williams, a Democratic businessman who once raised money for Attorney General Jim Mattox, faxed a note to Rove during the 2000 presidential race mentioning Bush's association with religious conservative Marvin Olasky, suggesting the campaign replace the bumper sticker "W 2K" with "W 1K."

"Four days later, I get a fax from Karl, handwritten on the same paper as my original fax to him, asking, rhetorically, what Clinton's bumper sticker should read in light of Dick Morris or what Gore's bumper sticker should read in light of Naomi Wolfe."

Then, in an aside that chilled Williams because he had not identified himself other than to sign his fax "Mr. J. Williams," Rove scribbled a paragraph about the 1990 governor's race, mentioning a national Democratic consultant and the fact that Jim Mattox had leveled a vigorous, self-destructive attack against fellow Democrat Ann Richards. How would Rove have known or even remembered Williams' role in that race? It seemed oddly excessive and strangely intimidating at the same time.

"He didn't say, 'I know who you are.' He simply let me know that he knew who I was."

Kim Ross, a lobbyist with the Texas Medical Association who over the years has found himself both an ally and an adversary, said anyone who engages Rove in a fight must be prepared to face a ferocious and implacable foe.

"It is in Karl's nature to engulf and devour and control and to rule."

Even Rove's neighbor, a dentist named Joe Neely, came to understand that. Neely was a fit and youthful-looking baby boomer with a good practice in Austin. He and his wife built a house among the hills and cedar breaks just west of Austin, along the pitch and turn of the Balcones Fault. It was a beautiful neighborhood, festooned with trees and divided into lots from two to seven acres, which assured some distance between the homes. Rove bought the lot next door, physically moved a century-old farmhouse onto the property and, with his wife, Darby, set about restoring it.

"One day, I'm coming home and right in front of our front door, in front of our house, there are a bunch of concrete forms up. I thought what the heck is that?" said Neely. "I mean dead on the property line as close to our property as you can get, set slightly before and looking into our master bath."

Neely knocked on his neighbor's door and Rove told him he was building a garage. Neely wasn't happy about it, but Rove assured him that he would plant trees to block the view. A construction crew laid the foundation, and then framed the first story. But when builders began erecting a second story, an apparent violation of deed restrictions, Neely had his lawyer call Rove to complain.

Rove directed that everybody meet at his house—Rove, Neely, the lawyers. He opened with an appeal to continue building the garage, but when it became clear that Neely wasn't going to budge, Rove's face grew dark.

"He started yelling and screaming and demanding I get off his property and never speak to him again. I'm just dumbfounded."

Eventually, after the lawyers talked, Rove dismantled the structure down to the slab. Neely planted some trees on his property to block the view of the concrete and figured the matter was ended.

One day, several months later, Neely got a call. One of the trees had died and there was a message on his answering machine . . . *"Tear down that tree . . ."*

Neely did and heard nothing more. Karl, Darby, and son Andrew had been long-time dental patients, but no longer. From then on, the neighbors did not talk, not for years—and only spoke again after Neely veered too close to the property line one day trimming a cluster of bluebonnets that had gone to seed. Rove called to complain, saying Neely had encroached on his land by 30 to 40 feet. He ordered Neely to meet him at the property line.

"My kids are loving this. They think it's high noon. So I got out there and he will not walk across onto my property and has taken a bunch of little survey flags and has stuck the flags into the ground right in front of our house." Neely apologized and promised it wouldn't happen again.

"I'm sorry about what happened five years ago with your garage," Neely told Rove. "And I'm sorry about your bluebonnets. But I've had it with you calling and leaving pugnacious, vitriolic messages on my answering machine."

Then Neely remembered his neighbor saying something remarkable, something so unexpected he didn't know how to respond.

"You just don't get it," said Rove.

"Get what?"

"What you said to me five years ago."

Neely did not know what he was talking about.

"You said you moved out here to get away from people like me."

Neely was flabbergasted. He could not imagine ever having said that. He was surprised how Rove had internalized this squabble between neighbors and made it so thoroughly personal. Beneath all the bravura, Rove seemed deeply unsure of himself. People . . . *like me*. What could he mean? That he was not some yuppie Austin professional? That he lacked the ease and social skills of his modestly prosperous neighbors? Neely denied ever saying anything like that.

"Now you're calling me a liar, huh?"

Neely almost laughed. This was not about settling an argument. This was about winning, Rove winning. He seemed to be driven by a roaring internal engine to control every disagreement, rule every dispute, and dominate every contest. In everything he did, Karl Rove wanted to win.

When it turned out he was wrong about New Hampshire and Bush lost, it was something Rove seemed to take personally.

The early exit polls gave some measure of the size of the defeat. Shortly after noon, Rove went across the hall at the Residence Inn in Merrimack and gave Bush the bad news that the early numbers had McCain up by 19 points.

"What the hell happened?" Bush asked.

Rove didn't have an answer, not a good one. He was surprised by the huge number of independents who came into the primary, an unprecedented outpouring of people drawn by McCain's reformist themes. Rove reasserted confidence in his 50-state strategy. McCain could not keep up, he said. "He's done. He's got the positive side of it. Now we'll see if there's much more positive side. I don't think there is."

That assurance didn't make the phone call to John McCain's hotel suite any easier, especially when the likelihood was "Sunny" John Weaver might be there. Weaver's message . . . *Consultants don't concede to candidates* . . . was crystal clear. Bush had lost and Weaver had won and on this night, Karl Rove had been outworked, outmaneuvered, outpolled and outthought. Weaver had been largely out of sight since Phil Gramm's ill-fated presidential race in 1996, working races in states other than Texas, where Rove controlled the gears and levers of political campaigns. As it turned out, Gramm's national co-chairman was John McCain. Weaver and McCain struck up a strong friendship and it was Weaver in 1997 who persuaded the Arizona senator to make his bid for president.

Now the political architecture of the 2000 presidential primary had taken on a new form. It was Bush against McCain all right, but it was also Rove against Weaver.

The McCain victory shook the Bush camp, which flew directly to South Carolina and Bush's speech on the vast, red-carpeted stage of the Amphithorium at Bob Jones University. For the first time, the ever-positive Karen Hughes allowed herself to express to a reporter the possibility of defeat, that the appeal of McCain's *Straight Talk Express* might be more than a brief splash of publicity. Following the speech at Bob Jones, Bush and the campaign staff gathered at a hotel in downtown Greenville for a strategy session where Ari Fleischer, reading from a memo, mentioned the university's ban on interracial dating. It was the first time anybody had briefed Bush about the rule and it came after he'd already appeared. At a news conference in the hotel, Bush fended off a few questions about the interracial dating ban, which in the days ahead was to grow into a problem for the campaign.

The strategy for beating McCain in South Carolina came in two parts. First, Bush needed to invert the formula that McCain was the reformer and Bush the politician. Hughes proposed a new slogan for Bush—Reformer With Results—and a new emphasis on the idea that McCain was the true Washington insider. The other part of the Bush strategy was darker and had a more mysterious genesis. It resembled the sour mash tactics of the Lee Atwater days, a hard, negative assault on the opponent, sometimes directly and sometimes under cover. It was the approach favored by Rove . . . *Attack, Attack, Attack* . . . only now, apparently, Bush was very much on the program.

Battered in New Hampshire and fighting back in South Carolina, Bush remembered how, in his 1978 campaign for Congress in Texas, Democrat opponent Kent Hance took him to task because some Texas Tech students served beer at a "Bush Bash."

"I thought people would see through that," Bush said one day, recalling his first campaign. "I learned my lesson. I learned that I need to respond. While I abhor the politics of tearing people down, I understand the need to counterpunch."

A new Bush television commercial branded McCain a hypocrite, a champion of reform who filled his treasury with thousands of dollars in contributions from corporate political action committees. Meanwhile, Bush inadvertently previewed another part of campaign strategy during a rally in a conversation picked up by a C-Span microphone.

"Y'all haven't even hit his soft spots," said state Senator Mike Fair, a Bush supporter.

"We're going to," Bush replied, but added he was "not going to do it on TV."

What followed were two weeks of slaughterhouse politics in Dixie.

The Bush camp launched saturation TV and radio attacks. It sent direct-mail warnings that McCain wanted to remove the pro-life plank from the GOP, which wasn't true but stirred the attention of the state's sizable population of antiabortion voters. Rove had recruited Ralph Reed, formerly of the Christian Coalition, to help bring out religious conservatives. Surrogates accused the Arizona senator, a former prisoner of war, of abandoning his Vietnam veterans. A professor from Bob Jones sent out an e-mail claiming McCain had fathered illegitimate children. Bush's polling firm made several hundred so-called "push-poll" telephone calls asking harsh questions about McCain. And other calls, which the Bush campaign declared were not its doing, presented even darker warnings: Cindy McCain had drug problems and the McCains had a black child.

The succession of attacks—some clearly from the Bush camp, some from supporters likely acting alone in the superheated political stew of South Carolina—angered McCain, who believed them a betrayal of the high campaign standards that Bush had so publicly proclaimed. Before the South Carolina debate, as the two men stood awkwardly next to each other in the studio, McCain turned on his rival.

"George," he said, slowing shaking his head.

"John," Bush replied, then added as if by explanation, "It's politics."

"George, everything isn't politics."

During a commercial break, McCain complained that Bush supporters had leveled a savage direct-mail and phone campaign against him. Bush expressed innocence. He reached over to grasp his rival's hand and said the two should put their acrimony behind them.

"Don't give me that shit," said McCain, pulling away. "And take your hands off me."

Although Rove denied responsibility, there clearly resonated in the dirty tactics a pattern familiar in Rove's history. The push polls in South Carolina recalled the survey back in Texas to damage Attorney General Dan Morales in the tobacco case. The phone calls spreading gossip resembled the virulent whisper campaign against Governor Ann Richards.

The practice of negative campaigning, the old Sun-Tzu ("All we need to do is throw something odd and unaccountable at the enemy."), was something Rove not only practiced but taught at the University of Texas. Bill Israel was a teaching assistant with

Rove one semester and recalls him instructing students how negative campaigning can turn voters quickly and decisively.

"It's better to narrowcast," Rove said in class one day, explaining the technique of passing powerful messages to small groups without stirring the larger public.

"Radio is really good for a negative attack," he said, because it's "tough to figure what the opposition is doing."

"The only thing worse to face is mail." Direct mail, Rove assured, is "immune from press coverage."

Bush beat McCain by 11 points in South Carolina. Rove was expansive in victory.

"People in this state wanted to know that he was willing to fight for it. Was he a guy who had the ability to pick himself up off the mat, dust himself off, wipe off the blood, and go back in there."

The size of the victory could not be attributed solely to the power of the Bush counterpunch. It was also an object lesson in how the Bush campaign could retool on a dime, seizing every good aspect of the McCain campaign and making them its own. Gone were the photo-ops and stump speeches at a lectern, replaced by town-hall forums of the type McCain had used so masterfully. Behind Bush at every stop was a new banner with the new logo—Reformer With Results. Bush moved to the right, promoting his Christian conservative values and suggesting his opponent was just another member of the liberal, tax-and-spend Washington set. Those who had watched Bush for years were struck by his new accent, thicker and softer, a true son of the South.

. . . We're improvin' achievement . . . We're gettin' down to vote-askin' time . . .

As the Bush campaign remade itself, McCain committed a strategic blunder, airing a television commercial charging that Bush "twists the truth like Clinton." For the Southern Republicans and Reagan Democrats of South Carolina, to compare someone to Clinton was an unspeakable act. Rove seized on the mistake and the Bush camp accused McCain of negative campaigning. Suddenly, it was McCain who looked like politics as usual. Bush had drained him of his most appealing characteristic. Exit polls showed that a majority of voters saw Bush as the "real reformer," a remarkable achievement by a team that only two weeks earlier had been steamrolled by the *Straight Talk Express*.

Rove was the architect of Bush's sharp turn to the right. But the move carried consequences, most notably the primary three days later in Michigan, where McCain forces were already trumpeting Bush's embrace of Bob Jones University, which not only had restrictions about interracial dating but also a distinct anti-Catholic bias. A big bloc of voters in Michigan were Catholic and Rove watched as Weaver and the rest of the McCainiacs launched their own counteroffensive, effectively dubbing Bush an anti-Catholic bigot.

Even a cab driver in politically active Austin chided Rove at the airport. After dropping off a reporter for the *Fort Worth Star-Telegram*, the cabbie spotted Rove and delivered some unsolicited political advice.

"Your guy," he said, walking up to Rove. "Your guy is a dead frat boy walking. He's so far to the right that we'll need John McCain to win in November."

Bush lost, but Michigan was McCain's last stand. The general election, Bush and Rove knew, would require the candidate to move back toward the middle. The first step was to shore up Catholic support with a letter to Cardinal John O'Connor apologizing for the Bob Jones visit, which Bush solemnly read before a battery of TV cameras.

"On reflection, I should have been more clear in disassociating myself from anti-Catholic sentiment and racial prejudice. It was a missed opportunity causing needless offense, which I deeply regret."

After the mea culpa, Bush boarded the campaign plane for Seattle and the upcoming primary in Washington. Rove stayed behind. From now on, Rove was to spend less time on the plane and more time steering the campaign's successful course from headquarters in Austin. Now, Rove assured him, things looked bright. The 50-state strategy would prevail. It was just like Rove told his business friends at lunch in Austin two months before the New Hampshire primary:

"They don't have the organization, they don't have the infrastructure, they don't have the resources."

Still, Bush was miffed by the McCain insurgency in Michigan. He said as much, chatting casually with a couple of reporters on the plane.

"I couldn't believe anybody who would think I'm an anti-Catholic bigot," Bush said.

The reporters questioned whether the letter to the cardinal was sufficient. In a startling gesture, Bush pulled out a penknife, opened the blade, and put it to his throat.

"What do you want? I just ate crow on national TV?"

"Jim Crow, I believe," one reporter fired back, and everyone laughed, Bush most of all.

Bush was two days from his win in the Washington primary, and about a week from Super Tuesday, the mother of all primaries, which was to seal his nomination. George W. Bush, sailing aloft at 40,000 feet, was a very happy man. He was about to become the Republican nominee for president.

And Karl Rove, back in Austin, was already thinking ahead to the fall campaign.

14

A Win's a Win

Through all those years, that which you most wish to win was waiting for you.

Ayn Rand

The smart guys said Bush was toast, couldn't win. Seven professors, all armed with elaborate statistical models, arrived in late August at the 96th annual meeting of the American Political Science Association in Washington with the same message—all the numbers point to Al Gore for president.

"They were all right," said Karl Rove, who proved them wrong.

Even James Campbell of the University of New York at Buffalo, a Republican conspicuously wearing an "Alpha Males for Bush" button, said his vote was wasted because Bush wasn't going to get more than 47.2 percent of the vote. Six of the seven statistical models said Gore would win with anywhere from 52.9 percent to 60.3 percent of the vote. A seventh model had the race a tossup. Nobody was betting on George W. Bush of Texas.

The Cartesian tellers of truth were all saying to pack it in, game over, fait accompli. The strong economy, the high approval numbers of the incumbent president, the history of the "in" party in post-World War II presidential elections where the second-quarter domestic product growth has topped 2 percent—all the formulas gave the race to Gore. (There have been exceptions to the in-party, good-economy thesis. In 1968, Democrat Hubert Humphrey was defeated amid acrimony over Vietnam and in 1976, Republican Gerald Ford was swept away in the post-Watergate tide. But these were special cases.) This year, the nation's leading political scientists had imposed mathematics on social science and confidently predicted the future.

"The economy is the answer to every question," said Campbell.

Rove loved this because the forecasts were grounded in statistics and eminently defensible. The academics had dumped every number known to man into a box—the number of refrigerators sold in the last quarter, the president's popularity rating, the candidates' historic standing in pre-Labor Day polls—and produced a precise and reproducible answer.

"Every one of those models predicting victory for Gore by between 4 and 18 points were right," Rove said two years later, long into his tenure at the White House.

While the geniuses of academia delivered their eulogy at a Washington hotel, Rove had his own models and his own history and his very own distinct strategy for the general election. To beat the odds, the Bush campaign was to be guided by two themes: character not policy and play on the other guy's turf.

Rove must have recognized that whatever gifts Bush had, an historically grounded command of the issues was not one of them. Gore, the geeky technocrat and long-time habitué of the Washington scene, would beat Bush every time in a showdown over Medicaid formulas or federal park funding. Moreover, the winds were all wrong for the Bush camp on the dominant policy issue: the economy. The key was to make character an issue, Gore's character. Rove understood that in Gore's self-defense of the Buddhist temple fund-raiser, he had sown the seeds of doubt about his credibility. He was Mr. No-Controlling-Legal-Authority. Rove decided to accelerate the drumbeat against

Gore, deriding him as a politician who "says one thing and does another" and reinvents himself to suit the political moment. But he needed poll numbers to chart the path.

In February, Bush campaign pollster Fred Steeper conducted a survey to gauge voter attitudes about Gore. Steeper surveyed 800 people nationwide. About half of those polled said they thought Gore would "say almost anything to get elected," fewer than half felt he had "questionable integrity" and less than one-third considered him a negative campaigner. Then the voters were told unfavorable things about Gore; that he misrepresented Bill Bradley's Medicaid plan, that he exaggerated his accomplishments and distorted his congressional voting record on abortion. They were reminded of the Buddhist temple.

The information had instant, damaging effect. After hearing the negative comments, more than two-thirds in the survey now believed Gore had questionable integrity and would say anything. Although few originally felt Gore was a negative campaigner, now more than half did.

On March 12, campaigning in Florida, Bush rolled out a new campaign line.

"The vice president is someone who will say anything to get elected," Bush said, repeating the phrase "say anything to get elected" four times during a 20-minute news conference.

Making character an issue was a strategic decision. Competing in the blue (Gore) states was a tactical one.

"You've got to play on the other guy's turf," said Rove. "Everybody knew we had to play in Michigan and Pennsylvania. But playing in Washington, Oregon, New Hampshire, Iowa, Minnesota, Wisconsin, Maine, Arkansas, Tennessee, and West Virginia, that was playing on the other guy's turf."

Tennessee, Gore's home state, was an inspired choice. Who was the last presidential candidate to lose his home state? And winning Bill Clinton's home state of Arkansas would be a deliciously symbolic victory. But what better illustrated the old Sun-Tzu ("Attack the enemy where he is unprepared, and appear where you are not expected.") than West Virginia? No decision Rove made in the 2000 general election more clearly illustrated his political genius than the decision to compete in West Virginia. Rove pored over the political maps, calculating electoral votes and precinct results and available calendar days. He knew Bush could win the West and the South, Gore would take the Northeast. The battleground would become the Midwest—Iowa, Michigan, Ohio, and Illinois. And in the mix, in the true rogue spirit of the Atwater days, Rove added West Virginia because it seemed impossible, but wasn't.

West Virginia was rock-solid Democrat, home of the United Mine Workers Union, a state that didn't even vote for Nixon or Reagan their first time around. What's more, it was part of the Democratic political myth, the place where John Kennedy went in 1960, straight into the ragged heart of Appalachia, into the coal fields where the fog hung like a necklace over the mountains—the sainted Jack Kennedy went to West Virginia to reassure the state's skittish Protestant voters and he emerged the guaranteed Democratic nominee for president.

When Rove pitched the idea of competing in West Virginia, Joe Allbaugh, the hulking Oklahoman and campaign manager, tilted his head down and looked skeptically over his glasses. Allbaugh's job was to manage the money and keep the political trains running, and the idea of squandering time and money in a small state with five electoral votes and a political history that looked like a Democratic party pamphlet didn't seem particularly smart. Allbaugh peered out over his glasses with his head down so that the full length of his flat-top showed, like a landing turf. This would take some convincing, Rove knew.

"First of all, the state had been hammered. It has the largest number of members of a pro-life organization per capita than any state in the union. It has a huge number of outdoor hunters, and the mountaintop mining decision of a Clinton administration appointee to the bench absolutely devastated the state's economy.

"If you looked at the demographics of where Clinton-Gore was in trouble and thought about the electoral map, what part of the electoral map fit this and was not part of our normal calculations? The answer is pretty damned obvious: West Virginia."

Dave Tyson, an old pal from College Republican days, was chairman of the Republican party in West Virginia. He read about Rove in *Newsweek* and called, offering assistance. Rove plugged Tyson into the "front-porch campaign," adding him to the wave of GOP notables traveling to Austin in early 1999 to visit Bush at the Governor's Mansion. Tyson was delighted by the company. There were a couple of members of Congress, some business types, Rove and Bush, the candidate, in full bonhomie. Tyson looked around the room and he recalled something Rove told him 25 years earlier when they were College Republicans.

"I remember Karl mentioning to me the people our age will probably be the ones running the party and running government."

Tyson told Rove the polls were soft for Gore and the issues were right for Bush, especially gun-control and the environment.

"You're not going to support somebody who wants to abolish the combustible engine like Al Gore," Tyson said.

This was a message Rove could sell not only in West Virginia, but also in Pennsylvania and Michigan. This was McKinley 1896 all over again, only instead of appealing to a new immigrant class in an emerging industrial age, Bush would reach out to mine workers and steel workers and auto workers caught in the post-industrial shift of the global economy. These were solid, working-class Reagan Democrats whose religion was under assault by Hollywood, freedom under attack by antigun forces and jobs were all being shipped overseas. Tap the anxiety of this group and you win. The winning issues were wedges—guns, abortion, and the environment. This was McKinley meets Atwater. The voters of West Virginia were ripe for picking and Rove had a plan.

"The key was to make a sustained commitment to it. This was a state without any infrastructure. The candidate flew in three times,

Dick Cheney went twice. We ran television, Barbara Bush and 41 also went. We sent surrogates. We went up with television. It was one of the first states we went up on with television in the general election and we stayed on. We built a grassroots organization."

In the spring of 2000, Rove met with a few organizers. He had a matrix that he applied from state to state to establish a minimum budget: how much it would cost for phone calls, for headquarters, for yard signs and direct mail. Rove proposed more than the minimum. He invited the organizers to envision an ideal campaign, one in which money was no object. What would it take? he asked.

"You would have thought we were from the planet Zercon. They couldn't believe we were talking about this. They were excited, but it was also, are you serious? When are the cameras going to come in and you're going to say, smile, you're on Candid Camera."

The initial goal was to establish five campaign headquarters in the state. They ended up with 24. Charleston lawyer Tom Potter, the former GOP state chairman, and Buck Harless, a wealthy surface-coal mine operator, set a goal to raise $30,000. They raised nearly 10 times that amount.

"It was clear they were contesting the election here," said Potter. "On the other side, Gore and the Democrats clearly took us for granted. They paid little attention to West Virginia as far as I could tell."

Overseeing the political operation was Bill Phillips, a long-time Republican who once worked for the late Congressman "Vinegar Bend" Mizell of North Carolina and had close ties with the current Republican governor, Cecil Underwood. Underwood was the state's youngest governor when he was elected in 1956 and the state's oldest governor when he was re-elected 40 years later. He provided his own campaign apparatus to assist the Bush-Cheney effort.

A more recent Republican governor, Arch Moore, stayed largely out of sight. Moore's daughter was running for Congress, but Moore was a convicted felon who served three years in prison after pleading guilty to extortion, income tax evasion, mail fraud, and obstruction of justice. When Bush flew into Charleston in August for a rally on the Capitol grounds, Moore watched from the back of the crowd. Afterward, back on his campaign plane, Bush learned that Moore had been in the audience.

"Arch Moore was there? Why didn't he come up on stage?"

Prison, a reporter reminded.

"Oh," Bush said, and then his face brightened. "Club Fed?"

Here, in Bush's bright optimism, was a new definition of compassionate conservatism: If a Republican politician commits a crime, it is conservative to put him behind bars. But it is compassionate to send him somewhere with tennis courts.

Team Bush sent a steady stream of troops to West Virginia: House Majority Leader Dick Armey to Martinsburg, Representative J.C. Watts and Senator John McCain to Charleston, Dick Cheney to the beleaguered steel town of Weirton, Bush's father to Bluefield and mother to Parkersburg. West Virginia had never seen such an embarrassment of riches from a Republican.

When Bush himself landed in Huntington in October for a rally on the banks of the Ohio River, 50 coal miners joined him on stage. A 63-year-old union miner named Dick Kimbler declared, "The Democratic administration shut my mine down" and he said the time had come to put somebody in the White House who cared about jobs.

"These good folks standing behind him—and their wallets— cannot stand four more years of Gore," Bush said and the roar of the crowd bounced across the broad stretch of river to Ohio and back.

But nothing galvanized a crowd like Charlton Heston, who arrived to a hero's welcome a week before the election at a National Guard armory in the deep, deciduous mountains of southern West Virginia. If Christian conservative groups were working with anti-abortion forces and the coal industry had stirred up the workers, nobody had more effect on the state's 350,000 hunters than Heston, the voice of the National Rifle Association (NRA).

"This is the most redneck, gun-loving state in the union," said James Haught, editor of the *Charleston Gazette*. "Heston had these huge rallies and they were almost like a revival meeting."

Hundreds of people crowded into the armory in Beckley to hear Heston. Hundreds more gathered outside, where the NRA erected video screens.

"You must forget all else and remember only freedom. Not what some shop steward or news anchor says. Just freedom," Heston boomed.

Gore showed up in late October, then again three days before the election. But it was too late. Bush won the state with 52 percent of the vote. And as Republicans in the Mountain State are a quick to point out, without West Virginia, he wouldn't have been elected president.

Two years later, an old political friend from Austin named Elton Bomer was talking with Bush and, learning the president was about to visit West Virginia in advance of the midterm elections, asked why.

"They don't elect Republicans do they?" Bomer asked.

"Well, they've got one congressman."

It seemed to Bomer an exotic political locale, but clearly one that had proved beneficial in the 2000 election and, presumably, in 2004.

"How the hell did you end up in West Virginia?" he asked the president.

"Karl Rove."

John McCain campaigned for Bush and the Republican ticket. But it was obvious to Team Bush he was doing so with all the conviction of the second runner-up in a teen-age beauty contest.

McCain appeared on stage with Bush in Oregon in the closing month of the campaign and dutifully praised the GOP nominee as a capable leader and the next president. Still, it didn't escape Rove's notice that McCain told a group in New Hampshire, "If you don't vote for Governor Bush, I understand and respect it." He then said much the same thing on Chris Matthews' television show "Hardball."

In these and other breaches by McCain, Rove must have seen the faint outline of his political enemy . . . *Weaver.* After the primary, McCain put John Weaver in charge of negotiations aimed at political rapprochement between the two camps, presumably just to screw with the Bush folks. Rove stayed away, intentionally keeping his distance whenever Weaver was around. Campaign manager Joe Allbaugh took the lead on the Bush side in coordinating appearances.

Rove won the battle against John Weaver in the primaries, and now he was to win the war. He had effectively forced Weaver out of Texas, had passed on virulent personal rumors to damage him, had outmaneuvered him in the GOP presidential primaries—and even after winning the White House, Rove clearly did not forget his one-time adversary. Once Rove took his place in the West Wing, in an office that previously housed Hillary Clinton, word spread that Weaver was persona non grata, according to several Republicans. Weaver told colleagues Rove had blackballed him in GOP circles and not just with political campaigns but corporate clients, including an airline, some computer companies and a television network.

"The problem with Karl is that his enemies list never ends," said a Republican friend and staunch Bush ally. "Once you're on it, it does not end."

Weaver wasn't the only McCain aide alone on the high wire— McCain campaign manager Rick Davis told an associate that he feared Rove was behind efforts to limit his business—but Weaver was the richest target because of the length of their blood feud. After a quarter century in GOP politics, the string had run out. Weaver was out of business. Eventually, he abandoned the party altogether and signed up with the Democratic Congressional Campaign Committee. He said the party no longer represented the values he believed in.

"He was made totally unwelcome in the Republican party," McCain told Roll Call. "I'm sorry, it's regrettable. I can't deprive a guy of making a living or feeding his family."

The shadow of Rove's political persona was now so long that it was tempting to see him in every undoing, even when there was little or no evidence to support it. His friend and former teaching partner, Bill Israel, was once so close he had dinner at Rove's home and he hosted the Roves for dinner at his. Israel stayed in their vacation home on the Guadalupe River in the scenic Texas Hill Country. He enjoyed Rove's sunny, energetic nature, the voluble great-grandson of a Norwegian counsel who was forever bubbling over with ideas about history and politics. And he appreciated Rove's nimble mind, although he was struck by his tendency to reduce even the most arcane intellectual argument to political warfare.

"He would cast ideological arguments around what's right and wrong, but in the end, the issue was always what's going to win," Israel said.

When he saw Rove on television during the hectic scramble of the Florida recount, Israel was concerned about the physical toll the campaign seemed to have taken on him. When Bush won, he e-mailed a quick congratulatory note. Rove responded as he usually did, in 12 to 16 hours, in a single sentence.

But the politics of the Bush administration, especially in the Middle East, bothered him. And following the September 11 terrorist attacks, Israel wrote an editorial suggesting the attacks were the predictable outcome of a failed American foreign policy. He e-mailed it to several friends, including Rove, and to the college newspaper at the University of Massachusetts where he was now teaching, which published it. He followed this up with another e-mail a few days later, but got no response.

Instead, when he opened his e-mail, he found scores of vituperative messages—*"How do morons . . . ," "My god, are you an idiot . . . ," "I'm glad I'm not a student"*—filling his mailbox. Page after page of angry, obscene messages. Israel discovered that 14 hours after his e-mail to

Rove, the editorial had been posted on a right-wing Web site by someone with a cyber-identity only as Thor, the Scandinavian god of thunder.

The idea that the senior adviser to the president was forwarding items for posting on right-wing Web sites seemed ludicrous, Israel knew. It seemed almost irrational to consider such a possibility. Why would he have the interest? Where would he find the time? "It could have been some other egocentric, one-liner e-mailing right-wing Scandinavian politico who answers me in 12 to 16 hours, who directed the pack of wild dogs to my door."

There was simply no way of knowing, not for sure. It was like Rove used to say in the classroom, Israel recalled, some direct political communication is immune to scrutiny.

It was 5 A.M. and George W. Bush couldn't sleep. He had been on the road more than year in pursuit of the presidency, traveling from city to city, waking up in the indistinguishable dark of yet another hotel room. Bush got up, put on some running clothes and poked his head out the door.

"Can't sleep," he said. "I want to work out now."

The security contingent, stationed overnight outside his door, followed the candidate outside for a brisk, three-mile morning run. A faint red sunrise streaked the sky and nothing was moving, just Bush, running through the streets of yet another city, turning now along a river where the moon rode as its reflection on the water.

Returning to the motel, Bush asked a member of his security detail about his travel aide, Logan Walters.

"Have you seen Logan?"

Walters, the diminutive, exceedingly attentive aide, was sleeping in the room directly across the hall. The schedule wasn't set to start until 10:30 A.M.

"Do you want me to wake him up?" asked a member of his security.

"No," Bush said and went into his room.

He emerged two minutes later, walked directly to Logan's room and began loudly knocking. The sleepy-eyed travel aide fumbled to open the door, then stood blinking in the doorway.

"Logan, are we at war?" Bush said.

Logan struggled to comprehend the question, and then his eyes grew wide.

"What? We're at war?"

"Logan, this is war. We've been at war for 12 months. And when I'm ready to go, you've got to be ready to go."

Bush then turned, and with the wry grin of a fraternity prankster winked at his security detail, disappeared into his room and went back to bed. A few minutes later, Logan stepped out into the hallway, freshly bathed, and fully dressed, packed and ready to go. He waited, patiently, for three hours for the events of the day to begin.

This became a refrain between Bush and his aide—"Logan, are we at war?"—more banter than call to preparation. In the wake of 9/11, the exchange has an odd, discordant feel. Bush the future commander in chief at war, pretending to be the commander in chief at war.

At the time, in the heart of a political campaign, the remark was more about camaraderie than statecraft. It was Bush the DEKE, having fun on the trail while Rove the drudge, back at headquarters in Austin, worked the phones.

And Rove was always on the phone.

The Bush for President Headquarters was a vast warren of cubicles and office spaces on the second floor of a red granite bank building in downtown Austin. There was a guard desk and a full security force protecting against anyone who lacked the proper credentials and electronic access cards. Rove had a small office cluttered with boxes and files where he walked around with the receiver to his ear, gesticulating wildly, pealing orders with the brisk authority of a general.

Stashed in one of the boxes was a framed picture of himself—rail-thin and wearing a Madras sports coat—with Bill Clements, his first big candidate in Texas. On the wall above the paper shredder was his portrait of Theodore Roosevelt, patron saint of vigorous, hard-charging Republicanism.

Even as the campaign fell into what McKinnon called "Black September," the post-convention period in which Gore rose in the polls and the attacks on Bush seemed to be working, Rove wore a confident look. He bought ice cream every week for the campaign staff. He presided over meetings with a cheery optimism. In the Gore attack designed to portray Bush as dense and dangerously ill-prepared, Rove saw a history lesson. Ronald Reagan vs. Jimmy Carter, the insurgent and the status quo.

"In 1980, it's a relatively close race. The party in power was not able to take advantage. People are inclined toward the challenger," Rove said one day at campaign headquarters. "There's a ceiling to what Carter is going to get. The question in the end is whether people need to be reassured that Reagan is acceptable."

Rove said the Gore campaign understood the analogy. "That's why they are trying to duplicate the language of 1979 and 1980, that Reagan was risky. Carter used similar terms to attack Reagan as an extremist that could not be trusted with the Oval Office."

The key, then and now, was reassurance. Voters, not just the party's conservative base but Midwestern soccer moms and moderate suburbanites, had to feel comfortable with Bush. The first step was visual, large crowds and bursts of confetti, a Latino rally in Philadelphia to open Bush's arrival for the Republican National Convention, a speech in which his largest national audience might see him as presidential.

"It's all visuals," Rove told campaign finance chief Don Evans. "You campaign as if America was watching TV with the sound turned down. It's all visuals."

By late summer, Professor James Thurber of American University, an expert in presidential politics, saw in the Bush campaign some evidence that its emphasis on personality and its appeal to a wider audience was working.

"George W. has very simple messages, but they're remembered to a certain extent by those who are watching the campaign," Thurber said in an interview. "He might not be the brightest guy around, but we've had a lot of presidents who weren't. He's not scaring people as much as he was at the beginning."

After tacking so far to the right in the primaries, Bush needed to steer a course back to the center—or at least appear to do so. He obviously understood the campaign had to send signals that would keep the conservative base in the line and still expand Bush's appeal among moderates. The conservatives would sign off on Bush's policies; the moderates needed reassurance about his record. "Political heuristics," Rove called it.

In his September 1985 memo to Bill Clements, young Karl Rove displayed a precocious understanding of how to send political messages to important voter groups. He had written that touting a pay raise for teachers was about reassuring suburban voters with children, not winning the vote of teachers' unions, and emphasizing the appointment of women wasn't to win the backing of feminist and minorities, but to bolster support among urban independents.

When Bush took the stage in 2000, he spoke forcefully about the need to protect the border with Mexico, but compassionately about the reality that immigrants will continue to enter so long as they can earn $5 an hour in America instead of 50 cents in Mexico. It was a message to two separate groups. Conservatives heard the part about protecting the border and the superiority of America. Moderates saw a Republican who recognized immigrants as people. The sentiment was Bush, but the political packaging was pure Rove.

Through three sessions of the Texas Legislature, Rove advised Bush with an eye on cultivating his conservative base without alienating voters in the middle. The Bush record was about large tax cuts, stronger student testing, greater local control for school districts. He preached personal responsibility. He never had to deal with a hate-crimes bill opposed by Christian conservatives, thanks to Republicans who bottled up the measure in committee.

Rove even tried to manage the results of the 1998 reelection race in Texas to enhance Bush's appeal in 2000, even if it meant sacrificing fellow Republicans in the process.

In 1998, Bush was assured of re-election. His popularity ratings were high, his Democratic opponent was weak and Rove was tapping an ever-larger national network of financial contributors. While Bush was far ahead in the polls, Republican ticket mate Rick Perry was locked in a very close race. Worried they were about to lose, the Perry team produced a television commercial late in the campaign attacking his Democratic opponent.

Rove, who was not even Perry's consultant, ordered the commercial killed.

"You're not going to run this spot," Rove instructed. "And if you run this spot, we're going to pull the Bush 41 endorsement spot that you'd planned to run at the end."

According to a Perry campaign aide, Rove's primary goal was to drive the numbers for Bush as high as possible, not only among White voters but also among Hispanics and African Americans who typically vote Democrat. To do that, Rove decided he only wanted positive commercials by Republican candidates on TV in the campaign's closing weeks.

"Their thinking was we want to get 68 percent of the vote instead of 67 percent or 66 percent of the vote," the Perry aide said. "We don't want to fuck up the political environment. It's the ultimate calculation on Karl's part that says Perry doesn't need to do that, that he can still win."

The Perry team feared Perry could not win, not without airing the attack spot against his Democratic opponent. But they also needed to close with the televised endorsement of former President George Bush, and Rove controlled the Bush commercial.

Perry, fearing he was about to be sacrificed, had no choice but to follow Rove's orders.

On Election Day, Bush won with 68 percent of the vote, swamping his opponent by 1.4 million votes—a testament to Bush's broad appeal that Rove trumpeted in the presidential race.

Perry also won, barely, by 68,731 votes.

"It was either calculated genius or arrogance," said the Perry aide.

Either way, it turned out Rove was right.

I 've won," said George W. Bush, one week before Election Day.
A couple of reporters on the plane appeared unconvinced. But Bush was supremely confident, leaning against the bulkhead with a Buckler near-beer in his hand.

"I have access to more information."

As it turned out, the Bush campaign righted itself in October after the September slide. Karen Hughes had produced a new slogan—Real Plans for Real People—which had the twin benefit of suggesting there was something unreal not only about Gore's ideas, but about Gore himself. More importantly, Bush exceeded expectations in three televised debates.

"People wanted to know if he could share the stage with Gore," said media chief Mark McKinnon.

Now the campaign rolled into its final days, pursuing what the Bush team called the DFIU strategy—don't fuck it up. Then the DUI story hit.

In September 1976, at age 30, Bush was arrested for drunken driving while in Kennebunkport visiting his parents. News of the two-decade-old arrest broke first on a television station in Maine, and then Fox News went with the story. Bush pleaded guilty in the case, paid a $150 fine and had his driving privileges suspended in Maine. Throughout his campaigns for governor and for president, Bush had sought to keep the episode secret, saying only that he had made unspecified mistakes in his youth.

Word of the arrest shot through the Bush press corps. Hughes, realizing her boss needed to confront the issue, gathered reporters outside the brick cattle barn at State Fair Park in West Allys, Wisconsin, for a late-night news conference.

"I'm the first to say what I did is wrong and I corrected that," Bush said, blinking into a blazing bank of TV lights. "I think the people of America will understand that."

Bush had concealed his arrest, but had he lied? That was the question reporters were asking. To conceal might simply be prudent, but to lie was to reveal an aspect of character. And in the rules of journalism, a candidate's character is fair game.

Although Bush had fended off questions about his past with a vague reference to youthful indiscretions, on one occasion he specifically denied being arrested. In an interview in 1998, Wayne Slater asked whether he had been arrested other than for stealing a Christmas wreath as a college student. Bush said no, and then appeared to reconsider his answer, indicating he had more to say. But Hughes cut him off. The reporter suggested that if Bush had something more to tell, he ought to tell it now, not risk having it emerge at an inopportune time in some future campaign.

After Bush withstood the barrage of questions outside the cattle barn and the media retreated to file its stories, everyone gathered at the hotel for the night. The luggage had not yet arrived and Hughes ordered a glass of wine as she waited.

"I know," she said, turning to the reporter. "You say we should have gotten this out before now."

One of the rules of politics is to release the bad stuff on your terms, not allow your opponents to do it on theirs. Hughes had violated that rule.

Hughes said she shut off the exchange between Bush and the reporter because she didn't know where the conversation was going.

"The governor was talking and winking at you, and I didn't know what was going on. I don't think I knew then."

When Bush did tell her about the arrest, they made the decision not to make the matter public.

Bush understood the potential political damage of his drunken-driving arrest. He had already headed off public disclosure of the arrest once. Two years earlier, when the governor was summoned to jury duty in 1996, Bush and his general counsel, Alberto Gonzales, took steps to keep the episode secret. Publicly, the governor pronounced himself eager to fulfill his obligation of citizenship by serving on a jury. Privately, Gonzales met in chambers with the judge and the attorney for the accused and urged that Bush be stricken from the jury pool. The case involved a drunken-driving charge and the defense attorney in the case said he was eager to question the governor under oath about his "young and irresponsible" years. Gonzales moved quickly to head off such a prospect.

In chambers, Gonzales raised an ingenious legal argument: putting Bush on the jury would be a conflict of interest. Governors, he argued, should not be deciding the fate of people in legal cases in which they might eventually be called on to consider pardons. The judge agreed and dismissed Bush from jury duty.

Even with the judge's action, some evidence of Bush's 1976 arrest still might have become public had the governor completely filled out a questionnaire required of potential jurors. The document asked "Have you ever been accused, or a complainant, or a witness in a criminal case?" The space was left blank. A spokesperson said later that an aide had filled out the document and didn't know the answer. Whatever the reason, the episode remained secret.

Gonzales' legal work won high praise from Bush. The young attorney had come from one of the powerful Houston law firms with Rove's blessing and with strong recommendations from influential business interests. Bush was impressed by Gonzales' intellect and conservative politics. The governor named him secretary of state in 1997 and, a year later, to an open seat on the Texas Supreme Court. Gonzales was bright, accomplished and Hispanic—Exactly the credentials rove knew would help expand the appeal of the Republican party. When Gonzales ran for election to a full term on the state's high court, Rove made sure that business interests contributed several hundred thousand dollars to assure victory. When Bush went to the White House, he took Gonzales with him as general counsel.

Both Gonzales and Hughes had been successful keeping the lid on Bush's arrest while he was governor, but now the episode had burst full-force into public view in the final days of the presidential race. Now it was up to Karen Hughes alone.

Hughes had an unassailable integrity in dealing with the media, but her first loyalty was to Bush and her natural instinct was to protect him. The morning after word of the arrest leaked, she worked to tamp down the story, which was shifting from one of concealment to one of credibility. On the airplane, Hughes first suggested Bush's remarks in 1998 had been off the record, then said Bush didn't remember making them at all—at least not as the reporter recalled them.

When the plane landed in Grand Rapids, Bush took the stage in the basketball arena of a Christian college and offered an oblique mea culpa to a cheering crowd of supporters.

"It's become clear to America over the course of this campaign that I've made mistakes in my life. But I'm proud to tell you, I've learned from those mistakes."

Journalists churned the drunken-driving story for another day, exploring Bush's effort to conceal the episode and questioning whether he'd been completely honest about it, but in the absence of new developments, the story ran dry and the media moved on. On the plane, the ever-ebullient Bush approached the reporter and laughed. "You ran me through the paces," he said.

Election Day was now less than 100 hours away. There was some evidence in the polling that the race was now tightening, but Team Bush was confident it had weathered the storm.

Now Rove was back, joining the campaign the final Sunday in Florida.

"I'm out!" he declared, bursting into the breakfast room at the hotel in Jacksonville where the media were having early-morning coffee. "They've let me out of the cage."

Rove had done the math and was pleased with his answer. He predicted that Bush would beat Gore by six percentage points with 320 electoral votes, 50 more than needed to win the White House.

Could you lose? a reporter asked.

Rove paused.

"We could lose," he said slowly, as if considering the possibility for a fleeting moment, then flashed a confident smile and repeated his prediction of victory.

As it turned out, Rove was wrong, at least in the short term. For all his skill, sometimes the numbers betrayed him. He had been wrong about New Hampshire in the primary and was wrong about winning California in the general election, squandering time and money better spent elsewhere. He engaged in the campaign too late in Minnesota and Wisconsin. And he was wrong about Election Day.

But he was right about West Virginia, and without West Virginia there would have been no recount in Florida and without Florida, no 5–4 decision by the U.S. Supreme Court. Florida was mostly a legal fight with James Baker III leading the effort, although Rove did help provide some political ground troops and did monitor affairs from headquarters in Austin and from a makeshift transition office opened in suburban Washington to give the impression during the legal fight that the outcome was inevitable. In the end, Rove did not win as planned, but he did win. After 36 days in Florida and 18 months on the road and a decade of planning and a lifetime of expectation— finally, Karl Christian Rove made it to the White House.

With Bush's victory as president, the "Iron Triangle" that had long competed for Bush's ear—Rove and Hughes and Allbaugh— headed for Washington. Rove and Hughes landed jobs in the West Wing; Allbaugh, whose wife was a lobbyist, was placed elsewhere at the Federal Emergency Management Agency.

Within two years, two of three loyalists who made up the triangle, announced they were leaving. Hughes was the first, saying she was moving back home to Austin where she would offer her advice from long distance. Then Joe Allbaugh announced he was quitting. Rove was not the instrument of their departure, but the result was still the same—only Rove remained for the 2002 midterm elections as the architect of a historic Republican sweep, then the mastermind of a subsequent coup in the Senate that dislodged Trent Lott and put a close Bush ally in charge.

As the year ended, the *New York Times* reported, "President Bush has created one of the most powerful White Houses in at least a generation, prominent Democrats and Republicans say."

With Mr. Bush's allies in place on Capitol Hill, "the president has consolidated what even Democrats say is a stunning degree of authority in the White House at the halfway point of his four-year term. The perception that Mr. Bush and his chief political counsel, Karl Rove, orchestrated a coup in the Senate—not withstanding the official White House denials that it had anything to do with Senator Trent Lott's decision on Friday to give up his leadership post— has only enhanced what veteran political strategists say is the political potency of the White House."

Back home in Austin, long-time political ally David Weeks was not surprised by Rove's ascension to power.

"I always said from the day he got to Washington, he'd own it."

15

General Rove

There is no truth in politics. There is only winning.

Ken Vest, Washington, DC, consultant

In the quiet corner of a five-star restaurant, where a light breakfast for three approaches a hundred dollars, it is difficult to make a credible argument for the sacrifices required by war. But Karl Rove was trying. He was trying very hard as waiters hovered at the side of the table with extra butter and fresh coffee and his secure White House cell phone kept ringing interruptions.

Rove had been asked to clarify distinctions between the president's approach to dealing with Cuba and his stated intentions toward Iraq. An English muffin had stopped halfway to his mouth while Rove sought to convince his two questioners that the embargo of Cuba was not about domestic political considerations. In Cuba, the White House was willing to wait for its citizens to overthrow Fidel Castro. No such patience had been communicated in the Iraqi problem.

Opening up trade with the island would be of immense economic help to the people of Cuba. But it would also anger an active constituency of President Bush: the Cuban-American voter. The president will have a difficult task gaining re-election if he doesn't win Florida and carrying Florida without the Cuban vote borders on the impossible. So, Rove chooses not to alienate South Florida Cubans by lifting the embargo of Castro.

But he insisted that has nothing to do with the policy.

"You can't say that Cuban-Americans in Florida aren't part of the equation, can you?"

"Well, here's the deal with that," Rove said. "That's a slippery slope. Because, like, for example, when I had my meeting with the four Republican leaders, which I talk about only because they talked, [Congresswoman] Jo Ann Emerson [Missouri] made the argument that the attitude of the Cuban community is changing because, politically, attitudes of the second and third generation were more open and attuned to this kind of relief. And you can make a legitimate case, cite polls, you can talk about people, you can talk about groups, but again, you're making a utilitarian argument. You're saying, 'Let's decide this on the basis of what's best for us, not based on what is the right policy for Cuba and the right policy for the United States.'"

What Rove called "a meeting with four Republican leaders," an almost innocuous description, was given a considerably different characterization by the attending members of Congress and a lobby group of Cuban exiles. The hard line Cuban exiles reported that Rove "read the Republican congress members the riot act and they went out with their tails between their legs." Rove's performance in the meeting was referred to as "mildly threatening" by the Cuba Policy Foundation, an organization promoting normalized trade with Castro.

The four Republicans were all from farm states and had been pushing to sell produce to Cuba, expanding markets for their own political constituencies. But Rove and the White House will clearly have nothing to do with it.

George Nethercutt, a Republican representing a farming region of Washington, said Rove's message was unmistakable: Cuban trade is not as important as Florida's electoral votes.

"There are people from all regions of the country who don't think Florida should set the policy. It ought to be a national policy."

The Rove-run White House has shown no flexibility on Cuba policy, even though the House of Representatives has voted to lift the ban on travel and limits of cash payments to the island. Jeff Flake, a conservative Republican representative from Arizona, has been one of Castro's most energized critics. But Flake thinks flooding the island with U.S. business prosperity can topple the Castro regime. After meeting with Rove twice, Flake and his republican colleagues said Rove was "unyielding."

While enjoying his Saturday breakfast on the shores of Austin's Town Lake, Rove insisted his position, and the president's, were based on strong principles, not craven electoral politics.

"Look, we're talking about a moral issue. We're talking about what is the best way to bring democracy to Cuba. Best way to bring democracy to Cuba is to make the people of Cuba live under the system that their leader has chosen for them."

Morality is also a good reason to begin doing business with Cuba.

The founder and director of the Center for Presidential and Congressional Studies at American University, James Thurber, was asked by an agency of the U.S. government to meet with dissidents in Cuba. After traveling to the island, he talked with 31 political prisoners who had been jailed by Castro for 15 years.

"It was the most moving thing I've ever done in my career. And to talk to them about it, [normalized trade relations with the United States] in the underground, so to speak, and bring back a manifesto of lifting all the embargo. They are all against the embargo and I am also."

Thurber, who edited a book on political consultants, and their influence on elections, said the only remaining reason for not trading with Cuba is domestically driven politics.

"I think Castro is awful. But everybody down there, among the dissidents, but also other elite that I met, even within their legislature, sort of directly and indirectly feel that if you open it up a little bit the regime will not last. If you open it up economically you bring more freedom."

But the Rove doctrine is in disagreement with Thurber's assertions. Rove has put a moral face on the creature of his Cuba policy, but its heart thumps to a political beat. There is no longer an economic or international political value to prohibiting U.S. trade with Castro. Angry, anti-Castro Cubans in South Florida are the only reason America is not doing business with Cuba. If goods and money flowed back and forth between the two countries, and President George W. Bush lifted the embargo, he would be certain to lose the South Florida Cuban vote. Karl Rove will not allow that to happen. A second term for his client, the president, is unlikely without Florida's 25 electoral votes. In a nation that was evenly divided in the last presidential election, Rove is unwilling to consider a policy that puts any votes at risk as 2004 approaches. That is Karl Rove's standard. Politics. Not morality.

Morality is the costume his politics wears.

And it is also the guise Rove has given the president to use in dealing with Iraq. Cuba must change from within, an eventuality caused by the suffering of the Cuban people, who Rove insists are obligated to overthrow Fidel Castro. For Iraq, Rove applies a different standard and envisions a revolution that will arrive in the form of U.S. Army battalions and laser-guided bombs. Of course, Cuba does not sit astride the world's second largest known reserves of oil. Iraq does. And Cuba is not a threat to Israel, one of the United States' closest allies. Rove's America will not wait for the people of Iraq to turn out Saddam.

"Iraq has developed and acquired from the North Koreans and expanded its ability to deliver weapons in the region, whether it's Ankara, or Tel Aviv, or Riyadh, or the oil fields," Rove said. "All of these things are now within easy distance of his intermediate range weapons. We've got a bad actor. We've got a really bad actor."

Rove knows what he wants. He knows what the president wants. He knows what the U.S. military wants. And he knows what corporate America wants. His job is sharply defined as creating a political climate that turns those wants into the public's demand. Keeping it simple does that. We are good. Iraq is bad. We love freedom. They do not. A clear, accessible message for an electorate too busy to read deeper into the story. The language must not be bloody. It's regime change. Not war. Clean and antiseptic. More of a procedure than a battle.

It's a bad thing that Saddam has all that oil.

But for Rove's political goals, it's a good thing that Saddam is such a bad man.

"Here's a guy who has been actively pursuing, for the better part of two decades, radiological, biological, chemical, and nuclear weapons," Rove argued. "There's very strong belief, absent the Israeli raid on the reactor, that he was within a couple of years of developing nuclear. We don't know. At least the people who do know aren't saying."

Nothing had changed about Rove's ideas. Saddam was still the Bush White House's bad guy. They needed a substitute because Osama was elusive. Saddam was just sitting there, buoyed on a sea of oil. He wasn't the evildoer they wanted. But Saddam would serve the current purpose.

Less than a mile away from the restaurant where he was sliding his chair out from the breakfast table, Rove had first suggested, at the beginning of the year, the "run-on-the-war" strategy in a speech to fellow Republicans gathered in Austin.

He rose and offered his hand to two journalists who had been reporting on him and his candidates for 20 years. His friendliness was sincere. He had been gracious with his time, giving up a Saturday morning from a calendar that likely shows no empty, unscheduled days. He didn't trust journalism any more than he ever had. But a book was being written about him. This was something new Rove had to manage. His involvement could shape its editorial direction and control the impact. If he was worried about anything, it was arguably that his own story might turn him into a political liability to the president, instead of an asset. This had not happened to Karl Rove before. Obviously, he intended that it should never happen.

Rove left the restaurant with a long list of important tasks ahead of him. A mid-term election was approaching and the president needed a mandate, the kind of support he did not earn in 2000. There were also difficult races in key Senate and House elections. The Republicans wanted to control the U.S. Congress. The party was looking to Karl to show them the way. He was expected to develop a strategy that would defy history and he intended to do precisely that. Karl Rove was always the man with the plan.

But he was also a part of another plan.

And this time it wasn't his. The terrorist attacks of September 11 had created a new environment for polices that were once considered radical. Rove's strategy for Election Day 2002 was aimed at building support for these new policies. The plan was already being rolled out on a global stage but it would be harder to execute without Republican power and a mandate for the president. But that was okay. Rove could handle the responsibility. What he liked about politics was that everything was a contest. He liked a good fight. A tough race. A contest.

And no contest had greater stakes than war.

On the campaign to the White House, Rove had made sure his client kept the electorate assured they were not going to be in any military and political tar pits overseas. George W. Bush frequently told crowds his would not be "an administration that gets involved in nation building" and that, if the United States sent troops anywhere, "I won't let it happen without an exit strategy." But America was attacked. And suddenly President Bush was nation building in Afghanistan. U.S. forces were also moved toward Iraq and no one has mentioned an exit strategy. Because there is none. A new world appears to be taking form. And Rove is an instrument of its creation.

Karl Rove has become the man with someone else's plan.

The meeting was at a secret location. No one was supposed to tell their staffers where they were or who they were with. Only Republican leadership from Congress and top lobbyists, who had supported GOP causes, had been invited. Karl Rove was set to present his plan for the mid-term elections of 2002. It was almost spring of election year, a good time for optimism. Rove was going to tell party leaders what he thought and they would get a chance to shoot at his ideas. He liked this. Rove always expected to win the day.

The technique Rove outlined for the midterms was to run on social security and education, fight the Democrats on their own ground, and let taxes and terrorism push the GOP across the finish line. The presidential advisor felt Republicans could take away Democratic party advantages on social issues, make it a breakeven proposition, and then wrap it up with talk of the tax cut and the president's leadership in the war on terrorism. The fundamental principle guiding Rove was that voters always think that Republicans are better on matters of defense and taxation. If they took Democratic territory on social issues, Rove thought the Republicans would win.

"When Karl walked into the room and said this stuff," a participant related to an associate, "the place went bat shit. Half of them were for him and half of them were against him. This one big time Republican lobbyist just got up and said, 'screw this. We can't run on education and social security and prescription drugs and all that other shit. We've done that. Let's run on taxes and terrorism. Fuck, we don't want to engage on that other stuff. We'll get killed on that.'"

Almost instantly, Rove's ideas were in trouble. The larger plan of the president, Cheney, and Wolfowitz could go nowhere if Karl couldn't even get this part right. The lobbyist, who represented large corporations that had been generous to Republican causes, got angry and confronted Rove as the gathering dissipated into pointless debate.

The exchange was described as heated.

"Are you outta your fuckin' mind?" he asked Rove. "Fuck these issues. The Democrats will run us to death on those issues. It's taxes and terrorism and nothing else."

Rove argued his position but he knew there was elegant simplicity in what he was being told. Maybe he should just bluntly emphasize the war as the lead issue, not the one to close the deal with voters. The Republicans didn't need to talk about social security and the economy. People don't fret over their retirement when America is engaged in a shooting war. History, Karl Rove's hobby, taught him that much. Americans are motivated by sacrifice during times of war. That took social security off the table. Prescription drugs and education were issues for another day, backburner stuff. What Rove was hearing was right. Voters would not cast their ballots based on positions on social issues as long as we were at war. The Republicans could run on the war and, if the economy got too bad and Democrats started to advance, Rove would have the president start talking about his tax cuts. The Democrats would be crazy to argue against tax cuts. In his controversial speech earlier in the year, Rove had suggested the war as one of the important issues to help Republicans. But, clearly, he was beginning to see it as the engine that drove the entire election.

Rove got the angry lobbyist's message and made it his own.

Ever since that speech in Austin urging candidates to run on the war, Rove's plans for using the war on terrorism to help Republican candidates were publicly apparent. The braying of Democrats, demanding an apology for politicizing the war only confirmed the conflict's political value to the Republicans. Americans have historically supported wartime presidents, regardless of how failed they may be on domestic matters. The strategy might be daring, risking the president's political capital at mid-term, but Rove was unable to resist using such an advantage. By midsummer of 2002, the tactic was verified when a computer diskette was discovered in Lafayette Park, across from the White House.

Political scientists thought Rove was once more changing the rules of the game.

"I pick up the Lafayette Park Manifesto written by Karl Rove and I see Republicans should take advantage of the war. They should speak about the war and the president's leadership therein. Does that translate into a deliberate effort to schedule this to pretend you're doing it for policy reasons but say we have to do it before the election because we need to maximize our chances in the election?"

Presidential scholar Bruce Buchanan was talking about slide number 20 in the political presentation put together by Rove and White House Director of Political Affairs Ken Mehlman. The Powerpoint show fell into the hands of Democrats when a Republican worker accidentally dropped it in the park and the diskette had been picked up and made public. Slide number 20 is headlined "Republican Strategy" and lists six methods for winning the election. The first bullet point says, "Focus on War and the Economy." Education was simply an issue to "promote." The slide show made the case that the president's enormous wartime popularity could be effectively deployed in the 2002 congressional contests.

Even impartial observers like Buchanan were taken aback by the audacity of the politics.

"I think in their own minds they're conflicted about it to some degree. But I think the way they rationalize it . . . Rove would rationalize it, is to explain to the President the consequences . . . the political consequences of each of the choices he is considering, and that so long as policy is not disturbed by doing something that helps us politically, we should feel free to do something which helps us politically."

And so the Rove policy was in place: to fight the war on terrorism, which was a just cause, and use that pureness of purpose to advance the Republican political agenda. The president had an obligation to talk about terrorism and the war, didn't he? And what was wrong with him asking for support for candidates who backed his policies on the war and domestically? Nothing, in Rove's estimation, was misguided about his approach. Another plan was in place.

Except the war on terrorism wasn't going so well.

Osama bin Laden was invisible. The most powerful government in the world was unable to find a six-foot, four-inch tall, bearded Muslim, who's on dialysis, clanking around attached to medical equipment. U.S. intelligence didn't even know if the chief evildoer was alive or dead after the attack on Afghanistan. Tapes purporting to contain his face and voice were surfacing and appeared both real and untraceable. Bin Laden was almost incorporeal, slipping across borders undetected, taunting the U.S. military and the American president. Meanwhile, suicide bombers were still attacking Israelis and U.S. allies, the most notable tragedy being the explosion at a nightclub in Bali.

Very little progress was being made. A few top al-Qaeda operatives were taken into custody. But not their leader. U.S. intelligence agencies kept getting mixed signals about potential attacks against Americans. Alarming warnings were issued and then retracted or revised. Americans were getting uneasy. No one had any real sense of what to expect. How do you fight an enemy you cannot see? The president could claim progress but was unable to prove it. The public believed in George W. Bush but it did not like the way things were going. And this discontent was rising as the fall elections loomed. Unchecked, these kinds of sentiments had the potential to harm the president and his party's hopes of gaining power in Congress.

Karl Rove needed a better, simpler, more marketable war.

Another moment of convergence had presented itself to Rove and he knew how to take advantage of it. On a much lesser scale, this kind of thing had been happening throughout his professional political career. In Texas, he had helped to facilitate a federal investigation that led to his client Rick Perry getting elected agriculture commissioner and, ultimately, to become governor. And whether he planted it or not, finding a bug in his own office was a defining moment in another Rove client's run for re-election as governor of Texas. Rove's political vision was never limited to normal horizons.

A political operative who has closely observed Rove's tactics for many years described the rationale Rove employed for what was coming next.

"What if we haven't avenged the Twin Towers? How do the president and Rove not suffer from that? And it was starting to look like we couldn't win the war on terrorism. Rather than lose that war we redefine that war. Suddenly it wasn't the people who were terrorists who killed us. It was evil itself. They can apply that to anyone they want. Tom Daschle or Hussein."

And this approach melded nicely with an agenda Vice President Dick Cheney and Deputy Secretary of Defense Paul Wolfowitz had been pushing for a decade to expand American influence and military abroad into a form of empire. Rove's political strategy for the president transformed a policy whose scope and tenets were unprecedented in American history.

All it needed was a little justification.

And Iraq was handy.

Although providence has been a close ally of his, Karl Rove is more than just lucky. He is also disciplined and methodical. The protocols and tools of modern political influence are not just known and mastered by him; they have also been refined by Rove. Constantly polling and analyzing data, he explores trends he thinks might be developing, tests specific demographics for variations in opinions, and deconstructs regional economies for underlying political influences. Rove generally knows the course a political river will follow long before the first trickle of change begins to flow.

But he never uses politics as persuasion when he makes his arguments to the president and the Cabinet. Rove is aware of how unseemly that would appear in a setting that is supposed to be about serving the country and not the ambitions of a political party or the president. Nonetheless, the president can have absolute, unwavering confidence, based upon his long record of experience with Rove, that, if Karl Rove is pushing a particular policy in a senior level staff meeting, he has already gone deep into that policy's political impacts, and they are good. Bush has been saying, since he first ran for governor of Texas, that he doesn't need polls to tell him what to think.

And he does not.

He has Karl Rove to tell him and Rove has the polls to figure it all out.

If Rove is encouraging a policy alteration, the unspoken fact is he has figured out the new position serves the president, the Republicans, and the conservative cause. Consideration of how that policy will impact the nation is almost ancillary to its political influence.

That's how Rove got his free-trader president to impose steel tariffs.

But Rove conceded only one half of the truth in his political calculus on steel.

"The discussion has been, 'okay, this was a political calculation by Rove to get Michigan, Ohio, Pennsylvania, that's what this was all about.' There is, if you will, a political consideration. But the political consideration is this: we want to get trade promotion authority. It's a tool that allows us to broadly expand free trade."

Only Karl Rove could argue he had found a political solution to improve free trade by imposing tariffs on imported goods.

Trade promotion authority was not the end product of the controversial steel tariffs. The congressional vote to give the president executive authority to construct deals with other countries was to be decided by a very narrow margin. Winning was impossible for Bush and Rove, unless they picked up support from members of Congress in the Ohio River Valley steel country of Pennsylvania, West Virginia, and parts of the industrial Midwest. And those elected representatives were not going to give the president their votes unless he was willing to trade with them. They wanted the steel industry and its unionized workers to be protected by tariffs from cheaper, imported steel.

More convergence for Karl.

Here was an issue that could increase the power of the president's office, put traditional Democrat-voting unions into the Republican column, and improve both midterm election performance and Bush's chances at a second term by securing more support in Pennsylvania, Ohio, and West Virginia, key electoral votes needed to win the presidency. The opportunity came along when the U.S. International Trade Commission voted unanimously that U.S. steel producers were experiencing substantial harm from imported shipments of less expensive foreign steel.

Rove recognized an important moment.

"That was the political calculation. You had a 6–0 vote. If you ignore that 6–0 vote and took no action whatsoever, you were in essence saying, 'we're not gonna uphold the laws that were already on the books.' And there would have been a lot of ramifications to that, the most practical ramification of which would have been we lose free trade."

The other ramification, the one Rove avoided talking about with his interviewers, was that Bush would have lost the opportunity for political gains in an industrial region that has been historically Democratic. Positioning President Bush on this blatant contradiction to his campaign pledge of protecting free trade would take some finesse. Rove had the president suggest he was buying time for U.S. steel producers to re-organize. Thirty-one of them were in bankruptcy proceedings. He also was able to argue that what the free trade effort lost to steel imports could be more than regained by the president's newly acquired trade promotion authority for the Executive Office.

Democrats were amazed by what they saw as the brazen hypocrisy.

"This guy is single-handedly dismantling the Democratic party," said a national party organizer. "He has analyzed the funding base and is picking off our core constituencies one by one. He's setting them against each other to choke off the money. We're dead. When did unions ever have a reason to support a conservative like George Bush before steel tariffs? Now they think he's protecting their jobs."

The premise Rove used to guide him on steel was sound but cynical. Rove has always relied on the high-profile moment as an integral device, an announcement or ceremony, to steer political support. In his analyses, the public does not follow detailed aftermath, unless it becomes widespread discomfort. If the president can protect steelworker jobs, get union votes, and argue trade promotion authority will improve their industry, then the choice is simple.

In an interview with Radio Free Europe, Ann Florini, a trade specialist at the Carnegie Endowment for International Peace implied that the domestically driven politics of the steel tariffs were more important than their effects on free trade.

"The problem with trade is that losses are concentrated and benefits are diffuse across the population. So the fact that all of us end up paying slightly higher prices for steel isn't enough to get anybody roused up to go out and vote Bush out of office. Losing jobs, even in demonstrably inefficient industries like the big steel mills that we have—those costs are very clear. And so those kinds of costs do mobilize people to get up and vote."

She was right.

In the midst of the fall 2002 election campaigns, major steel producers announced they were increasing prices to U.S. automakers. But voters were not likely to blame the president for that, if they noticed at all. Auto manufacturers were certain to pass along the additional costs of steel to consumers. Prices for new cars will go up. But President Bush will escape harm from that, as well. Car buyers will simply think the carmakers are trying to increase their profits. Displaced anger will be directed at the auto manufacturers instead of the actual cause of the higher prices, which were the president's steel tariffs.

Karl Rove wins. Again.

He has created a politics of pretense. Neither Rove nor the Bush administration give the electorate credit for being sophisticated enough to call them to account. If they were concerned about being caught, Rove would reduce the president's exposure to claims of hypocrisy and broken campaign pledges. Instead, Bush signs his education bill, the "Leave No Child Behind Act" with a smiling Ted Kennedy over his shoulder. This is the TV moment the electorate remembers, a president appearing to create bipartisan coalitions and endeavoring to "change the tone" in Washington while helping our children. When Bush proposed a federal budget, however, funding for education was cut with the president authorizing only $22 billion of the $28 billion the measure called for. America needed money to increase military strength and pay for the president's tax cut.

Children will be left behind.

When he is caught constructing these awkward alliances, Rove is known to run and hide. As he was pushing the president's faith-based initiatives, early in the Bush administration, a memo was leaked about Rove's dealings with the Salvation Army. The White House needed charitable organizations to spend time and money lobbying to let Congress know there was widespread support for the proposal to send taxpayer money to charities funded by religious groups. As one of the largest charities, Salvation Army was on Rove's radar to get them involved in the political process. The organization, however, was hesitant.

The Salvation Army has a policy of not hiring homosexuals. Under the bill being prepared for Congress, government money was to be restricted from flowing to charities that discriminated against individuals based on sexual orientation. The Salvation Army was not likely to support such a bill and Rove needed their resources to win. An international charity, the Salvation Army had the ability to spend tens of thousands of dollars monthly on a lobbying effort for the faith-based initiative.

So Karl constructed a deal.

In the leaked memo, the Salvation Army agreed to spend $90,000 to $110,000 monthly on public relations and political lobbying, if Rove would make a "firm commitment" to get the charity an exemption from the nondiscrimination clauses in the new bill.

When the memo went public, both the White House and the Salvation Army denied being involved in any such deal. If there were no deal, why then, a short time later, did the White House say no "senior officials" were involved? Before too long, Rove conceded he was the first person to be contacted by the Salvation Army when it decided to seek the exemption. The next iteration of the Bush team's response was that a deputy assistant to the president said Rove "doesn't think he was told the specifics of what" the Salvation Army wanted and that he had "no substantive discussions about the matter."

The Salvation Army flap showed that compassionate conservatism is only compassionate to people who are conservatives. Rove's goal was to get money for religious charities and if it meant excluding gays and lesbians from employment with the Salvation Army, he would take the tradeoff. You can't be compassionate to everybody. But you can be a conservative all the time.

Compassionate conservatism is an inverted form of Nixonian politics. Rove has recognized that Bush's smile and his charm are the sugar for the bad medicine being dosed out by the administration's policies. Behind what one Democrat calls Bush's "menacing smile," lives a derivative of Richard Nixon's governing style. With a wink and a nudge, Nixon's cabinet used to suggest, "Watch what we do. Not what we say." During Vietnam and the Cold War, Nixon's advisors understood that a president who talked tough would have great appeal to the electorate. Nixon talked tough. But he governed softly, especially on domestic policies. This was, after all, the president who breathed life into an idea known as the Environmental Protection Agency.

Bush talks soft and governs tough.

A Washington, DC, business and political consultant, who has worked for both parties, thinks Rove's politics are ingenious. And dangerous.

"Rove is Nixonian in his cynicism and manipulation of patriotic themes. The irony is that, W., in many ways, is the anti-Nixon. Nixon was brilliant but self-destructive. W. is dull but, in Rove's hands, maniacally disciplined. It's like Rove is Nixon's heir. Cold-blooded. Ruthless. Paranoid. But unlike Nixon, Rove has figured out how to mask it all behind Bush's smile."

To build a Republican dynasty, Rove needed more than just Bush's gleaming grin. He had to use a few stolen strategies. The GOP could control national politics if Rove nabbed an important concept from the Democrats. President Bill Clinton, whose strategic political skills approach Rove's, understood innately that voters did not follow the close details unless policy affected the daily course of their lives. During Clinton's two terms, Democrats learned to speak differently than they voted.

A Clinton organizer said Rove has taken that gun out of the Democrats' hands and turned it back on them.

"The thing is, we used to vote liberal but we would press release to our districts as conservative. At least, we positioned our votes that way, knowing our constituents didn't know any better. Karl realized he could use those tactics to advance the conservative agenda. Republicans are now voting ultra-right wing. But their press releases to their districts are that they care about people. These are just the rules of the game. They learned it from us and now Rove has applied it to us."

Every move Rove made was a considered choice to help the president become more politically powerful and put conservatives in a position to push on their favorite issues. Once more, just as in his Texas days, he was creating an environment for the right things to happen. They were all simple and obvious steps, each designed to strengthen support for Bush and broaden the base of the conservative agenda. That means if you have to pass a 190 billion dollar farm bill to gain votes of farmers and Democrats in the plains states and the Midwest, then that's what you do. It doesn't matter that your own party had been working for six straight years to wean the American farmer from price supports and senior elected members of your own party screamed about the spending. It is also irrelevant that the bill was more blatantly anti-free trade than even the steel tariffs. This was a political choice, a political need. And that's more important than policy. Besides, the legislation was designed to help giant, corporate growers more than family farms. The president, however, told the country that he had made the sacrifices necessary to preserve the family farm. And people believed him. He is such a charming and likeable man. Americans want to believe in their president.

And Karl Rove knows that, too.

So he devised another plan, a risky one that would make extensive use of the president's popularity. If he could execute this strategy, Republicans would drown out the Democrats on domestic issues and corner them into backing the president on taxes and the war. The Democrats would be mostly issueless. Republicans would be in control of the White House and Congress and the president could have the mandate he did not get on Election Day 2000.

But first Rove needed something to sell the electorate. And it wasn't the war on terrorism because that just wasn't going too well. It was time to roll out some new ideas, a different product. President Bush and Cheney had big plans of their own, a new American protocol for dealing with foreign threats and stabilizing the Mideast. The concept also had the potential to regulate oil prices and supplies for decades. Rove knew he was expected to help make that possible. But there was still a lot of lingering haze and political confusion over the war on terrorism. Rove intended to clear up all of that. If he did, the president could make history during midterm elections and the world might know a new kind of U.S. foreign policy.

The only thing in the way of the Bush and Cheney plan was Iraq.

But General Rove had an idea for turning Iraq into a political solution instead of a problem.

16

The Baghdad Road

Hey, we can't take over a country that doesn't exist, so fine we'll
go take over some country. We can't invade al Qaeda. We can't
occupy it. We can't even find it. Okay. Fine. But we do know
where Baghdad is. We've got a map. We can find it on a map. And
they've got oil and an evil guy. So let's go there.

Jason Stanford, Democratic Consultant

T he reporters were a bit confused. Not about the speech itself, which was well crafted. Context was the problem.
They were having trouble with the idea of George W. Bush
talking about U.S. military policy. Something seemed not
to fit.

"Hell," said Sam Attlesey of the *Dallas Morning News*, "I'm just
now getting comfortable with Bush as governor. This campaign for
president stuff might be too much."

The three veteran Texas political reporters were in Charleston,
South Carolina, to cover the Texas governor's speech on the military
to cadets at the Citadel. Afterward, they had found a rooftop bar
where locals gathered and watched the falling light throw shadows

across Charleston Harbor toward Fort Sumter. They had filed their reports already but still didn't quite know what to say to each other.

"At least somebody in this campaign has sense of history," said R.G. Ratcliffe of the *Houston Chronicle*, nodding in the direction of the island fort where the first battle of the Civil War was waged.

Earlier in the day, Bush, trailed by his strategist Karl Rove, had entered a gymnasium full of cheering cadets at the famed military academy. The speech was his first step in outlining policies for a potential Bush administration. The Republican hopeful, criticized by analysts and political opponents as a lightweight on foreign policy, was plowing straight into a field of questions about his capabilities. Bush had held only one public office, governor of Texas, and his credentials for assessing military capabilities and purposes were limited by experience. The text, written largely by the same people who had advised his father, former Defense Secretary Dick Cheney, former Assistant Secretary of Defense Richard Armitage, and former National Security Council official Condoleezza Rice, was an attempt to prove the younger Bush was packing the necessary intellectual gear on military affairs.

The Texas governor promised to protect Americans from terror and significantly increase military spending. He envisioned a more mobile U.S. armed force that would not be overdeployed, as he suggested was the case under the Clinton administration. Although many of the biggest cuts in military spending were begun under policies approved by his father, President George H. W. Bush, the son implied Clinton was the cause and that there would be new funds for a soldier pay raise and weapons research under a second Bush administration.

But the younger Bush had a lingering problem of credibility on military matters. And it was not just because he was without experience in federal office.

It began during his first campaign to become governor. Bush and incumbent Governor Ann Richards were debating in Dallas when the challenger was asked about his own military service. During the

Vietnam era, Bush had managed to land a coveted spot in the Texas National Guard's pilot training program. In most states, including Texas, the waiting list to become a part of the National Guard averaged three to five years. Actually, the wait would have been much longer were it not for the fact many young men did not bother to put their names on the list because they knew they would be drafted before getting accepted into the guard.

Getting a seat in a plane and learning to fly in the National Guard was even more challenging. Those were the most sought after commissions and were severely limited by available aircraft and excessive demand for the training. But George W. Bush did not spend any time on a waiting list.

He was first asked about his good fortune in the debate with Ann Richards.

"Mr. Bush, when you entered the National Guard's air wing in Houston, waiting lists in states around the country were three to five years, yet you just seemed to get into the Guard without any trouble. How did you move up the list? Do you think there was any influence used by your father, who was then a U.S. congressman from Houston?"

The question from the panelist was not unexpected and Bush had a smooth and rehearsed answer for the statewide broadcast.

"All I know is that a position opened up and I got to enlist," Bush said. "I knew I wanted to learn to fly airplanes and this was a great opportunity. If there was any influence exercised on my behalf, I sure didn't know about it. I know my unit could have been called up at any time and just flying airplanes is dangerous. I could have been killed. You think about that when you turn on those afterburners."

Actually, Bush's air wing at Ellington Air Force Base outside of Houston was not likely at all to be ordered to active duty in Vietnam. And he probably knew that. The pilots were gaining hours flying outdated technology, planes that were being phased out of Southeast Asia. The F-102, which Bush was flying, was part of a fleet the USAF had decided to stop flying on overseas missions and was to be completely out of commission by June 30, 1970. He also was far short of the requisite 1000 hours needed to fly the F-102 in combat or foreign missions. Bush knew that, as well, because he was told by a commanding officer.

Inexplicably, Bush's military service did not become an issue of any significance during the presidential campaign. There were many reasons it might have turned into a political quagmire for the candidate. Bush's records were incomplete. He missed a critical physical and lost flight status. He went to Florida and Alabama to work on political campaigns while still on active duty. But no matter how hard reporters searched for evidence of preferential treatment, they were unable to discover documented proof his family exercised influence to keep its eldest son clear of jungle combat.

But it is hard to believe they did not.

After the Texas gubernatorial debate had concluded, Karen Hughes, his media relations expert, approached the reporter who had asked Bush the National Guard question. Regardless of the fact that Bush's answer revealed he had been expecting the query, Hughes was outraged that her candidate had been confronted with his past.

"Exactly what kind of question was that?" she asked. "I really didn't see any reason for it. What were you getting at? There's no point in bringing any of that Vietnam stuff up in a race for the governor of Texas. I just don't understand."

"It was a legitimate question, Karen," she was told. "He and I are of the same generation. I was obligated to ask the question. I lost friends in Vietnam, friends who tried but were unable to enter the National Guard. I just wanted to know how he managed to pull it off."

"It's just completely irrelevant," she huffed, and then disappeared to catch up with her candidate.

Just the appearance of preferential treatment ought to have concerned the Bush campaign. Was it simply a statistical miracle that, out of all the young men waiting to enter the Texas National Guard, destiny just plucked George W. Bush out of a sea of names and gave him a chance to fly airplanes over the Texas Gulf Coast instead of the Central Highlands of Vietnam?

Not likely.

Because the statistical anomalies were even greater than the good fortune represented by Bush entering the guard. The same air wing at Ellington Air Force Base outside of Houston also included Lloyd Bentsen III, son of Texas U.S. Senator Lloyd Bentsen, as well as the son of Texas' other U.S. Senator John Tower and seven members of the Dallas Cowboys football team.

This was not about luck. It was about connections.

A few days after the debate had been broadcast, a press person in the campaign of incumbent Governor Ann Richards contacted the reporter who had asked the National Guard question.

"You need to talk to Ben Barnes about this National Guard thing," he was told.

Barnes, once the political wunderkind of Texas politics, was the youngest person ever to become Texas House speaker. He was still in his twenties. Barnes held that office when Bush entered the National Guard. During the Vietnam era, numerous requests were made of Barnes' office to get the children of the well connected into the National Guard and out of Vietnam.

On the telephone during the 1994 Texas governor's race, Barnes had an uncertain memory.

"I can't recall specifically what, if anything, we did on George W.'s behalf," Barnes said. "I think there were conversations, but my staff would have been more involved than I was."

An unapologetic Democrat, Barnes is a good friend of Ann Richards, the incumbent Bush was trying to defeat. Obviously, he had motivation to help the governor. However, Barnes was not likely to stand before cameras and countrymen and say he helped George Bush jump in front of other sons and get into the National Guard. As a lobbyist and political consultant in Texas, his future business might have been a bit limited by doing that.

What Barnes did admit was that the Texas National Guard, during the Vietnam years, maintained what was called a "political list." A limited number of people were able to exercise influence and political connections to get a name, either placed on the list, or moved up for service. It meant there were no rice paddies in that person's future, unless he chose to become a rice farmer on the Texas coastal plains.

"Look," Barnes said, "the fella who maintained that list for the Guard and General [James M.] Rose is still alive. Let me talk to him first and then I'll put you in touch with him. He'll know if Bush's name was on there and if it got moved up so he could take pilot training."

After two weeks of phone calls to Barnes, who was following up with the former Guard officer, a date was set for an interview. An hour before the reporter was to board a flight from Austin to Houston, Ben Barnes called and said the interview was not going to happen.

"You need to understand, this fella is widowed. And he's fairly old these days. He lives with his daughter and his son-in-law and they are both very big George Bush supporters. He was all set to do this until he told them about it, and they just urged him not to talk to anyone about this. He told me his life would be very uncomfortable at home, if he talked to you or anybody about Bush and the Guard. That's all I've got to tell you."

But the truth doesn't change just because it's missing a few details.

The appearance of what happened for George W. Bush in the Texas National Guard is very likely the truth of what happened. Bush was moved up into the pilot training program ahead of hundreds, probably thousands of other young Texas draft age men. His father was a congressman and could have easily called the Texas house speaker requesting such a favor. If he did, Barnes' or his staff would have almost certainly granted the request and the younger Bush would never learn, nor would he care to ask, how he got such a safe, precious spot in the Texas National Guard. George W. Bush was able to tell the gubernatorial debate panel that he knew nothing more than a position opened up and he got it. And that is probably, to him, the full scope of the truth.

In a lawsuit deposition, Ben Barnes did admit that he took a call from a Bush family friend seeking favoritism to move Bush up on the National Guard waiting list. Barnes said no one from the Bush family ever contacted him, but Houston businessman Sid Adger did call and urged Barnes to get George W. Bush a pilot position in the Guard. Barnes said he contacted General Rose of the Texas Guard to make the request.

Bush's military history ought not to be ignored as the American saber is rattled at Iraq. It provides important context.

By 2002, George W. Bush was comfortable in the role of a wartime president. With Karl Rove at his side, refining his image and politics almost daily, Bush had become the aggressive defender of American democracy against terrorism. As he talked about Iraq, the president seemed to be beating the breastplate of his chain mail and sounding very much like a warrior.

Except he has never heard the sound of a shot fired in anger.

And he was leading his country into perilous terrain.

Karl Rove had to be confronting unfamiliar frustrations. When your genius is built around a skill for seeing the far horizon, you can sometimes find immediate issues complicating. 2002 was to be the first big political test for the administration of George W. Bush and, domestically, the political dynamics were knocking around Rove and his president. The economy refused to get it up off of its knees and widespread corporate corruption continued to punish Wall Street instead of CEOs who had committed fraud. Political fault was sticking mostly to the Republicans, who the public historically associated with big business.

The war on terrorism was compounding the politics. Nobody knew if Osama bin Laden was dead or still clattering around remote mountains, dragging his dialysis equipment behind him and plotting more attacks. Something seemed to be going on. Intelligence agencies kept getting increased chatter on communications lines, which indicated more attacks might be imminent. That prompted increased terror alerts and then retractions and clarifications, only leading to more confusion. On top of that heap of problems, the Democrats were calling for a new agency to manage homeland security. George W. Bush was a Republican, and he didn't want to create a gigantic bureaucracy on his watch.

Control of the politics was slipping from Karl Rove's grasp.

Democrats were so optimistic that House Majority leader Richard Gephardt predicted his party might pick up as many as 30 or 40 new seats in the U.S. House of Representatives. The shine he put on the Democrats' future seemed to be based on more than just the dynamics of the moment. International and domestic developments were evolving in ways that benefited Democrats.

So Rove got to work. And he came up with a strategy that provided a turnkey solution to every crisis President Bush was confronting. The Democratic advantage went away overnight.

Jason Stanford, a national Democratic consultant who operates out of Texas, admitted his side was politically disarmed by Rove's ingenuity.

"It was just brilliant. They figured out real soon that Osama was going to be a hard guy to go and get. He can hide in a cave, right? So, what do they do? They just picked a war they could win. Hey, we can't take over a country that doesn't exist, so fine we'll go take over some country. We can't invade al Qaeda. We can't occupy it. We can't even find it. Okay. Fine. But we do know where Baghdad is. We've got a map. We can find it on a map. And they've got oil and an evil guy. So let's go there. They never stop and say that. But they know it's what they are doing. It has to be the most evil political calculation in American history."

A simplification but the rudiments of a plan.

Karl Rove did not, however, wake up one bright morning and say, "I've got it, Mr. President. If you'll just invade Iraq, we can take care of all of your domestic problems on the economy, corporate corruption, unkept campaign promises, and the war on terrorism." There was, though, a political judgment made about making Iraq the object of our national anger. We weren't just taking on terrorism. We were confronting evil itself. And, clearly, Saddam was evil and, as such, he was nothing more than a terrorist in charge of a country. Arguments were easy to make, whether substantive or not, that he likely helped the Arabs who attacked on 9/11.

Demonstrably, though, what had Saddam Hussein done to suddenly be moved up on the list of bad guys? In the decade since U.S. forces routed Iraqi troops from Kuwait, Baghdad had been dealing with poverty, disease, a deteriorating infrastructure, and an economy limited by an oil-for-food program established through the United Nations. Even the Central Intelligence Agency, in a 2002 report to Congress, said it was unable to offer evidence Saddam was connected to Islamic terrorists or was developing weapons of mass destruction. Containment and deterrence had worked with Iraq. Saddam feared doing anything rash because he knew retribution was certain to be swift and complete. His behavior has largely been consistent since the conclusion of the Persian Gulf War. Certainly not good. But not as evil as the White House needed him to be.

The "Suddenly Saddam" strategy came out of nowhere, a political curiosity arriving at the perfect time for Rove and Bush. How did it happen that Saddam Hussein became the most important matter in the world at just the right instant in an election campaign to help the president and his political party? President Bush barely mentioned the Iraqi dictator to the public when he was running for office. Nothing about Saddam had changed significantly in more than 10 years.

What had changed was the U.S. political climate under Bush and Rove.

American University political scientist James Thurber does not want to believe the urgency over Iraq was motivated by cynical political tactics of Karl Rove. But he did not deny Bush and Rove's Iraqi rhetoric obscured domestic problems like the economy and a lack of effectiveness in prosecuting the war on terrorism.

"Why is Saddam more of a threat this October and November election season than he was last year or the year before?"

"Well, that's a good question," Thurber answered. "Timing is everything in politics and it certainly is helping. I have to believe on faith because I wasn't sitting there, that this wasn't decided with Karl and the president and the vice president sitting in the White House saying, 'Let's go for it now because it's going to do the following.' I think it happened slowly through the Pentagon and [Paul] Wolfowitz leading and Cheney right there with him and Karl put his arms around it and said, 'Yeah, this is gonna help us.'"

Rove's own conservatism was cured through the years in a smokehouse of those hawkish Bush advisors. As he was formulating campaign strategy for the midterm election, Rove was gathering with senior Bush administration counselors who had been urging aggression toward Iraq for more than a decade. Deputy Defense Secretary Paul Wolfowitz and Vice President Dick Cheney were among the thinkers from the first Bush presidency that had pushed an expanded American presence around the globe. Under the second President Bush, this ideology gained political potency behind the leadership of Defense Secretary Donald Rumsfeld. While George H. W. Bush had been cautious and hesitant to move in military directions urged by this same group of advisors, his son was emboldened by the events of September 11.

And slowly, the shape of a political and military plan began to materialize.

The initial expression of this new thinking occurred the first day of June as the president spoke to the graduating class of cadets at West Point. In a commencement address, whose contextual importance was largely missed by the media, Bush's language revealed that deterrence had been abandoned as U.S. military policy. When reporters did not play the story prominently, the White House had staffers go out and re-spin the news. A single word, used only once in the text of the president's speech, characterized its important, underlying message: preemption.

"I will not stand by as peril grows closer and closer," the president told his West Point audience. "If we wait for threats to fully materialize, we will have waited too long."

"The war on terror will not be won on the defensive"

"We cannot defend America and our friends by hoping for the best."

The language was unmistakable and not subject to interpretation. The president was informing the wider world that America was assuming the office of global sheriff. There were good guys and bad guys. We were going after the bad guys. And anyone who did not think like America was very likely an enemy. Looking and acting suspiciously were now sufficient grounds for the United States to seek you out as an enemy of freedom and democracy. We were no longer waiting for trouble as a motive for intervention.

Due process is limited in this new American internationalism.

"All of a sudden," one Democrat suggested, "we're the cowboy who walked into the saloon with a gun, saying, 'get behind me if you're with me or we're gonna shoot ya.'"

The president had also laid his predicate for acting against Iraq. Suspicions were now enough, even if intelligence efforts were unable to substantiate allegations against Saddam. The ensuing debate over acting preemptively against Iraq, the timing of the public discourse and the moments of great decision, all show the trademarks of a disciplined campaign run by Karl Rove. Simply put, the president was to spend the summer shaking his sword at Saddam, thus drowning out discussions over record deficits, corporate corruption, and a tepid economy. Along the way, reputable voices would emerge to argue for congressional and United Nations' authorization. By agreeing to this approach, the president avoided polarizing the electorate with a definitive decision of his own before it came time to vote. He was tough, but reasonable.

"I think this entire discussion was perfectly orchestrated by Karl Rove," a Democratic consultant said. "He even framed the debate. At the end of the summer, they had guys like [James] Baker and

[Henry] Kissinger come out and urge a specific approach to dealing with Iraq. Then Bush looks conciliatory by going to the UN and by seeking congressional approval. If he is going to look conciliatory, Karl would much rather it is to Republican voices than Democratic. Suddenly, the debate goes from being about whether we should attack Iraq to one of whether we are going to go it alone. They advanced the issue by skipping over all the important parts."

There were other indications that Rove was on the job before the president took the discussion to the United Nations and Congress. A few days after the Bush speech at West Point, Congress had set a date to hear testimony from FBI agent Colleen Rowley. Rowley was the author of a memo to her superiors in the agency, which had indicated there was a probability of an event like 9/11. The memo had gone ignored. But her words before Congress were certain to dominate broadcast news on the day of her testimony and headlines of newspapers the next day. There was nothing in her story that would help the president or wary Americans worried about their safety.

So, the White House covered her up with news of its own.

On June 6, 2002, as Rowley was making her congressional appearance, the Bush administration rolled out plans for a Department of Homeland Security. Earlier in the year, the president had staunchly resisted the idea promulgated by Democratic leadership. But now he was offering his own proposal, hastily drawn, to prompt a huge reorganization of government. The story dominated news coverage and Colleen Rowley's chilling testimony of the failed FBI bureaucracy turned into a sidebar, a lesser event.

The Democrats, though, caught on too late.

Jim Jordan, the director of the Democratic Senatorial Campaign Committee, was considered prescient for comments he made in August 2002 as he was briefing political reporters. Energized by the war on terrorism having grown quiet, and Wall Street acting equally drowsy, Jordan felt Democrats would benefit from politics moving back to the pocketbooks of voters. Jordan said he thought something was happening in the American electorate and that it would accrue to the benefit of his party. But he was asked if he thought Republicans might regain political dominance over the agenda with the issues of terrorism and war.

His answer was widely quoted.

"You mean when General Rove calls in the air strikes in October?"

As cynical as the remark may have sounded, it had an underlying logic. Jordan, recognizing he had shocked a few people in his audience, added, "I hope I'm wrong. Certainly, none of us want to think that the administration, for domestic political reasons, would use the war. But I think the temptation will be strong."

Jordan was undoubtedly right that "something was going on out there," and Democrats were feeling better about the midterm elections. Polls indicated they had a chance to pick up seats in the House and, perhaps, even gain more power in the Senate. But Karl Rove wasn't oblivious to this trend. He had his own polls. He also had a plan for turning the political dynamics on their head.

But he was not going to launch until the time was right.

The calculated nature of what Rove and his president were doing was revealed in a *New York Times* article quoting Chief of Staff Andy Card. Card indicated the White House was resisting launching its public relations offensive on Iraq because, "from a marketing point of view, you don't introduce new products in August."

And so they did not.

But when Congress returned, Bush and Rove began to take control of the national debate by stepping up efforts to pressure Congress for a resolution authorizing the use of force against Iraq. The Democrats knew, immediately, Rove had them co-opted. War on terrorism had previously been declared, so effectively, the United States was already in a state of war. If the president had also identified Iraq as an enemy, any member of Congress who resisted the Iraqi resolution was in danger of appearing to not support the president in a time of national peril. Not a good place to be, politically.

However, the options for Democrats were equally perplexing. A lengthy debate in Congress, to clarify why the Iraqi resolution was foolish, would have the effect of covering up discussion of domestic issues, where Democrats had the edge. The political conundrum was proof that Rove had them outflanked. If Democrats helped to pass the resolution quickly, there was a chance that they could execute a political return to domestic affairs like the economy, corporate corruption, health care, and even pension reform. But the president still had a chance to keep eyes on the Iraqi controversy by pursuing a joint resolution before the United Nations. Between the United Nations and Congress, war talk with Iraq could be timed to fill the entire fall campaign schedule.

As Congress haggled over the syntax and importance of an Iraq resolution, the president addressed members in joint session to talk about possible war with Iraq and unveil his new National Security Strategy. Affirming the ideas first espoused at West Point, the president gave U.S. foreign policy an evolutionary shove to the right by claiming America was justified in striking preemptively against perceived enemies.

Now we were relying on perception, not proof, preemption instead of deterrence.

"The greater the threat, the greater is the risk of inaction," the president said. "And the more compelling the case for taking anticipatory action to defend ourselves, even if uncertainty remains as to the time and place of the enemy's attack. To forestall or prevent such hostile acts by our adversaries, the United States will, if necessary, act preemptively."

Even the timing of this speech to Congress was suspect. The stock market, which had been faltering consistently as the volume of war talk rose, closed at 7940 during the third week of September, the lowest point in more than a year. The president's National Security Strategy was outlined for Congress on September 20. The news media hardly took note of the paltry stock numbers. We were being told, as a nation, the president and his cabinet were changing the way America decides to go to war.

That was the news. Not the markets.

Making the case for war against Iraq was not easy, unless you judiciously avoided the facts. The president filled his campaign speeches with fears that Saddam Hussein was on the verge of acquiring a nuclear weapon while the esteemed International Institute for Strategic Studies reported that Iraq was years away from developing a bomb of its own. The White House also conveniently ignored the fact that radical Islamists like the al Qaeda viewed Saddam with almost as much loathing as they did America. His regime is secular, not Islamist and that makes him the enemy of al Qaeda. A member of a minority sect of Islam, the Sunnis, Saddam has no reason to conspire with the terrorists who attacked the United States. Getting rid of Saddam will do nothing to alleviate terrorist threats to America, and presidential rhetoric cannot change that.

As he campaigned around the country for Republican candidates, Karl Rove kept the president lasered on to message. The world was a dangerous place. Saddam was only one of many despots America needed to confront. Bush's National Security Strategy, justifying preemptive action, was a bold template for dealing with the new threats. Voters appeared disinterested in domestic concerns and did not bother with envisioning where the president's policy of preemption might take their country.

But there were reasons to tremble. Even among conservatives.

Writing in Patrick Buchanan's *The American Conservative*, Paul W. Schroeder argued that, instead of stabilizing international politics, the president was about to make the planet a more tremulous and worried place with the concept of preemption.

"The American example and standard for preemptive war, if carried out, would invite imitation and emulation, and get it. One can easily imagine plausible scenarios in which India could justify attacking Pakistan, or vice versa, or Israel any one of its neighbors, or

China Taiwan, or South Korea North Korea, under this rule that suspicion of what a hostile regime might do justifies launching pre-emptive wars to overthrow it."

A conservative on the far right, Schroeder did not sound very different from Gore Vidal on the left, who posted a 7000-word deconstruction of the new Bush doctrine in the *London Observer*.

But the Democrats lacked the courage and the intellect to make these issues stick. And Karl Rove knew it. Within his own party, and expanding ever outward, Rove had the president cultivate an atmosphere where it was almost considered treasonous to question policy. Scott Ritter, a former arms inspector who had served his country as a U.S. Marine for 12 years, was the target of a Rove-like whispering campaign when he made high-profile claims that the White House was about to take the United States to war with Iraq based on erroneous information. Ritter, among the last U.N. inspectors to leave Iraq, said it was impossible that Hussein had weapons of mass destruction, chemical or biological armaments. For his frankness and courage, Republicans tried to discredit Ritter by referring to him as "the Jane Fonda of Iraq" and asking, "when will his exercise video be released?"

Whisper wars had already been used by Rove against U.S. Senator John McCain of Arizona in the presidential primary for the GOP. Although no one was willing to be quoted, a question was raised about McCain's mental health after being held prisoner of war in Vietnam for a number of years. Also, whispers of homosexuality in Texas had diminished Ann Richards in her race for governor against Rove's client, George W. Bush.

Regardless of the dubious tactics, the president's popularity did not falter. Everywhere he went, adoring crowds gathered to hear him speak for republican candidates. Karl Rove scheduled Bush into numerous locations where the GOP needed to win. And under the cover of war, nothing the president said seemed to cause him political harm. When he suggested during an East Coast trip that the Senate was holding up the Homeland Security bill because it was not "as interested in the safety and security of the American people as it needed to be," there ought to have been greater outrage and political backlash. Senator Daniel Inouye of Hawaii had known the darkness of war from World War II and Senator Max Cleland of Georgia, who had left two legs and an arm in Vietnam, both failed to speak in a public and personal manner about the president's insult.

As the president logged tens of thousands of miles on Air Force One, executing the Karl Rove midterm strategy, he appeared politically invincible. Using his popularity acquired through the War on Terrorism, Rove had the president concentrate on the threat posed by Hussein. Unflagging in his verbal attacks on Iraq, Bush expressed certitude, a confidence of cause, which drew people to him and his party's candidates. Americans like a president who can make decisions and believe in himself.

Karl Rove understood the political value of this key Bush characteristic.

"I've seen, even in this White House, I've seen people agonizing over decisions, but I've never seen him," Rove said.

The presidential advisor claimed Bush told him, during a private meeting in the Oval Office, that he has not regretted a single decision he has made since 9/11.

"So, I thought about it afterwards, because, you know, history is really littered with people who agonized over decisions, even great presidents sometimes found themselves agonizing over decisions, and I'm sure there will be some moments where there's a decision he'll agonize over, but you don't want a president who walks into the Oval Office every morning and says, 'Oh god, I've got to make decisions,' because that's what the job is all about."

The sense of being absolutely correct is a dangerous trait, especially when a president has a political advisor who edits the information used to arrive at decisions. In the case of Bush, it is made more treacherous by a president who dislikes data overload. During one particular staff meeting, Bush is reported to have told his advisors that they were "nuancing him to death."

"Checking a box decisively is a nice thing," said political scientist Bruce Buchanan. "Especially compared to wringing your hands endlessly, like Clinton did. But if it's a process where the deck is stacked in advance and you know what box is going to be checked, decisively wrong doesn't strike me as that much of an advantage over being confusedly right."

These kinds of convictions are political assets until contradictions arise, undermining their logic. The midterm campaign was an old-fashioned barnstorming tour to show off the president's strength and persuasiveness. In the Congress, he was on the verge of getting the Iraq resolution approved and the United Nations was slowly bending to his American will. The Bush bus seemed once more to be glory bound.

If only North Korea had not made the Iraqi crisis look silly and manufactured.

North Korea's leader Kim Jong-il acknowledged to the United States that his country had a maturing nuclear weapons program. And he told the president as Congress was debating the Iraq resolution. The timing was worse than even the hypocrisies the news made of the White House policy toward Iraq. How was North Korea less dangerous than Saddam? Kim had the long-range missiles to deliver nuclear warheads. Pyongyang had violated a 1994 weapons agreement by developing nuclear capabilities. According to the *Washington Post*, the president's own language may have prompted the violation. A source told the newspaper "the North Koreans decided to go ahead with the [nuclear] program after President Bush identified them as a member of the international axis of evil."

The strategy the White House used to deal with this troubling news appears to have come from the mind of Karl Rove. First intelligence reports on North Korea's nuclear assets reached the Bush administration during the summer, as efforts were being made to clarify support and causes for the war against Iraq. But the White House kept quiet. When Kim formally confirmed to Washington, through normal diplomatic channels, that he had nuclear strength, Congress was in the midst of debating the resolution demanding Saddam disarm or face the consequences.

But the White House kept the news from Congress for 12 days, until the debate on Iraq was closed.

Such a move is the political equivalent of holding up a sign reading, "Karl was here."

But the Democrats had no voice. No one expressed indignation with the White House's behavior, even though there was an abundance of questions worth asking. Democrats could hardly campaign against a war they had helped to declare. And no one has ever gotten elected by running against a tax cut, in spite of the fact that the Bush reductions mostly benefited corporations and the wealthy.

Democrats were cornered by Karl.

No politician emerged to discuss what the potential war against Iraq was really about. Nor was anyone speaking of the careful dismantling of environmental regulations or proposed reductions in education funding while military spending spiked into double digit percentage increases, the Bush failure to address his prescription drugs promise, a tide of red ink threatening the very government that holds the country together, unrepentant unemployment and record business failures, and Osama on the loose. The president was confident. The public believed. And the democrats cowered.

The campaign was brilliant.

The president swirled in and out of 15 states identified by Karl Rove as crucial to Republican gains in Congress. Bush was almost mythological, descending from the sky in the world's command center called Air Force One, possessed of a relentless level of approval from the people who were enduring hard times caused, in part, by his leadership. In the closing days, it was obvious voters were deciding to give the president what he wanted: congressional control for republicans and a mandate to clear out Saddam.

The final hours of the election show scattered signs of Karl Rove and his operatives. In the Florida governor's race and the Texas senate campaign, automated calls were being made against the Democrats. Texas U.S. Senate candidate Ron Kirk and Florida gubernatorial hopeful Bill McBride were the targets of phone messages from purportedly gay rights groups. The callers told voters Kirk and McBride were supporters of gay marriage. It is no coincidence the tactic was used in Texas and Florida, two of the most important electoral regions of the country.

"It is almost eerie, what Rove has done," one Washington consultant said. "He dismantled the Democrats so effectively they just stood there, dumbstruck. He silenced their opposition with intimidation, picked apart institutions, just basically destroyed dissent, and he wrapped all of this in patriotic hues. I'm telling you, it's scarily phenomenal."

The Republicans won the battle by obscuring the domestic issues with Iraq and terrorism, just as Karl Rove had advised almost a year earlier. But Rove knew the truth about the Bush policy toward Iraq. He simply ignored it. Just as the Democrats stood back, afraid to speak about what was unfolding.

There was one person who articulated the facts. Of course, Karl Rove had him cornered, too. No one was listening to Iraqi foreign minister Tareq Aziz because he worked for Saddam Hussein. But in one, short sentence, he captured the issues no American politician had the courage to confront.

"This," he said, "is all about oil and Israel."

At the dawn of the New American Empire, if it comes, U.S. troops, a swiftly moving mechanized infantry, will cross the border from Turkey into Iraq. To the south, other battalions will invade from Kuwait. They will approach Baghdad, roughly, along the valley and course of the Tigris River. Invasion will happen under cover of darkness after weeks of air bombardment. Most of Iraq will be without electricity or any electronic communications. Resistance by Iraqis will inevitably turn to slaughter. A nation starved and bled by its own leader and international sanctions will have little will to fight against American gun ships and bombs that appear to think before they kill. But the Iraqis will claim many casualties before they fall.

Nothing Saddam can say is likely to abate the White House's determination to take control of Iraq. The evidence presented to UN arms inspectors, or independently gathered by them, will probably not measure up to an impossible standard of proof set by the Bush administration. As Baghdad comes under U.S. military rule, talks will begin with oil field service companies like Vice President Dick Cheney's former employer Halliburton. Halliburton, and the other multinational in the same business, Schlumberger, can be expected to win lucrative contracts to rebuild Iraq's energy infrastructure. American troops will be standing atop what may be the world's' largest oil reserves at 200 billion barrels. As it begins to flow, more than a regime will have been changed.

To the east, Israel will have new protection with its staunchest ally posting guard in the midst of the Arab world. The United States, according to Iraqi opposition leaders in London, would get first considerations in regards to the oil supply. Saudi Arabia's uneasy relationship with the United States will be almost co-opted. Americans are unlikely to be as compelled to keep the Saudis happy to get access to their fossil fuels. We would have our own ocean of crude, secured by our troops and our resources. The Saudi royal family will become more cautious about sending back channel funds to terrorists. They might lose more than just an oil market in the United States. America may cast its covetous eyes toward the sweet, light crude of their part of Persia as a second step to expand the empire.

But there may never again be peace.

"It's a war without end," one analyst said. "I don't think this thing will ever be resolved. We'll create about 10 generations of new terrorists in the Arab world. We have to go in and occupy Baghdad and that is a true disaster. There will be soldiers coming back in body bags and that will destroy his presidency. You go into Iraq and you will have tens of thousands of casualties. And who in the hell wants their kid to die for a tank of cheap gasoline?"

There will be many perils as America deploys its Bush doctrine of preemption. New bases in foreign lands will be subject to attack. Soldiers and diplomats exercising "constabulatory duties" under the new policy will be easy targets. Other nations may imitate the Bush doctrine. Chinese troops might cross the gulf to end the political debate over the future of Taiwan. What will President Bush be able to say? Political complications will be many and manifest.

But there will be someone who has looked ahead. He will have analyzed the dynamics and found a medicine to heal the crisis. An advantage might even be gained from his insight and obsession. He will be there trying to figure out how to make it all work politically. Just like he always has.

The president's future is controlled by a reliable and facile mind. Karl Rove will always be the man with the plan.

17

Yonder Goes Justice

In politics, nothing ever happens by accident. If it happened,
you can bet it was planned that way.

Franklin Delano Roosevelt

West of Del Rio, Texas, U.S. Highway 90 rises imperceptibly toward the continental divide, about 500 miles distant in southern New Mexico. At the Pecos, after pulling over to stretch, Pete McRae stood on a ledge and looked down into a deep canyon where the historic river emptied into the great reservoir of Lake Amistad. Goats, which the distance made appear as small household pets, were grazing far below on a green strip of land along the river's edge. McRae seemed to have little on his mind outside of the grandeur of the Texas west. But he was thinking. He is always thinking.

Pete McRae lifted his eyes across the gorge to where the sky and land are endlessly seamed. He has the horizon eyes of someone who has lived too long on the high plains, a gift from his family, which has been farming the vast open spaces near Amarillo since the 1930s. They do not reveal the resolve that has sustained him through years of being a casualty of someone else's political ambitions. Every day of the rest of his life, Pete McRae will, in some manner, be trying to make up for time and opportunity he believes was taken from him by Karl Rove.

"I went to prison mostly because of Karl Rove and this mysterious connection he had to an FBI agent. I don't know if that relationship existed before the bugging incident or if it started afterward, but that was what caused me, and everyone else in the Agriculture Department, all of our problems."

The day he left for prison, August 19, 1996, has lingered in McRae's consciousness for more than just the obvious reasons. It was also the day Bob Boyd died. Boyd was the agriculture department consultant whose fund-raising tactics had prompted a federal investigation. A judge had ruled Boyd and another consultant did not have to stand trial because of poor health. McRae, however, along with Deputy Agriculture Commissioner Mike Moeller and agriculture department manager Bill Quicksall, were all tried and convicted of improperly using federal funds.

And McRae is still being punished.

"I am a convicted felon and I'll never be able to hold a job in government or really a visible political consulting role because folks running for office really can't employ me. So, something that I am particularly good at, I've lost the ability to do that. And you know, part of it is my doing. You know, we did make mistakes. But once again, I don't think they were the kind of mistakes that should have sent three guys to prison."

McRae will always retain a detailed memory of his trip to the Bastrop, Texas, federal correctional minimum-security prison. He can still feel the weight of the Texas heat. The leaves on the cottonwoods along the Colorado River were distinct and graphic in a manner he had never before noticed. To the east, broken clouds were thinning against the August sun. A common summer morning had turned profound. Pete McRae, with his steely idealism and country boy flattop haircut, had become a victim of politics.

The experience has left him clinging, almost desperately, to his American optimism.

"I realize there are people who can, in some ways, manipulate the process. Generally, the process works the way it's supposed to, both the judicial and the political process, but I've been around long enough to know that there are people who can manipulate those processes, if they use enough deceit, and sometimes there are folks who can get hurt by that."

Crossing the bridge over the Pecos and heading into the Chihuahuan Desert, McRae was pursuing work he had begun while waiting out his appeals and final sentencing. He had taken on a project to help rehabilitate historic forts in West Texas. The forts, McRae later discovered, held deep symbolic value for African Americans because the facilities had once housed the Buffalo Soldiers. Respectfully named by Native Americans, who said the Black soldiers' hair felt like a buffalo's fur, the Buffalo Soldiers were given much of the responsibility for civilizing the Texas West and keeping stage and rail routes safe from raiders.

McRae drew up a plan to use the forts and their histories to inspire and educate at-risk youth from Texas cities. The state government funded the idea during George W. Bush's first legislative session as governor in 1995. An estimated 1000 students have gone through the Buffalo Soldier program and funding for the curriculum is renewed each legislative session almost without political resistance. McRae's trip to West Texas was to explore the possibility of developing a nonprofit travel company to provide family tours of the Buffalo Solder forts.

Fort Davis was the most strategically located of the Buffalo Soldier outposts. Situated near the Great Comanche War Trail, the two ancient Apache trails, and the El Paso-San Antonio Road, soldiers from Fort Davis were easily dispatched to provide protection for settlers and travelers in the region. The fort was built in a box canyon against high basaltic rock cliffs. Wild roses, sustained by the cool waters of Limpia Springs, proliferated in the little valley. The springs fed a creek that had carved a naturally protective setting at the base of the Davis Mountains.

McRae walked around the fort with a comfortable familiarity, pointing out the barracks that had bivouacked the Buffalo Soldiers, the infirmary where many of them lay ill and died on the frontier. As he sat on the wooden walk, speakers played the sound of a bugler calling for "boots and saddles," the musical notes the Buffalo Soldiers would have heard more than a century earlier, which ordered cavalrymen to put on their riding boots and saddle their horses. After being drawn to Fort Davis, McRae discovered it had a history that was about much more than just the Buffalo Soldiers. The fate of one man in that remote outpost has provided a context for McRae's personal travails.

Fort Davis may be American history's most glaring example of how politics and perception can be used to ruin an honest man.

In 1880, a young second lieutenant was transferred to Fort Davis and given the duties of Acting Assistant Quartermaster and Acting Commissary of Subsistence. Henry O. Flipper, who had become the first Black to graduate from the United States Military Academy at West Point, was also the first Black officer commissioned in the Regular Army. Lieutenant Flipper's troop of Buffalo Soldier cavalrymen had been serving out of Fort Concho, Texas, under orders to pursue and capture a notorious Apache chief, Victorio, whose warriors had been raiding on both sides of the Rio Grande.

Flipper's Troop A was part of the 10th U.S. Cavalry, one of two Black regiments established after the Civil War. Born a slave in Thomasville, Georgia, on March 21, 1856, Lieutenant Flipper discovered books and education and learned to read in the wood shop of another slave. After attending schools operated by the American Missionary Association, the future officer in the U.S. military entered Atlanta University the year it was founded, 1869. Through a series of letters he wrote to his Georgia congressman, Flipper's nomination to West Point was sent to the Secretary of War. After passing the rigorous entry examinations, he entered the academy on July 1,

1873. At West Point, Flipper excelled in Spanish, French, engineering, and law.

But his education did not help him avoid racism and political persecution.

A new commander took over Fort Davis in the spring of 1881. Colonel William R. Shafter was a stern man with a reputation for dealing severely with his subordinates. After taking control of the post, Shafter chose to relieve Lieutenant Flipper of his quartermaster duties. Unfortunately, the change was announced just as Flipper discovered commissary funds missing from his trunk. Flipper, who was noticeably intimidated by Shafter, tried to conceal the loss of the money, hoping it could be found before a new quartermaster was named. To secure more time to search for the missing cash, Flipper resorted to lying to his commanding officer.

In the Fort Davis chapel, Flipper was court-martialed for embezzlement and conduct unbecoming an officer and a gentleman. Before the trial, other White soldiers and local residents had warned the lieutenant that Colonel Shafter was leading a conspiracy to drive the Army's only Black officer out of the service. Flipper was acquitted of the embezzlement charges, but his lying resulted in a conviction on the allegation of conduct unbecoming an officer. President Chester Arthur signed an order upholding the dishonorable discharge of U.S. Army Second Lieutenant Henry Ossian Flipper.

Though he spent the rest of his life trying to win reinstatement to the Army, Henry Flipper continued his record of achievement outside of the military. Not surprisingly, to those who knew his character, much of his time was in service to his country. For eight years, Flipper worked for the Department of Justice as a special agent in the court of Private Land Claims, translating Spanish documents into English. In El Paso, he acted as a translator for a U.S. Senate subcommittee on foreign relations and eventually became a special assistant to the Secretary of the Interior, who used Flipper's skills and education on the Alaskan Engineering Commission.

Always maintaining his innocence, Lieutenant Flipper made eight different attempts to have his name cleared and his military record reinstated. His rank and status could not be restored without an act of Congress. The first bill to correct the wrongs done to Henry Flipper died in a congressional committee in 1898. None of them ever gained enough interest or support to reach a floor debate. But Flipper did not stop trying until 1924. Second Lieutenant Flipper died in 1940, at age 84, and went to his grave stripped of his military honors. It was not until February 1999, that he was pardoned, 59 years after his death.

"That guy was a fighter."

Pete McRae was looking at a historical display of Lieutenant Flipper in the Fort Davis Museum. He would never compare himself to the determined officer of the Buffalo Soldiers. And he will be embarrassed to learn anyone has. But there are some inescapable similarities between their cases. Both are victims of politics and abused power.

The struggle of the U.S. military's first Black officer was not just about racism and politics. Flipper, and the Buffalo Soldiers were part of the early beginnings to the Civil Rights movement and the rise of a Black middle class in America. Military service was the first institution to provide African Americans with opportunities to be judged for their character and performance. That door was opened by the persistence of Lieutenant Flipper.

But Flipper represents something else, too.

For Pete McRae, Henry Flipper's treatment is proof that the wrong person with the right amount of political power can harm innocent people.

That's why he sees danger in Karl Rove's White House role.

"I don't think he should be there. I think that the White House is not a place for a political consultant. I don't argue that he could be doing the exact same thing outside the White House and visiting the Oval Office daily, but actually having the guy with his ability to manipulate those levers of power, it's just wrong to have a guy with those political motivations in the White House. I just think, generally, it's a bad precedent, a bad situation, to have your political advisor on the government payroll. The Pentagon's gotta listen to you. The Justice Department's gotta listen to you. And that's bad. And I don't think Karl's motivations are pure. Ever."

McRae knows that Karl Rove probably doesn't even remember who he is. Rove's disconnect from what happened at the Texas Department of Agriculture is as complete as McRae's conviction that Rove ran the political assault that sent him to prison. McRae believes Rove is oblivious to the consequences of his political skills, nor does he care. And that, too, is annoying, considering all that McRae has lost. McRae, however, refuses to whimper and play the part of a victim.

There is something he wants, something he is willing to fight for. Second Lieutenant Henry O. Flipper finally got it. And Pete McRae, and his friend Mike Moeller, want it, too.

O n Mike Moeller's ranch near Fort McKavett, Texas, a two-track wagon road, about 150 years old, still provides the best path through the live oak and cedar. In a few locations, the limestone has been graded. But it is still a rough road and even the tires and suspension system of a twenty-first-century four-wheel drive pickup failed to smooth the passage. Moeller wondered aloud what the trip must have been like in the nineteenth century, on a wagon with steel wheels and wooden spokes.

His task on this day was to check on a new solar powered pump. A well was drilled on a portion of his acreage where cattle have no access to water. Rather than install another windmill to lift the water from underground, Moeller has chosen to try a more technological approach.

His family has farming and ranching interests spread across central and south Texas. Moeller's time is spent managing their operations, not exactly what he thought he would be doing with his life.

"No, this is not what I had in mind 15 years ago."

Mike Moeller earned his masters degree at the prestigious LBJ School of Public Affairs at the University of Texas in Austin. A combined knowledge of government and agriculture made it almost inevitable he would find his way to the state agency that oversees farm and ranch production in Texas. When he was hired by the Agriculture Commissioner to the agency's number two position, Moeller found he liked the work and was excited by the prospects of running for election to succeed his boss.

Until he encountered Karl Rove.

"I was a public servant. And I thought I was a public servant in the best sense of the word. That's really what I wanted to do with my life. The last of the bleeding hearts. I really wanted to make a difference. I wanted to help folks. So, that's gone. For better or worse, that's gone. And there's no way I'll ever be back in that arena again."

Moeller was working for Jim Hightower, who was the opponent of a Karl Rove client. Moeller is certain Rove worked with an FBI agent to conduct a ruinous political and legal barrage on him and others at the Texas Department of Agriculture.

"A lot of it is more obvious in hindsight. But you know, we had people inside the agency, who were working for us, who told us they were being approached and told to go see Karl Rove if they thought they had damaging information on the commissioner or anyone at the agency."

A couple of deer, who had been sleeping beneath a live oak tree, scrambled to their feet and ran as Moeller's pickup approached the new water well. A dark solar panel, leaning in the direction of the southwest sun, was the only indication man had ever passed this way before.

"How about that? Look at that," Moeller said. "I'm not sure but this may be the functional end of the windmill. But I guess we'll have to keep them just to look like a ranch."

Getting out of his truck, Moeller walked over to the wellhead, an eight-inch diameter pipe rising about a foot above the limestone and caliche dust. He and a visitor lifted an aluminum trough out of the bed of the truck and sat it near the well. Moeller attached a plastic hose to the valve, hooked it over the side of the trough, and then flipped the breaker on the solar panel to operate the pump. He had to kneel down in the white dust and place his ear next to the pipe to hear the electric pump lifting the water from the Edwards Aquifer, 360 feet below.

"Well, it sounds like it's working. I guess all we can do is wait and see if water comes out of the pipe."

Mike Moeller's life has not been diminished by his political conflict with Karl Rove. He has simply had a forced change of course. Moeller has become a successful agribusiness man instead of an elected state official running an agency that regulates Texas farms and ranches. A choice was taken away from him by Rove's political machinations. And he was sent to a federal prison camp. But Moeller has never let his political prosecution define his existence.

"In terms of my personal attitude and so forth, life goes on. And you find a way to survive and get on with your life. In my case, it's been dedicating myself to my family and to my family's business and helping folks closer to me. I lost a career and it had been a good career up to that point and it would have continued to be a good career."

Instead, Mike Moeller, like Pete McRae, went to prison on a federal conviction that they had used government money to pay a consultant to raise campaign funds. Moeller has long argued that he did not know that consultant Bob Boyd was shaking down business people in agriculture to make donations to Democrats like former commissioner Jim Hightower. And when he found out, Moeller said, he put an end to it. That was not, however, good enough for a federal court jury.

"Did you ever feel like you did anything criminal?"

"No. I read that indictment. And I never found anything in there that I knowingly and willingly did. To find you guilty, they have to say you knowingly and willingly broke this law. And in our case, it was conspiracy and that just didn't happen. Nobody ever sat down and said, 'We're gonna send these two old guys out and drag the sack for Hightower.' That just never happened.

"You know what? Let me be more specific. At the end of 1989 and the beginning of 1990, when they were raising money for Hightower, nobody knew. Period."

Waiting for the water to rise into the cattle trough, Moeller found himself contemplating matters he had long ago put behind him. This was a strange place, with the black-eyed susans blooming along the fence line and a rare fall show of bluebonnets on the range, for him to be thinking again of Karl Rove, and what he had done to Moeller's plans. He still blamed Rove for the viciousness with which he and the agriculture department workers were pursued. But he also thinks he should have been more vigilant.

"I don't think I knowingly and willfully committed a crime, which is what I was convicted of. But I was negligent. I don't think there's any question I didn't pay attention. And if I had it to do over again, I would have paid attention. And I would have snuffed it out before it started."

Dressed in a golf pullover, shorts, and athletic shoes, Moeller hardly appeared as a Texas rancher. And he also wanted to make certain no one viewed him as embittered and ruined, a victim unable to recover.

"That's a phase you go through. There definitely was a time in my life that I felt like I'd been robbed and cheated."

He did lose 19 months to a federal prison camp in Three Rivers, Texas. The experience, Moeller claimed, was absurd. Three Rivers was operated on an honor system. Inmates were often allowed to come and go from the camp on their own to outside jobs in the community. And there were constantly convicts, who simply walked away, never to return. Moeller walked a quarter mile every day to teach classes at a local community college near the prison grounds.

"It certainly did not seem like a good use of taxpayer money. We had a gym, an all-weather track, basketball courts, and an unbelievable weight room, croquet courts, even. I took tennis lessons while I was there. You know, they spent 30 to 40 thousand dollars a year incarcerating people. We could have been back in our communities, doing something valuable, a little more worthwhile."

Water splashed in the cattle trough. A steady stream was flowing out of the black plastic pipe. The silent solar pump had performed.

"That's a hell of a deal, ain't it?" Moeller asked. "That is just way cool."

While the trough filled, Moeller drove around the ranch and looked over his land. Slowly, he is turning over operations to his son. The grasslands are leased to another rancher and this location serves mostly as a retreat, a place to get away and hunt deer and turkey. If he wanted, Moeller could sit outside the door of the cabin and take his limit of wildlife. But the ranch has scattered deer blinds, where hunters wait for animals to pass into view.

He contemplated where he might be, if Karl Rove had not gotten involved in Texas politics. Moeller undoubtedly would still be involved in agriculture. But he might not be spending time driving his fence lines along the edge of the Edwards Plateau, where the live oaks and cedar breaks open up to the Chihuahuan Desert, just west of his ranch.

As removed as he is from politics, Moeller has not stopped worrying about how Karl Rove may one day use his accumulated influence and control.

"Given where he is, ya have to think he will use his power. I'm a lot more concerned now that Karen [Hughes] is gone, that he'll fill that void. I can't imagine any good coming from anything Karl touches. He fills the void left by Karen. Heaven knows what we are in for.

"Besides, how would you know if he abused his power? I think he is a very mean-spirited man, who has his own interests at heart. The country's well-being is about as far from his consciousness as it could be."

When the truck returned to the site of the new well, less than six inches of water filled the bottom of the trough. The solar pump worked, but not quickly. Moeller planned to call the rancher leasing his land and have him turn off the pump the next day.

"I'm just happy to have this well," he said. "You should have seen it. The driller used a water witch to find this spot. He walked around with that dowsing rod for a long time and then told him to drill here. It's deeper than the other wells we have. But we've got water."

Mike Moeller has not spent the years since the investigation bitterly contemplating Karl Rove. He spoke of the president's counselor only when pressed, and not with any obvious pleasure. But there was something that grated on him about the knowledge that Rove has never considered the consequences of his own behavior, the way he ran the agriculture commissioner's race, the people he harmed with what Moeller will always see as political persecution.

"I guess I have to say it doesn't surprise me that he wouldn't think about any of us, given the type of person we're talking about. He's not gonna accept responsibility for the bad things he did, at least not any time soon. It's never been a shock or surprise to me that he has that attitude."

While his passenger was locking the last of the three ranch gates behind the pickup, Moeller climbed out from behind the wheel and tossed a large board into the bed of his truck.

"Might find some use for that around the home place," he explained.

He turned left, down the wide dirt road, in the direction of Fort McKavett. Graders have cut through the caliche gravel and limestone and made a road that follows the course of the old Butterfield Stage route. A century and a half ago, travelers from San Antonio rode a commercial stage, pulled by horses, across this same range, bound for the desert and the Franklin Mountains of El Paso. The trip took them weeks. On either side of the fences lining the roadbed, there are undoubtedly bones of angry Comanches and naïve Anglo-European settlers, who had no idea the world could not change without shedding their blood across this plateau.

In minutes, Moeller's truck covered a distance that would have required a day's worth of hard riding by nineteenth-century travelers. He knows the history of this place, and feels very close to it. As a graveyard appeared on the right, Moeller spoke of a man who had brought his family to Fort McKavett after the Civil War. There was amazement in his voice as he tried to articulate how alone it must have been out here.

He was quiet for a few minutes and then Karl Rove came back into his consciousness again. Mike Moeller sounded like he was concluding a conversation he had just conducted with himself, and he only gave voice to the final thought.

"I think he played the game a lot better than us. Causing a person to lose an election and go to prison are two very different deals. He just doesn't care."

Behind the pickup, the white dust rose from the road and curled into a large plume, which reached over the tailgate and chased it easterly. But Moeller didn't see it. Mike Moeller's eyes, as they always are, were fixed on the road ahead.

Karl Rove materialized. The two reporters waiting to meet with him were going over a list of questions when he appeared in the lobby of Austin's Four Seasons hotel. The president's advisor smiled and led the way to a table in the corner of the café at a lower level. It was a Saturday morning and the luxury hotel's elegant restaurant was relatively empty. Beyond the outdoor terrace behind Rove's table, two swans moved slowly along the flat water of Austin's Town Lake.

Rove was, as he always is, very busy. He had come to Austin after a series of meetings at the Bush ranch in Crawford. The president's problems were obvious to the electorate and his advisors. The American economy was stubbornly refusing to get better and move again and Osama bin Laden was still at large, his terrorist network hindered, but not dead. The Bush administration had turned attention away from these failures and on to the matter of Iraq and Saddam Hussein. The strategic redirect of policy interests was designed to help Republicans in midterm elections who might take a hit if there was too much talk of the economy.

There was, of course, another purpose. A president always gets the blame or credit for the health of the economy on his watch. Positive campaign predictions of George W. Bush had not been proved by economic developments. His tax cut and the war on terrorism had created a federal deficit that loomed over the nation with more potency to harm than any Iraqi weapon of mass destruction. Mr. Bush had done little about controlling the costs of prescription drugs for seniors and low-income groups, one of his key campaign promises.

Things improved when Karl Rove started repeating two words that absolved the president of domestic challenges: Regime change.

Rove has conceded that he is involved in all of the president's policy development and political efforts. But he has ceaselessly denied that his closeness to the president means he has excessive influence on what happens in the United States and the rest of the world. He is, Rove insisted, doing nothing more than a job that has already been defined by tradition.

"If you look back, there are a number of instances, even in modern times, where somebody has done the role of political advisor and then came in and played a policy role. I'm nowhere near the stature or the level of the example, but remember we had Gerald Ford's campaign manager in 1976 and the George H. W. Bush campaign manager of 1980 becomes the White House chief of staff in 1981, James A. Baker, III."

Over breakfast, Rove tried to down play his impact on the Bush administration and the president's decision-making process. But it was not an easy argument to make, even for a champion debater. He has known Bush so well for so long, and the relationship is so critical to the political character of the president, that there is no way to conceive of anything of consequence happening under President Bush without intimate involvement on the part of Rove. The political advisor to the president, the president's friend, his confidante, dinner partner, traveling companion, a man whose destiny is tightly wrapped in Bush packaging, described himself as nothing more than one of many advisors President Bush listens to before taking action.

Rove offered a description of the president that seemed to confirm suspicions Bush was not capable of carrying the office with his own abilities. He needs things. And Karl Rove is his great provider.

"He doesn't make decisions alone. That is to say, you know, you get a sense of some people. They are self-contained. They are totally self-contained so they need nothing in order to arrive at a decision. He respects, he honors the process that gives information."

In those words, Rove inadvertently portrayed Bush as a man smart enough to know that he is not smart enough. But he is well equipped for making decisions, and no one knows this better than his long-time associate Karl Rove. Who, then, is better able to influence Bush's decision making than someone like Rove, who has been a part of it for almost 30 years? By now, Rove has an elaborate understanding of how the president thinks, when is the best time to provide him information, and how he arrives at his conclusions. Combine that closeness with Rove's control over the flow of information going to President Bush and the case is overwhelmingly strong that Karl Rove also has his hand on the wheel.

Which may be why Rove has generally emphasized the president's ability to choose rather than the process that delivers Bush information.

Because Rove is in control of most of that information and its interpretation.

The boundaries of Karl Rove's world are easy to see. And he lives and works on the side of the line where the Republicans are. Anything that happens across that border, in Democrat territory, is of no interest to him, except in terms of how he must develop his plans and strategies. There is nothing else over there for him. No policy ideas. No friends. Just people who must be viewed as enemies for the choices they have made. There's them. There's us. Karl keeps it simple. And so do his candidates.

Not many years after Rove had moved to Austin, his neighbor approached him about introducing Rove to a friend. This person had gotten a job at an oil and gas firm with the assistance of his new friend. He told Rove the man he wanted him to meet was very much like Rove because he was active in politics. When Rove asked his neighbor the party affiliation of his friend, he was told the man was a Democrat. For that reason, Rove said he did not want to meet the individual. The man that Rove's neighbor was talking about turned out to be Pete McRae, who, 10 years later, ended up in prison because he was on the losing side of a fight against a Rove client.

That is still how Karl Rove conducts his politics.

"I guess one of the things of politics is you do things that benefit your friends. And when given a choice between some amount of friends and a larger group of friends, you go with the larger group of friends. The problem is that treats everything as an economic calculus and you have no moral commitment."

Of course, even within the GOP, Rove chooses the president's friends, and his own, very carefully.

A few weeks after the relaxed conversation at Austin's Four Seasons, Rove was on a campaign trip to California with President Bush. This was a tricky one, a series of events and appearances that required Rove to use both his strategic and interpretative talents. Otherwise, the president risked appearing overtly hypocritical and involved in lost political causes.

The campaign tour was designed to help California Republican gubernatorial candidate Bill Simon. An investments manager, Simon was not the first choice of the Republican National Committee. Rove and the rest of party leadership had backed moderate Richard Riordan in the primary. But he lost. And President Bush very quickly traveled to California and raised $5 million for Simon. Unfortunately, even for meticulous planners like Rove, bad things can happen to excellent operatives.

Bill Simon's investment company was hit with a $78 million civil judgment for fraud, after he had won the primary.

And suddenly Karl Rove was confronted with one of those co-nundrums he resolves in order to earn his great fees and his reputa-tion. For a while, Rove was mulling over the idea of keeping the president away from Simon and California. This made obvious sense. Every newspaper reader and TV news viewer in the nation was agitated over corporate fraud scandals, CEOs who had made millions while destroying retirement accounts of their companies' employees. Putting President Bush in front of California cameras with Bill Simon at his side would dilute the White House's message that it intended to crack down on CEOs who acted illegally. There was no way the president could sell corporate accountability and show up on California and network newscasts enthusiastically back-ing a man whose company a trial court had said defrauded investors in a manner that led to a $78 million ruling.

But California was too important to be ignored. One out of eight Americans lives there and the Republican party has many big dollar donors who call the state home. George W. Bush will need their cash to help pay for his political future. Regardless of Bill Simon's legal challenges, Rove knew the president had little choice but to travel to California. And so, when cornered, aboard Air Force One, he began to explain the tactic.

"It's a big state, where the political situation is very fluid and, you know, a lot of things happen first in California, politically and culturally. And it's not a state that you can and should ignore."

Ultimately, Rove, as he generally does, figured out a method for dancing dryly through the storm. In the setting of private fund-raisers, Rove had his client speak fondly of Bill Simon. This was to keep happy the Republicans with willing wallets. But at the public rallies, with thousands of Bush believers cheering for the president, he did not mention Simon's name, nor was Simon anywhere to be seen. Rove agreed to a breakfast, lunch, and reception to help Simon's efforts. These were private; doors closed to the media kinds of affairs. Limited television coverage was allowed late in the day, timed to keep Bush-Simon shots and sound bites off of the network news, which was on a deadline three hours ahead of the west coast.

When the president's plane landed at Stockton, Simon was in a row of local dignitaries lined up to greet Bush as he stepped down from the aircraft. Simon got the same, quick handshake as the others, undoubtedly because Rove knew there were numerous cameras taping the president's arrival. When he spoke before the subsequent rally, Bush praised local congressional candidates by name and delivered his standard stump speech decrying corporate fraud. He did not mention Bill Simon nor was Simon present at any of the president's public events.

The strategy changed among the wealthy supporters who attended the private luncheon. The president was warm and complimentary about Simon's achievements.

"I'm so proud to be here and embrace his candidacy," Bush said.

There was, however, no embrace until the president was away from the public stage and the doors to the luncheon were closed.

Although Simon was not named in the judgment against the investment firm that he controls with his brother, Rove was cautious about allowing the president to become too closely associated with the GOP's gubernatorial choice. Rove told the White House press corps that Simon was welcome to attend the public rallies, "if his schedule permitted." This remark suggested, implausibly, the Republican gubernatorial hopeful might have something more important to do than hang out on stage with a popular president and be photographed. Obviously, nothing could have been more important to Bill Simon's campaign. But he was not visible at the big public rallies with Bush because Rove had told Simon to stay away.

"He's welcome to attend, and would be encouraged to attend, if it doesn't conflict with his schedule," Rove said. "But I really don't know whether he'll be there or not."

Actually, Rove did know.

There had been almost daily communication between the White House and the Simon campaign prior to the California trip, according to the Simon campaign. Karl Rove leaves nothing to chance. Undoubtedly, he knew exactly where Bill Simon would be when the president was on stage, in front of adoring crowds. And Simon was not going to be near the president and the television cameras. Rove did not know if the fraud conviction would be overturned and Simon's association with Bush conflicted with the White House theme of corporate accountability.

The Bush team expected that the media, making the campaign tour with the president, would notice differences between the California events and other stops. Aboard Air Force One, traveling to California, the decision was made to offer reporters a rare session with the president's political advisor. The questions were all about Bill Simon and the extent of the president's connection to his campaign, as Rove had anticipated.

"At previous stops, where we've been raising money for candidates, you've had separate film crews there, taping footage for ads. Will Simon have the same arrangement? Has Bush agreed to let . . ."

"I'm not aware that they have a film crew," Rove answered. "They may have a film crew. But my sense is, talking to the Simon campaign people that they, their feeling is that they've got a limited amount of time and, while they might have a picture or something of the president, their focus is on Simon and Simon's message, and Davis and Davis' record."

More accurately, Karl Rove knew the shooting schedule of every film crew in California and the Simon campaign had been informed there were to be no political commercials filmed during the president's visit, especially ads that showed Bush and Simon together. Rove had zero believability when he suggested he did not know if Simon had a film crew on the scene. The detail is exactly the kind of information Rove does not let escape him. Besides, he had no intention of letting there be such a political ad and he had, undoubtedly, already made that known to the Simon campaign.

"Does the president have any objection to Simon using the president in Simon's ad campaigns?" Rove was asked.

"Well, we'd have to see what, first of all, I think it's hypothetical. I don't think they have any interest in the president being the focal point of an ad. So, I don't think . . .

"But, does the president have any objection to being in an ad?"

"We'd have to see what they propose, if it would be appropriate. But you know, we want to support the Republican ticket across the country. This is a big state, an important race, a race that a couple of years ago people would have thought would not have been a race, and yet it is."

Rove's answer to that question contradicts what he said about a possible film crew awaiting the president when he got to California. He either mischaracterized the truth or he simply lied for political expediency. By saying, "We'd have to see what they propose," Rove revealed that either nothing had been brought up about a commercial with the president, or, if it had been, was already slapped down. The answer turned his previous one—"I'm not aware"—into a completely misleading statement.

Of course, he knew. He had just said he would want to see what Simon's people might propose, which meant, clearly, nothing had been proposed, so there was no film crew. And there was no film crew because Rove had ordered it that way. The Simon campaign, told to keep clear of the public events, knew better than to ask for a TV commercial with the president.

As adroitly as he always had on other controversial issues, Rove turned the questions away from Simon and toward the general politics of California. This trip, he argued, wasn't so much about Bill Simon as it was rebuilding the Republican grass roots of the state, energizing the faithful GOP voters with the president's appearance.

"This is a state that has a tendency to be very apolitical and to swing widely from certain election cycles to other election cycles. So, it's a state that, if you ignore, you get what you play for: nothing. But if you play in the state, all kinds of things are possible."

Rove concluded his political discourse on California politics with a reference to progressive electoral reforms instituted in the early twentieth century. He explained the state's lack of partisan offices for candidates to pursue, how there is a small number of state senators compared to California congressmen, the fact that most city and county officeholders do not get to run under party affiliations, and why this nonpartisan commitment in local politics means the appearance of a president is of more importance for California Republican grassroots. After concluding, Rove returned to his small private office aboard Air Force One.

Karl Rove had other things to do

The country was worried about the economy and the president was pushing war with Iraq. North Korea's admission to having nuclear weapons turned the president's war policy on Iraq into blatant hypocrisy. Polls in the Florida governor's race involving the president's brother were beginning to trouble Rove and a few senatorial campaigns were not playing out precisely as he had anticipated. Opinion leaders were starting to complain loudly about a lack of progress in the war on terrorism. These matters were all of grave political consequence for Rove's client, President George W. Bush.

But Rove could handle them. He intended to get the situation under control.

He always did.

In these settings, President Bill Clinton was always at his best. Other speakers might have approximated his language. But his presentation was without equal. As Clinton walked into the Roosevelt Room of the White House, everyone in attendance knew, emotionally, what was about to transpire. The president, almost certainly, was going to take them to the edge of tears, fill them with regret and American pride, then conclude with suggestions of hope and redemption by righting a great wrong.

More than 117 years after Second Lieutenant Henry Ossian Flipper was dishonorably discharged, President William Jefferson Clinton intended to deliver a full pardon to the first African American graduate of West Point. In the wan light of a February afternoon in 1999, Clinton stood before descendants of Flipper, selected members of Congress, African American leaders, and aged Clarence Davenport, the sixth African American to graduate from the U.S. Military Academy.

The event, small and private by White House standards, attracted almost no media attention. But this was an American story, rich with the kind of poignancy modern journalism usually rushes to convey. And Clinton knew it. He understood what a privilege he had in bestowing the pardon on Flipper. The president also was aware of the political value of his executive decision. He was always his finest when there was a convergence of issues of social justice and political advantage.

"I want to welcome you all to an event that is 117 years overdue," he said.

"We must be candid and say that the special quality of American freedom is not always extended to all Americans. A word like 'freedom,' to be more than a slogan, requires us to acknowledge that our 'more perfect union' was created by imperfect human beings . . ."

Clinton described Flipper as an "extraordinary American" who chose to serve his country, in spite of being born into slavery in a land of freedom. The president detailed the U.S. military's political prosecution of Flipper at Fort Davis, Texas, and then he listed the lieutenant's numerous accomplishments, mostly in service to the U.S. government, after he had been dishonorably discharged. Flipper did not quit. His hope was a hard thing to kill.

"The army exonerated him in 1976, changed his discharge to honorable and reburied him with full honors. But one thing remained to be done, and now it will be. With great pleasure and humility, I now offer a full pardon to Lt. Henry Ossian Flipper of the

United States Army. This good man has now completely recovered his good name."

"Lieutenant Flipper's family teaches us," the president added, "that we must never give up the fight to make our country live up to its highest ideals."

As Flipper's family members dabbed tears from their faces, the president moved through the small gathering, congratulating and consoling with his special skills of empathy. Pardon had been the family's final challenge. After the Army had cleared Flipper of all charges, a bust of his likeness was unveiled at West Point. In the lieutenant's honor, the military academy also annually presents an award named after Flipper for the graduate who best exemplifies "the highest qualities of leadership, self-discipline, and perseverance in the face of unusual difficulties while a cadet."

Pete McRae certainly did not speak of any of this during his Sunday afternoon visit to Fort Davis. Even though he has great appreciation for the Buffalo Soldiers and their history at Fort Davis, McRae does not draw the obvious parallels between his own problems and those confronted by Henry Flipper. The lieutenant was mentioned only in passing, and admirably, almost as a student might talk reverentially of a favored teacher. But McRae had more in common with the proud soldier than he would have ever acknowledged.

He had also asked Bill Clinton for a pardon.

Twice.

Jesse Oliver, the former general counsel for the Texas Department of Agriculture, wrote a petition to the president. He asked Clinton to commute the sentences of McRae and former Deputy Agriculture Commissioner Mike Moeller. In the document, Oliver argued that the investigation leading to the indictments was "steeped in politics," but U.S. District Judge Sam Sparks had "refused to allow the introduction of evidence that would have demonstrated to the jury the government's political motivations for the investigation."

The appeal to Clinton described the alleged relationship between Karl Rove and FBI Special Agent Greg Rampton, who Oliver said timed his federal investigation for political effect, and who was working with Rove.

"Rove, with the assistance of the Rampton investigation and its attendant leaks, crafted [GOP agriculture commissioner candidate Rick] Perry's campaign around the issue of ethics and unsubstantiated allegations of improper and unethical activity at TDA."

Oliver pointed out that Rove had admitted in federal documents that he met with Rampton and discussed the TDA investigation and also told a state senate committee that he had two or three conversations with Rampton. And he related the exemplary involvement of McRae and Moeller in issues of social value, having created programs like the Buffalo Soldiers Heritage Program for young African Americans, the Vaquero Heritage Program for Hispanic youth, and the Texas Agriculture Youth Congress. These were all products of their initiative and sense of social conscience.

But President Clinton did not respond.

When he was leaving office, succeeded by Karl Rove's marquee client George W. Bush, President Clinton received another petition, this one asking for executive clemency and a complete pardon. A number of controversial pardons were granted in the closing days of the Clinton administration, including one given to wealthy financier and Democratic party donor Marc Rich. Journalists wrote widely of the potential abuse of the powers of executive clemency by Clinton. But there was never any indication that the appeal from lawyers for McRae and Moeller, delivered to the White House counsel, was even read.

There was no reason to think any of this was on Pete McRae's mind as he walked across the parade grounds at Fort Davis. He does not exhibit bitterness or any trace that he is being consumed by unfairness and rejection. In the mile-high air at the base of the Davis Mountains, McRae seemed to be enjoying the pleasant touch of the sun and talking about the Fort's history. Only when pressured, did he return to questions about himself. Pete McRae clearly considers himself the least interesting subject in his life.

"You know, you get up in the morning and do the best you can, and if things don't work out, then it's because it's something out of your control. And that's the way I feel about what happened. They just won that battle, the bad guys, the way I characterize them, as the bad guys. It's just time to move on. It was time to move on years ago."

On the way over the mountains, the cottonwoods along Limpia Creek filled the truck window with a blurry wall of green. The front range of cliff faces was shadowed and darkening, only the tops of the great mesas still glowing in the long light of the west. Climbing toward Wild Rose Pass, McRae was trying to get others to do what he had already done: close the door on the past.

"We made mistakes and shouldn't have gone to prison for those mistakes. But it's kind of the breaks of the game. A lot worse happens to people every day than has happened to me."

A presidential pardon, in his lifetime, is unlikely for Pete McRae or his friend, Mike Moeller. And they have both stopped even contemplating the idea. There is a different future for both of them to live now. It is not one either of them had imagined. But they did not know they were going to run headlong into the politics of Karl Rove.

Rolling down the mountainside from Wild Rose Pass, McRae saw the prairie expanse of the Permian Basin filling the distance. The stretch of land symbolized all the promises of Texas. Oil flowed out of the ground there and filled the state with prosperity. George H.W. Bush started his own oil company in this part of West Texas. Coming home a war hero, he developed a successful production operation, and, eventually, became president. His son, George W. Bush, spent his childhood, played baseball, and took his own failed turn at the energy business in that same landscape, hovering in front of Pete McRae.

But none of that mattered.

This was also Pete McRae's place. He was born in Texas. Has always lived there. And Pete McRae understands how the land can make you feel anything is possible. There is no better place than Texas to keep a man moving toward the horizon, always believing there is something better up ahead.

Notes

Introduction: Mr. Co-President

Page 4   "'Jimmy, my boy . . .'" Author interview, press plane (August 1999).

Page 6   "'Of all the kids . . .'" KHOU-TV interview.

Page 7   "'The thing that's unique . . .'" Bruce Buchanan interview, University of Texas (2000).

Page 7   "'He [Bush] wouldn't have . . .'" Bruce Buchanan interview, University of Texas (2000).

Page 8   "'Bush began to think . . .'" American Enterprise Institute, Rove seminar (December 2001).

Page 8   "In a joking . . ." American Enterprise Institute, Rove seminar (December 2001).

Page 8   "'It's a 24-hour . . .'" McKinnon interview (Austin 2002).

Page 8   ". . . first book he remembers . . ." American Enterprise Institute, Rove seminar (December 2001).

Page 9   "The pamphlet, written . . ." American Enterprise Institute, Rove seminar (December 2001).

Page 9   "As a colleague . . ." *Time* (April 2001).

Page 9   "'It's a great run . . .'" Author interview with Rove (Austin, 2002).

Page 10   "'Karl Rove is . . .'" *Time* (August 11, 1999).

Page 10   "'I think he's . . .'" Bruce Buchanan interview, University of Texas (2000).

Page 10   "'The politics at the . . .'" Author interview with Rove (Austin, 2002).

Page 12   "'We're a group . . .'" Author interview with Rove (Austin, 2002).

Page 13   "The duties keep . . ." *Wall Street Journal* (August 2002).

Page 13   "'Yeah, I think he's . . .'" interview with Mauro (Austin, 2002).

Page 14   "Jim Hightower, the Democratic . . ." *Dallas Morning News* (February 1990).

Page 14   "Unfortunately, the political bullet . . ." *Dallas Morning News* (September 1993).

Page 14   "When the 'Brooks Brothers . . .'" Salon.com (August 5, 2002).

Page 16   "An amateur historian . . ." American Enterprise Institute, Rove seminar (December 2001).

Chapter 1: Battles and Wars

Page 20   "The *Washington Post* reported . . ." *Washington Post* (August 13, 1973); "GOP Probes Official as Teacher of Tricks."

Page 22   "'Karl just dominates . . .'" interview with Republican anonymous source.

Page 23   "And among Bush family . . ." *New York Times* (March 2000).

Page 28   "'The playing field . . .'" interview with anonymous Democratic source.

Chapter 2: Timing Is Everything

Page 31   "For almost seven . . ." FBI incident report (October 10, 1986).

Page 31   "Gary L. Morphew . . ." Texas Department of Public Safety incident report, October 7, 1986.

Page 31   "'It wouldn't surprise me . . .'" FBI incident report (October 10, 1986).

Page 32   "'There have been a number . . .'" *Houston Chronicle* (October 12, 1986).

Page 32   "'I'm not picking up . . .'" FBI incident report (October 10, 1986).

Page 32   "Scott said that . . ." FBI incident report (October 10, 1986).

Page 32   "This time, Scott . . ." FBI incident report (October 10, 1986).

Page 33   "Scott said he called . . ." FBI incident report (October 10, 1986).

Page 33   "The bug was found . . ." Texas Department of Public Safety incident report (October 7, 1986).

Page 33   "'Turn it off . . .'" *Austin American-Statesman* (October 12, 1986).

Page 33   "Morphew said he told . . ." *Austin American-Statesman* (October 12, 1986).

Page 33   ". . . contacted that agency . . ." Texas Department of Public Safety incident report (October 7, 1986).

Page 33   "In the interim . . ." FBI incident report (October 10, 1986).

Page 34   "By 9:00 A.M. . . ," Texas Department of Public Safety incident report (October 7, 1986).

Page 34   "Rampton and the DPS officers . . ." FBI incident report (October 10, 1986).

Page 34   "'Rove and Clements . . .'" FBI incident report (October 10, 1986).

Page 35   "Bayoud hired Knight . . ." FBI incident report (October 10, 1986).

Page 35   "'Checking my office . . .'" Author interview with Rove (Austin, August 2002).

Page 36   "'Are you sure . . .'" Author interview with Rove (Austin, August 2002).

Page 37   "'Tactically, they ran . . .'" Republican anonymous source interview.

Page 37   "After reporters arrived . . ." author present at event.

Page 37   "'Obviously, I do not know . . .'" *Austin American-Statesman* (October 7, 1986).

Page 38   "'How do we know . . .'" KPRC-TV report.

Page 40   "'Well, I was surprised," *Dallas Morning News* (October 8, 1986).

Page 40   "'I don't know anything . . .'" *Dallas Morning News* (October 8, 1986).

Page 40   "'Mark White got word . . .'" Author interview with Alofsin (August 2002).

Page 41   "'If they found a bug . . .'" *Austin American-Statesman* (October 8, 1986).

Page 41   "'Whoever thought . . .'" *Houston Chronicle* (October 12, 1986).

Chapter 3: Perception Is Reality

Page 43   ". . . the bugging as 'Texasgate' . . ." *Houston Chronicle* (October 12, 1986).

Page 44   "'And we got this . . .'" interview with Republican anonymous source.

Page 45   "'I told them to do . . .'" *Dallas Morning News* (October 13, 1986).

Page 45   "'I removed that device . . .'" FBI incident report, October 10, 1986.

Page 45   ". . . results were, 'satisfactory' . . ." *Austin American-Statesman* (October 21, 1986).

Page 45   ". . . only after he had spoken . . ." FBI incident report.

Page 45   "'I have no legal . . .'" *Austin American-Statesman* (October 1986).

Page 46   "'I can tell you . . .'" *Austin American-Statesman* (October 19, 1986).

Page 46   "Results of the FBI lab . . ." FBI incident report.

Page 46   "'It seems to me . . .'" *Houston Chronicle* (October 1986).

Page 46   "'I don't know why . . .'" *Austin American-Statesman* (October 1986).

Page 47   "'Why didn't they just . . .'" *Houston Chronicle* (October 1986).

Page 47   "'That's a bunch of . . .'" *Fort Worth Star-Telegram* (October 1986).

Page 47   "'Later that day . . .'" Author interview with Rove (August 2002).

Page 48   "When he was interviewed . . ." FBI incident report.

Page 48   "'We haven't placed a buy . . .'" Author interview with Rove (August 2002).

Page 49   "'Diamond advised that . . .'" FBI incident report.

Page 50   "Five minutes after . . ." FBI incident report.

Page 50   "... It appears that ..." FBI incident report.

Page 51   "'The other thing ...'" Author interview with Rove (August 2002).

Page 52   "'I wouldn't quite call it ...'" Davis interview (July 2002).

Page 52   "'Did Karl know ...'" Republican anonymous source interview.

Page 53   "'We were completely aware ...'" FBI anonymous source interview.

Page 53   "'I have no idea ...'" Author interview with Rove (August 2002).

Page 54   "'The numbers show ...'" McKinnon interview (August 2002).

Page 54   "... convivial talk about ..." *New York Times* (March 14, 2000).

Page 55   "'I mean what was ...'" Author interview with Rove (August 2002).

Page 55   "The movie showed up ..." *New York Times* (March 2000).

Page 55   "'That's why it was ...'" Author interview with Rove (August 2002).

Page 56   "... received a 'target letter' ..." Morphew interview with Pete Slover *Dallas Morning News* (2000).

Page 56   "'At this time ...'" *Dallas Morning News* (October 29, 1986).

Page 56   "'At this writing ...'" Texas Department of Public Safety memo (February 10, 1987).

Page 57   "... Morphew was asked again ..." Morphew interview with Pete Slover *Dallas Morning News* (2000).

Page 57   "'Of course, Rove knew ...'" Author interview with Alofsin (August 2002).

Page 58   "'I don't remember ...'" Author interview with Alofsin (August 2002).

Chapter 4: Suspicions and Clues

Page 61   "'Bob, this is Ken ...'" interview with Mike Moeller.

Page 62   "... announced the following ..." interview with Pete McRae.

Page 62   "Boyd and Boatwright made ..." interview with Moeller.

Page 62   "'I never meant to ...'" interview with Moeller.

Page 63   ". . . Sheila Jackson Lee . . ." interview with Jesse Oliver.

Page 63   ". . . contacted top Texas . . ." interview with Boatwright.

Page 63   "'I remember him saying . . .'" Author interview with Rove.

Page 64   "'I think I had . . .'" Author interview with Rove.

Page 64   ". . . series of suicide . . ." *Houston Chronicle* (June 23, 1990).

Page 65   "Hamilton County Sheriff's . . ." *Houston Chronicle* (June 23, 1990).

Page 65   "'The information we received . . .'" *Houston Chronicle* (June 19, 1990).

Page 65   "A few days before . . ." *Houston Chronicle* (June 23, 1990).

Page 65   "'How the hell . . .'" *Houston Chronicle* (June 23, 1990).

Page 65   "Cullick's article . . ." *Houston Chronicle* (June 23, 1990).

Page 65   "'The Perry campaign . . .'" *Houston Chronicle* (June 23, 1990).

Page 66   "'I have a lot of . . .'" *Houston Chronicle* (June 23, 1990).

Page 66   ". . . pick him up in California . . ." *Dallas Morning News* (June 19, 1990).

Page 66   ". . . inspector general at the regional . . ." *Austin American-Statesman* (August 11, 1991).

Page 67   "Although USDA's internal . . ." USDA letter to Larry Beauchamp (November 2, 1989).

Page 67   "Before joining the Travis County . . ." Beauchamp resume, job application to Travis County District Attorney (March 2, 1987).

Page 68   "Beauchamp had become . . ." *Austin American-Statesman* (August 11, 1991).

Page 68   "'To question my . . .'" *Austin American-Statesman* (August 11, 1991).

Page 69   ". . . former Dallas Cowboys' . . ." *Waco Tribune-Herald* (January 3, 1990).

Page 69   "When that didn't work . . ." *Austin American-Statesman* (January 9, 1990).

Page 69   "'It's a continuation . . .'" *Austin American-Statesman* (January 9, 1990).

Page 69   "The chairman of the Republican . . ." *Albuquerque Journal* (July 11, 2002).

Page 70   "'We did not investigate ...'" USDA letter to Larry Beauchamp (November 2, 1989).

Page 70   "When asked by a reporter ..." *Austin American-Statesman* (August 11, 1990).

Page 70   "'Ol' Ronnie Reagan's idea ...'" Hightower stump speech (1990, various).

Page 71   "'At that time ...'" Pete McRae interview (July 2002).

Page 71   "The next morning ..." USDA letter to Larry Beauchamp (November 2, 1989).

Page 72   "'And I furnished him ...'" *Austin American-Statesman* (August 11, 1990).

Page 72   "'I'd heard about ...'" interview with Buck Wood (July 2002).

Page 72   "'He showed up in ...'" interview with Garry Mauro (July 2002).

Page 73   "'You gotta understand ...'" interview with Garry Mauro (July 2002).

Page 73   "'You think Rove ...'" interview with Garry Mauro (July 2002).

Page 73   "Byron Sage, the special ..." Byron Sage interview (July 2002).

Page 73   "'He worked for Gramm ...'" anonymous Democrat interview (July 2002).

Page 74   "Assistant U.S. attorney ..." Jesse Oliver interview, based on conversation between Oliver and TDA defense attorney's phone call with Mills.

Page 74   "... were not inappropriate ..." Texas State Auditor's preliminary report (November 1989).

Page 76   "Hightower had spent ..." *Dallas Morning News* (October 31, 1989).

Page 76   "'In terms of how it worked ...'" Jesse Oliver interview.

Page 76   "'I can't tell you for ...'" David Elliot interview (July 2002).

Page 77   "The headline was ..." *Dallas Morning News* (November 13, 1989).

Page 77   "The chief fund-raiser ..." Moeller, McRae, Oliver interviews, Texas Secretary of State records.

Page 77   "'I actually engineered . . .'" McRae interview.

Page 77   "They did their fund-raising . . ." Moeller, McRae, Quicksall trial court testimony; Moeller, McRae interviews.

Page 78   "Boyd and Koontz intended . . ." Moeller, McRae, Oliver interviews; court documents.

Page 78   "Boyd got nearly . . ." *Dallas Morning News* (November 13, 1990).

Page 78   "'If he is not . . .'" *Dallas Morning News* (November 13, 1990).

Page 79   ". . . prearranged verbal cue . . ." McRae interview; trial court testimony.

Page 79   "Reporters, like Debbie Graves . . ." Moeller, McRae, Oliver interviews.

Page 80   "'I do know that I became . . .'" Texas State Senate Rove testimony (March 26, 1991).

Page 81   "'I don't recall . . .'" Texas State Senate Rove testimony (March 26, 1991).

Page 81   "'I can't remember . . .'" Texas State Senate Rove testimony (March 26, 1991).

Page 82   "'This summer [1990] I met with agent . . .'" U.S. Senate, Committee on Foreign Relations, sworn affidavit to Board for International Broadcasting (August 27, 1990).

Page 82   "While charging that Texas-Federal . . ." Texas State Auditor's final report on Texas-Federal Inspection Service (December 1, 1989).

Page 82   "The day the report . . ." McRae, Jesse Oliver interviews.

Page 82   "'We were drinking . . .'" McRae interview.

Page 83   "'That was the pivotal thought . . .'" Oliver interview.

Chapter 5: A Number Two Mexican Dinner with One Taco Missing

Page 85   ". . . Perry had told a rural . . ." *Mineral Wells Index* (December 4, 1989).

Page 86   ". . . 'USDA officials are not . . .'" *Austin-American Statesman, Dallas Morning News* (December 6, 1989, various).

Page 86   "Unannounced, Rampton arrived . . ." Moeller, McRae, Oliver interviews, trial documents.

Page 86   "'I do know he played . . .'" Moeller interview.

Page 87   "'I will just tell you . . .'" Author interview with Rove.

Page 87   "'Debbie Graves had . . .'" McRae, Moeller, Oliver interviews.

Page 87   "On the same day that . . ." Trial documents, McRae interview *Amarillo Daily News, Austin American-Statesman, Dallas Morning News* (January 24, 1990).

Page 87   "Rampton informed numerous . . ." Oliver interview, anonymous Agriculture Department sources.

Page 88   "Christy Hoppe interviewed . . ." *Dallas Morning News* (February 14, 1990).

Page 88   "'The problems at TDA . . .'" *Houston Post* (June 27, 1990).

Page 88   "'I am the one who called in . . .'" Moeller interview.

Page 89   "Hightower Consultant Investigated . . ." *Austin American-Statesman* (February 15, 1990).

Page 89   ". . . said Boyd 'coerced' him . . ." *Austin American-Statesman* (February 15, 1990).

Page 89   ". . . numerous agency workers . . ." Moeller interview.

Page 90   "Vernie R. Glasson, executive . . ." Copy of Glasson letter (February 7, 1990).

Page 91   "Executive director of the American . . ." Copy of Datt letter (February 23, 1990).

Page 91   "According to numerous agriculture department workers . . ." Moeller, McRae, Oliver, anonymous Agriculture Department source interview.

Page 91   "'There are a lot of . . .'" Byron Sage, FBI agent interview.

Page 92   "'That's like saying . . .'" *Houston Post* (September 28, 1990).

Page 92   "'Let me think . . .'" *Texas Observer* (August 25, 2000).

Page 93   "'Nixonian dirty tricks' . . ." *Austin American-Statesman* (September 28, 1990).

Page 93   "The chairman of the Texas . . ." Slagle Democratic party press release (September 27, 1990).

Page 93   "'He did everything . . .'" Rick Perry interview (September 2002).

Page 94   "'I'm one hundred percent . . .'" McRae interview.

Page 94   "On January 8, 1991 . . ." *Austin American-Statesman* (January 9, 1990, various).

Page 94   "The man he named . . ." *Austin American-Statesman* (August 17, 1991).

Page 94   "'This begins to appear . . .'" *Austin American-Statesman* (August 17, 1991).

Page 95   "The closest Karl Rove . . ." *Houston Post* (June 27, 1990).

Page 96   ". . . the prosecution of Moeller . . ." Buck Wood interview (July 2002).

Page 96   "'I told Mike Moeller . . .'" Buck Wood interview (July 2002).

Page 96   "Pete McRae felt . . ." McRae interview.

Page 96   "Eleven growers and processors . . ." Trial court documents, Wood, McRae interviews.

Page 96   "'I had a little hope . . .'" McRae interview.

Page 97   "'That's kind of like . . .'" Wood, McRae interviews, trial court documents.

Page 97   "'I know we made . . .'" McRae interview.

Page 98   "'I was just going through . . .'" Kenneth Boatwright interview.

Page 98   "'Yeah, he contacted me . . .'" Kenneth Boatwright interview.

Page 98   "'I think it's ridiculous . . .'" Kenneth Boatwright interview.

Page 99   "'Oh yeah, sure . . .'" Kenneth Boatwright interview.

Page 99   "Spence was defending . . ." *Idaho Statesman* (May 26, 1993).

Page 100   "The shell came from . . ." *Idaho Statesman* (May 26, 1993).

Page 100   "You knew before the trial . . ." *New York Times* (May 28, 1993).

Page 100   "One of Rampton's colleagues . . ." *New York Times* (May 28, 1993).

Page 101   "He had conducted enough . . ." Buck Wood interview (July 2002).

Page 101   "'That's a bunch of crap . . .'" Byron Sage interview.

Page 101   "'These are phony . . .'" *Idaho Statesman* (May 26, 1990).

Page 102   ". . . but Maurice Ellsworth said . . ." *Idaho Statesman* (August 11, 1993).

Page 102   ". . . U.S. Marshal for Idaho . . ." *Idaho Statesman* (August 11, 1993).

Page 102   "'I think that there's . . .'" *America Newsnet,* conservative radio network interview (November 23, 1999).

Chapter 6: The Confirmation

Page 104   "'Logan,' he announced . . ." author Slater present.

Page 105   "'This was a big moment . . .'" author Slater present.

Page 107   "'Bush is the kind . . .'" *Dallas Observer* (May 13, 1999).

Chapter 7: Never Young

Page 111   "The White House meeting . . ." Author interview with Bush administration associate.

Page 112   "'There were no ifs . . .'" Author interview with Ludlow (July 2002).

Page 113   "Long into their . . ." Photo displayed by Rove.

Page 114   "Classmate Rick Higgins . . ." Author interview with Higgins (June 2002).

Page 114   "'He was so . . .'" Author interview with Hargreaves (June 2002).

Page 114   "'He was task-oriented . . .'" Author interview with Higgins (June 2002).

Page 115   "Sorenson, Rove's opponent . . ." Author interview with Sorenson (June 2002).

Page 115   "He quoted Napoleon: . . ." Rove campaign memo, Governor Bill Clements papers, Texas A&M University (September 1985).

Page 116   "Suddenly, into the gymnasium . . ." Rove campaign memo, Governor Bill Clements papers, Texas A&M University (September 1985); author interview with Rove (August 2002).

Page 116   "When he was . . ." *New York Times Magazine* (May 14, 2000).

Page 116   "His sister, Reba . . ." *Dallas Observer* (May 13, 1999).

Page 117   "Growing up . . ." Author interview with Rove (August 2002).

Page 117   "The star of . . ." Author interview with student Susan Galprin (June 2002).

Page 118   "'I didn't think . . .'" Author interview with Roark (June 2002).

Page 118   "The thing was . . ." Author interview with Langeland (July 2002).

Page 119   "'Debate was a . . .'" Author interview with Jones (July 2002).

Page 120   "One was the . . ." Author interview with Jones (July 2002).

Page 120   "Fellow student Eric . . ." Author interview with Kriesler (June 2002).

Page 120   "Once, Rove put . . ." Author interview with Langeland (July 2002).

Page 120   "'We were all . . .'" Author interview with Higgins (June 2002).

Page 121   "He and classmate . . ." Author interview with Gustavson (June 2002).

Page 121   "He brought this . . ." Author interview with Gustavson (June 2002).

Page 122   "There is a . . ." *Odyssey 1969* Olympus High School yearbook (May 1969).

Page 122   "Eldon Tolman's history . . ." Author interview with Gustavson (June 2002).

Page 123   "He ran errands . . ." *Salt Lake Tribune* (July 31, 2000).

Page 123   "'Karl was down . . .'" Author interview with Ludlow (July 2002).

Page 123   "At school, Rove . . ." Author interview with Gustavson (June 2002).

Page 124   "'He annoyed a . . .'"author interview with Gustavson (June 2002).

Page 124   "'Karl was a . . .'" Author interview with Smart (June 2002).

Page 124   "'You know so . . .'" Author interview with Higgins (June 2002).

Page 124   "Rove leaped into . . ." Author interview with Gustavson (June 2002).

Page 125   "The first time ..." Author interview with Rove (August 2002).

Page 125   "And here came ..." Author interview with Gustavson (June 2002).

Page 125   "Tolman wanted his ..." Author interview with Gustavson (June 2002).

Page 126   "In Salt Lake City ..." *Utah History Encyclopedia* (University of Utah Press, 1994).

Page 127   "'I always viewed ...'" Author interview with Jones (July 2002).

Page 127   "Friend Mark Dangerfield ..." *New York Times Magazine* (May 14, 2000).

Page 127   "His father, Louis ..." Author interview with Rove (August 2002).

Page 127   "When Keith Roark ..." Author interview with Roark (June 2002).

Page 128   "Chris Smart remembered ..." Author interview with Smart (June 2002).

Page 128   "As a freshman ..." Author interview with J. D. Williams (June 2002).

Page 129   "Rove never got ..." Author interview with Rove.

Page 129   "'It was at the ...'" Author interview with Bob Kjellander (June 2002).

Page 130   "He assumed a ..." *Washington Post* (August 13, 1973).

Page 130   "'It was funny," Author interview with Kjellander (June 2002).

Page 130   "Dixon had a ..." Author interview with Dixon (August 2002).

Page 131   "Rove rose swiftly ..." application for Clements transition office, January 12, 1979, Governor Bill Clements papers, Texas A&M University.

Page 131   "At a seminar ..." *Washington Post* (August 13, 1973).

Page 131   "'So one of ...'" *Washington Post* (August 13, 1973).

Page 132   "'While this is ...'" *Washington Post* (August 13, 1973).

Page 132 "In March, Rove . . ." author Slater interview with Rove (July 1994).

Page 133 "'I introduced Lee . . .'" author Slater interview with Rove (July 1994).

Page 133 "In the end . . ." Author interview with Robert Edgeworth (July 2002).

Page 134 "It was a . . ." Author interview with Robert Edgeworth (July 2002).

Page 135 "The *Washington Post* . . ." *Washington Post* (August 13, 1973).

Page 136 "'He sent me . . .'" Author interview with Edgeworth (July 2002).

Page 136 "A few months . . ." author Slater interview with Rove (July 1994).

Chapter 8: Face Value

Page 137 "'He was . . . *cool*' . . ." Author interview with Rove (March 1999).

Page 137 "'I was supposed . . .'" Rove deposition in 1996 tobacco lawsuit.

Page 138 "'We're not alike . . .'" Author interview with Rove (August 2002).

Page 138 "'Lee had a . . .'" Author interview with McBride (July 2002).

Page 139 "At dinner one . . ." Author interview with Rove associate.

Page 139 "But by then . . ." Author interview with Rove (August 2002).

Page 139 "The Virginia Republican . . ." *Austin Business Journal* (September 2, 1985).

Page 140 "As it turned . . ." Application for Clements transition office, January 12, 1979, Governor Bill Clements papers, Texas A&M University.

Page 140 "'He's a personable . . .'" *Dallas Morning News* (June 2, 1978).

Page 141 "Although paid from . . ." Rove deposition in tobacco lawsuit (1996).

Page 141 "Contributions to the . . ." *Odessa American* (October 29, 1978).

Page 141 "'I am very . . .'" *Dallas Morning News* (June 2, 1978).

Page 142   "Turner said he . . ." Author interview with Turner.

Page 142   "Reese offered a . . ." *Dallas Morning News* (June 2, 1978).

Page 142   "The elder Bush's . . ." *Washington Post* (September 15, 1978).

Page 143   "In 1979, Valerie . . ." Harris County divorce records.

Page 143   "'Okay, here are . . .'" Author interview with Rove (August 2002).

Page 144   "At the turn . . ." *Law and Order* by O. Henry; *Everybody's Magazine* (September 1910).

Page 144   "Earl and Merle . . ." Earl and Merle Black, *The Rise of Southern Republicans* (Cambridge, MA: Belknap Press, 2002).

Page 145   "So Rove sat . . ." Rove campaign memo, Governor Bill Clements papers, Texas A&M University (September 1985).

Page 145   "'The whole art . . .'" Rove campaign memo, Governor Bill Clements papers, Texas A&M University (September 1985).

Page 146   "His job was . . ." Governor Bill Clements papers, Texas A&M University.

Page 146   "He arranged the . . ." Rove campaign memo, Governor Bill Clements papers, Texas A&M University (March 19, 1979).

Page 147   "'It can be . . .'" Rove campaign memo, Governor Bill Clements papers, Texas A&M University (April 16, 1979).

Page 147   "Even as letters . . ." Letter from Dr. C. J. Ruilmann, Governor Bill Clements papers, Texas A&M University (February 9, 1979).

Page 147   "'Enjoyed your letter . . .'" Rove letter to constituent, Governor Bill Clements papers, Texas A&M University (September 26, 1979).

Page 148   "'It was hilarious . . .'" Author interview with McBride (July 2002).

Page 149   "'It was a . . .'" Author interview with anonymous Republican colleague.

Page 149   "'Anti-White messages . . .'" Rove campaign memo, Governor Bill Clements papers, Texas A&M University (September 1985).

Page 150   "'It will go . . .'" author Slater interview with Rains (November 1987).

Page 150   "'That sort of . . .'" Author interview with Whittington (August 2002).

Page 151   "When a Houston . . ." Author interview with Wayne (August 2002).

Page 151   "'The greatest reward . . .'" Author interview with Rove (August 2002).

Page 152   "'Probably, it was . . .'" Author interview with Rove (August 2002).

Page 152   "At a reception . . ." *Dallas Morning News* (January 20, 1989).

Page 152   "Rove arranged meetings . . ." Author interview with Whittington (August 2002).

Page 152   "The White House . . ." *Associated Press* (April 28, 1989).

Page 153   "'He got Lee . . .'" Author interview with Perry (July 2002).

Page 154   "Luce remembered sitting . . ." Author interview with Luce (August 2002).

Chapter 9: Perchance to Dream

Page 156   "'Mr. Rove . . .'" Transcript of Senate Nominations Committee hearing (March 26, 1991).

Page 157   "'God, it was . . .'" Author interview with Weeks (August 2002).

Page 157   "Glasgow quizzed Rove . . ." author present.

Page 158   "'I was going . . .'" Author interview with Rove (August 2002).

Page 158   "He had gone . . ." Application for Clements transition office, January 12, 1979, Governor Bill Clements papers, Texas A&M University.

Page 159   "His teaching partner . . ." Author interview with McNeely (June 2002).

Page 159   "'That's 1896 . . .'" Rove presentation.

Page 159   "When asked in . . ." Rove deposition in tobacco lawsuit (1996).

Page 160   "'He'd always wait . . .'" Author interview with Johnson (January 2000).

Page 160   "His college transcripts . . ." *The New Yorker* (November 8, 1999).

Page 160   "'I wasn't exactly . . .'" *Texas Monthly* (May 1994).

Page 161   "Having a father . . ."   *Dallas Morning News* (February 25, 1990).

Page 161   "'These were our . . .'" Author interview with Bush (August 1998).

Page 161   "'The irony is . . .'" Author interview with Rove (August 2002).

Page 161   "'You know . . .'" *Midland Reporter-Telegram* (July 4, 1989).

Page 162   "In early 1993 . . ." Author interview with Toomey (January 2000).

Page 163   "They had visited . . ." Author interview with Whittington (August 2002).

Page 163   "'He didn't know . . .'" Author interview with Ratliff (August 2002).

Page 164   "'Now, I hear . . .'" Author interview with Bush aide.

Page 164   "At Harvard . . ." Author interview with Freeman (June 1999).

Page 165   "'You sent me . . .'" Author interview with Wayne (August 2002).

Page 165   "Phillip Morris and . . ." author Slater interview with Rove (March 1999).

Page 166   "Not so, said . . ." Author interview with Wayne (August 2002).

Page 167   "He was right . . ." Bush campaign finance reports filed with the Texas Ethics Commission.

Page 167   "Eventually, the tutorials . . ." Author interview with Toomey (January 2000).

Page 168   "'The sense was . . .'" Author interview with Rove (August 2002).

Page 168   "'He would go . . .'" Author interview with Bush aide.

Page 169   "'My first impression . . .'" Author interview with Toomey (January 2000).

Page 169   "'I was never . . .'" George H. W. Bush, Doug Wead, *Man of Integrity* (Eugene, OR: Harvest House, 1988).

Page 169   "Once, when a friend . . ." Author interview with Bob Thomas (September 2002).

Page 170   "'In addition to . . .'" *National Review* (December 21, 1998).

Page 171   "A reporter from . . ." author Slater present.

Page 171   "'He was shaky . . .'" Author interview with Bush associate.

Page 171   "'Look, you are the . . .'" Author interview with Bush aide.

Page 171   "At campaign headquarters . . ." Bush campaign news releases.

Chapter 10: Gain with Pain

Page 174   "He was one . . ." *Forbes* (October 8, 2001).

Page 174   "'I want the . . .'" *Dallas Morning News* (December 4, 1990).

Page 175   "'Forget about environmental . . .'" *Dallas Morning News* (September 1, 1991).

Page 175   "Two weeks into . . ." *Dallas Morning News* (September 1, 1991).

Page 175   "'I have very . . .'" *Dallas Morning News* (September 1, 1991).

Page 176   "'We needed to . . .'" *Dallas Morning News* (September 19, 1992).

Page 177   "Rove picked up the . . ." author present.

Page 177   "'Lena had $2 million . . .'" Author interview with McDonald (August 2002).

Page 178   "'Nobody's going to . . .'" Author interview with McDonald (August 2002).

Page 178   "'I have one . . .'" Author interview with Williamson (August 2002).

Page 178   "'I think that . . .'" Author interview with McDonald (August 2002).

Page 179   "First there was . . ." Bush for governor news release (June 19, 1994).

Page 179   "At the State-Federal . . ." *Austin American-Statesman* (May 21, 1994).

Page 180   "'He was constantly . . .'" Author interview with Republican associate.

Page 180   "'Do you have . . .'" Rove testimony in Travis County District Court, pretrial hearing (December 22, 1993).

Page 180   "Rove testified that . . ." author Slater present.

Page 181   "Not true . . ." Author interview with Elliott (June 2002).

Page 181   "'They mounted a . . .'" Author interview with Earl (November 2002).

Page 181   "In a political . . ." Texas Republican party news release.

Page 181   "His political investigators . . ." author present.

Page 182   "'The fact that . . .'" Author interview with Bonner (August 2002).

Page 182   "'They got what . . .'" Author interview with Ross (July 2002).

Page 182   "'I do my . . .'" Author interview with Miller (August 2002).

Page 183   "'You can't challenge . . .'" Author interview with Weeks (June 2002).

Page 183   "'You don't need . . .'" Author interview with Ogden (June 2002).

Page 184   "When Bush contacted . . ." Author interview with anonymous Republican colleague.

Page 185   "'For a while . . .'" Author interview with anonymous Republican colleague.

Page 185   "'There's something wrong . . .'" Author interview with anonymous Republican colleague.

Page 185   "'I'm going to . . .'" Author interview with anonymous Republican colleague.

Chapter 11: Born to Run

Page 188   "Thornburgh looked like . . ." *Los Angeles Times* (October 30, 1991).

Page 188   "Rove knew a . . ." *Texas Lawyer* (August 1, 1994).

Page 189   "Thornburgh went down . . ." *Texas Lawyer* (December 12, 1994).

Page 189   "'The guy owes . . .'" author Slater interview with Rove (July 1994).

Page 189   "'I had no . . .'" *Associated Press* (March 23, 1994).

Page 190   "The campaign was . . ." *Texas Lawyer* (August 1, 1994).

Page 190   "'Not a bad . . .'" *Texas Lawyer* (August 1, 1994).

Page 190   "The judge ruled . . ." *Texas Lawyer* (August 1, 1994).

Page 191   "'Outrageous,' Thornburgh said . . .'" *Associated Press* (June 19, 1993).

Page 191   "'A reasonable candidate . . ." *Texas Lawyer* (August 1, 1994).

Page 192   "Thornburgh's side approached . . ." *Texas Lawyer* (December 12, 1994).

Page 192   "Thornburgh, humbled and . . ." *Texas Lawyer* (December 12, 1994).

Page 193   "'Don't mess with . . .'" Author interview with Berry (November 2002).

Page 193   "'I will be . . .'" *United Press International* (June 5, 1993).

Page 194   "'Hey buddy . . .'" Author interview with Berry (November 2002).

Page 194   "Rove knew that . . ." Author interview with Republican colleague.

Page 195   "One day, a . . ." Author interview with Sipple (August 2002).

Page 195   "'He looked at . . .'" Author interview with Sipple (August 2002).

Page 196   "The Republican nominee . . ." *Dallas Morning News* (March 25, 1990).

Page 196   "Barbara Bush . . ." interview with Bush aide.

Page 197   "'They like her . . .'" *Dallas Morning News* (July 26, 1993).

Page 197   "It had Richards . . ." *The Texas Poll* (October 1993).

Page 198   "'If you have . . .'" Author interview with Berry (November 2002).

Page 198   "'He knew what . . .'" Author interview with Berry (November 2002).

Page 199   "His foray into . . ." *Houston Chronicle* (May 8, 1994).

Page 199   "'I like selling . . .'" *Time* (July 31, 1989).

Page 199   "On game nights . . ." *Midland Reporter-Telegram* (July 4, 1989).

Page 200   "He didn't even . . ." *Dallas Morning News* (May 2, 1989).

Page 200   "In promoting Bush . . ." *Dallas Morning News* (February 24, 1989).

Page 201   "'Am I going . . .'" author Slater interview with Bush (April 1994).

Page 201   "Bush turned and . . ." author Slater present.

Page 201   "'The sense was . . .'" Author interview with Rove (August 2002).

Page 202   "Rove suggested he . . ." Marvin Olasky, *The Tragedy of American Compassion* (Washington, DC: Regnery Gateway, 1992).

Page 202   "'The two issues . . .'" Marvin Olasky, *The Tragedy of American Compassion* (Washington, DC: Regnery Gateway, 1992).

Page 203   "'Limit GWB's public . . .'" Rove internal campaign memo.

Page 203   "'When you're developing . . .'" Author interview with Berry (November 2002).

Page 204   "'Bush puts down . . .'" Author interview with Berry (November 2002).

Page 204   "When Bush fumbled . . ." *Dallas Observer* (May 13, 1999).

Page 204   "'Is the Rove . . .'" author present.

Page 205   "'Now let me . . .'" Author interview with Berry (November 2002).

Page 206   "Sipple produced virtually . . ." Ad texts, ad tape recordings.

Page 206   "'Crime is crime . . .'" Author interview with Sipple (August 2002).

Page 207   "'Here's what I'll . . .'" Author interview with Berry (November 2002).

Page 207   "'We can put . . .'" Author interview with Sipple (August 2002).

Page 208   "'You just work . . .'" *Houston Chronicle* (August 17, 1994).

Page 208   "'You have been . . .'" author Slater interview with Richards (August 1994).

Page 209   "Bush set the . . ." Bush interview with Sam Attlesey (November 1993).

Page 209   "'There was clearly . . .'" Author interview with McDonald (August 2002).

Page 210   "Bush's East Texas . . ." *Houston Post* (August 26, 1994).

Page 210   "Richards' press secretary . . ." Author interview with McDonald (August 2002).

Page 210   "'This guy is . . .'" Author interview with Sipple (August 2002).

Chapter 12: Voices in the Room

Page 214   "'If Rove had . . .'" Author interview with Stiles (November 2002).

Page 214   "'We've got to . . .'" Author interview with Stiles (November 2002).

Page 215   "'If people had . . .'" Author interview with Stiles (November 2002).

Page 215   "Bush leaned defiantly . . ." Author interview with Sadler (September 2002).

Page 215   "'This will kill . . .'" Author interview with Rove (August 2002).

Page 216   "'In the history . . .'" Author interview with Sadler (September 2002).

Page 216   "Bush was stunned . . ." Author interviews with Sadler, Stiles.

Page 217   "'The politics of . . .'" Author interview with Rove (August 2002).

Page 217   "'Okay,' Bush said . . ." Author interview with Bush, Bullock aides.

Page 217   "He was open . . ." author Slater present.

Page 218   "In his capitol . . ." author Slater present.

Page 218   "'He didn't take . . .'" Author interview with Christian (November 2002).

Page 218   "'Evidentially, he must . . .'" author Slater interview with Bush (April 1995).

Page 218   "In Bush's first . . ." Bruce Buchanan interview with author.

Page 219   "'He had roles . . .'" Author interview with Christian (November 2002).

Page 219   "'Brian made the . . .'" Author interview with Bush associate.

Page 220 "Once, when a . . ." author Slater present.

Page 220 "Unlike the others . . ." Texas Ethics Commission finance reports.

Page 220 "'Our job is . . .'" Rove deposition in tobacco lawsuit (1996).

Page 221 "In his 1980 book . . ." Sidney Blumenthal, *The Permanent Campaign: Inside the World of Elite Political Operatives* (Boston: Beacon Press, 1980).

Page 221 "Under the permanent . . ." Sidney Blumenthal, *The Permanent Campaign: Inside the World of Elite Political Operatives* (Boston: Beacon Press, 1980).

Page 222 "'There's nothing scattergun . . .'" Author interview with Christian (November 2002).

Page 223 "Periodically, Bush would . . ." *Boston Globe* (June 21, 1995).

Page 223 "'No one will . . .'" Author interview with anonymous Bush aide.

Page 223 "'Thank you . . .'" Author interview with anonymous Bush aide.

Page 223 "Rove signed on . . ." Rove deposition in tobacco lawsuit (1996).

Page 224 "'Did you ever . . .'" Rove deposition in tobacco lawsuit (1996).

Page 225 "To head off . . ." author Slater interviews with Attorney General Dan Morales, Tobacco Institute lobbyist Mark Harkrider (March 1996).

Page 226 "The push poll . . ." Copy of the survey by Public Opinion Strategies (Alexandria, VA).

Page 226 "Late one morning . . ." Author interview with Mark Harkrider.

Page 226 "'My job advising . . .'" Author interview with Rove (March 1996).

Page 227 "Although he delivered . . ." Author interview with Rove (March 1996).

Page 228 "'You son of . . .'" Author interview with Pauken (June 2002).

Page 228 "'Lee was the . . .'" Author interview with Pauken (June 2002).

Page 228   "'You have to . . .'" Author interview with Pauken (June 2002).

Page 229   "'Somewhere between . . .'" Author interview with Sadler (September 2002).

Page 230   "'We've never met . . .'" Author interview with Sadler (September 2002).

Page 230   "'I'd go down . . .'" Author interview with Rugeley (July 2002).

Page 230   "'I made the . . .'" author Slater interview with Perry (July 2002).

Page 230   "Former Governor Clements . . ." Author interview with Sipple (August 2002).

Page 231   "'I started getting . . .'" Author interview with Sadler (September 2002).

Page 231   "Sadler had his . . ." Author interview with Sadler (September 2002).

Page 232   "'It's sit down . . .'" Author interview with Johnson (January 2000).

Page 232   "'I have absolutely . . .'" Author interview with Sadler (September 2002).

Page 234   "'What do you . . .'" Author interview with Sadler (September 2002).

Page 234   "'They've never been . . .'" Author interview with Sadler (September 2002).

Page 235   "'Where did this . . .'" Author interview with Sadler (September 2002).

Page 236   "'I'm ready . . .'" author present.

Page 236   "'They were long . . .'" Author interview with Berry (November 2002).

Chapter 13: He Shoots, He Scores

Page 237   "'Look here!' he said . . ." author Slater present.

Page 238   "'This was his . . .'" Author interview with McKinnon, first published in *American Journalism Review* (April 2001).

Page 239   "'Matthews,' Bush said . . ." author Slater present.

Page 239   "'Zip it!' he'd say . . ." author Slater present.

Page 240   "'I thought, that . . .'" author Slater interview with Hughes (March 2001).

Page 240   "'If you are . . .'" Rove speech in Austin (November 12, 1999).

Page 241   "At lunch one . . ." Rove speech in Austin (November 12, 1999).

Page 242   "New Hampshire may . . ." *New York Times* (December 19, 1999).

Page 243   "'He looked over . . .'" Author interview with Hughes (December 1999).

Page 243   "Company employees were . . ." author Moore present.

Page 245   "'Steve wrote this . . .'" Stuart Stevens, *The Big Enchilada: Campaign Adventures with the Cockeyed Optimists from Texas Who Won the Biggest Prize in Politics* (New York: Free Press, 2001).

Page 245   "In most campaigns . . ." Stuart Stevens, *The Big Enchilada: Campaign Adventures with the Cockeyed Optimists from Texas Who Won the Biggest Prize in Politics* (New York: Free Press, 2001).

Page 246   "Rove held firm . . ." author Slater present.

Page 246   "While Bush toured . . ." author Slater present.

Page 247   "'Consultants don't concede . . .'" interviews with campaign aides.

Page 247   "'Thanks for calling . . .'" interviews with campaign aides.

Page 248   "'Karl was really . . .'" interview with anonymous Republican colleague.

Page 249   "Colyandro called it . . ." Author interview with Colyandro (July 2002).

Page 249   "The column said . . ." *Chicago Sun-Times* (September 18, 1992).

Page 250   "After the column . . ." Texas GOP Victory, 1992 release (September 18, 1992).

Page 250   "'The thing that . . .'" Author interview with Colyandro (July 2002).

Page 250   "'John decided that . . .'" Author interview with Weeks (August 2002).

Page 251   "In everything Rove . . ." *New York Times Magazine* (May 14, 2000).

Page 251   "When Harvey Kronberg . . ." Author interview with Kronberg (August 2002).

Page 251   "When an article . . ." author Slater present.

Page 251   "Jack Williams . . ." Author interview with Williams (August 2002).

Page 252   "'It is in . . .'" Author interview with Ross (July 2002).

Page 252   "'One day . . .'" author Moore interview with Neely (August 2002).

Page 254   "'What the hell . . .'" *Time* (February 14, 2000).

Page 254   "Rove didn't have . . ." Author interview with Rove (February 2000).

Page 256   "'I thought people . . .'" author Slater present (January 2000).

Page 257   "A professor from . . ." CNN *Inside Politics* (February 14, 2000).

Page 257   "'George,' he said . . ." *The New Yorker* (March 20, 2000).

Page 257   "'Don't give me . . .'" *Time* (March 21, 2000).

Page 258   "'It's better to . . .'" Bill Israel article prepared for publication.

Page 258   "'People in this . . .'" interview with Karl Rove (February 19, 2000).

Page 259   "Even a cab . . ." author Slater present.

Page 259   "After the mea . . ." author Slater present.

Page 260   "'I couldn't believe . . .'" author Slater present.

Chapter 14: A Win's a Win

Page 261   "'They were all . . .'" Author interview with Rove (August 2002).

Page 261   "Even James Campbell . . ." *Houston Chronicle* (September 3, 2000).

Page 262   "'Every one of . . .'" Author interview with Rove (August 2002).

Page 263   "In February, Bush . . ." *ABC News* (March 2000).

Page 263   "'The vice president . . .'" author Slater present.

Page 263   "'You've got to . . .'" Author interview with Rove (August 2002).

Page 264   "'First of all . . .'" Author interview with Rove (August 2002).

Page 265   "Dave Tyson, an . . ." Author interview with Tyson interview (June 2002).

Page 265   "'The key was . . .'" Author interview with Rove (August 2002).

Page 266   "The initial goal . . ." Author interview with Potter interview (December 2002).

Page 267   "When Bush flew . . ." author Slater present.

Page 267   "When Bush himself . . ." author Slater present.

Page 268   "'This is the . . .'" Author interview with Haught (December 2002).

Page 268   "'You must forget . . .'" *ABC News* (November 2002).

Page 268   "Two years later . . ." Republican source interview (July 2002).

Page 269   "Weaver told colleagues . . ." interviews with Republican sources.

Page 269   "'The problem with . . .'" Author interview with Republican source (July 2002).

Page 269   "Weaver wasn't the . . ." Author interview with Republican source (July 2002).

Page 270   "'He was made . . .'" *Roll Call* (May 2002).

Page 270   "His friend and . . ." Author interview with Israel (August 2002).

Page 271   "'It could have . . .'" Bill Israel article prepared for publication.

Page 271   "It was 5 A.M. . . ," Author interview with Bush security officer (October 2000).

Page 272   "Stashed in one . . ." author Slater present.

Page 273   "'In 1980, it's . . .'" author Slater interview with Rove (June 2000).

Page 273   "'It's all visuals . . .'" author Slater present.

Page 274   "George W. has . . ." Author interview with Thurber (July 2000).

Page 275   "Rove, who was . . ." Author interview with Perry campaign aide (September 2002).

Page 276   "'I've won,' said . . ." author Slater present.

Page 276   "'People wanted to . . .'" Author interview with McKinnon (August 2000).

Page 277   "'I'm the first . . .'" author Slater present.

Page 277   "'I know,' she . . ." author Slater present.

Page 279   "'It's become clear . . .'" author Slater present.

Page 279   "'I'm out!' he . . ." author Slater present.

Page 281   "As the year . . ." *New York Times* (December 2002).

Page 281   "Back home in . . ." Author interview with Weeks (August 2002).

Chapter 15: General Rove

Page 284   "'Well, here's the deal . . .'" Author interview with Rove (Austin).

Page 284   "Rove 'read the Republican . . .'" Christopher Marquis, *New York Times* (July 28, 2002).

Page 285   "'There are people . . .'" Christopher Marquis, *New York Times* (July 28, 2002).

Page 285   "After meeting with . . ." Christopher Marquis, *New York Times* (July 28, 2002).

Page 285   "'Look, we're talking . . .'" Author interview with Rove.

Page 285   "'It was the most moving . . .'" Thurber interview with author Moore.

Page 285   "'I think Castro . . .'" Thurber interview with author Moore.

Page 286   "'Iraq has developed . . .'" Author interview with Rove.

Page 287   "'Here's a guy . . .'" Author interview with Rove.

Page 288   "The plan was already being rolled . . ." The White House, National Security Strategy document, WhiteHouse.gov (September 17, 2002).

Page 288   ". . . an administration that gets . . ." Bush stump speech, campaign 2002, author present, various.

Page 288   "The meeting was at ..." anonymous Republican source interview.

Page 289   "'When Karl walked into ...'" anonymous Republican source interview.

Page 289   "'Are you outta you're ...'" anonymous Republican source interview.

Page 290   "Ever since that speech ..." *New York Times* (January 19, 2002).

Page 290   "'I pick up the ...'" Bruce Buchanan interview, University of Texas.

Page 291   "'I think in their own ...'" Bruce Buchanan interview, University of Texas.

Page 292   "'What if we haven't ...'" anonymous Democratic source interview.

Page 293   "And this approach melded ..." *Atlanta Constitution-Journal* (October 6, 2002).

Page 294   "'The discussion has been ...'" Author interview with Rove (Austin).

Page 295   "'That was the political ...'" Author interview with Rove (Austin).

Page 295   "'This guy is single-handedly ...'" anonymous Democratic source interview.

Page 296   "'The problem with trade ...'" Radio Free Europe (March 7, 2002).

Page 296   "... major steel producers ..." *Detroit Free Press* (August 10, 2002).

Page 296   "... signs his education bill ..." President's remarks at bill signing, Hamilton, Ohio, White House.gov (January 8, 2002).

Page 297   "The Salvation Army has ..." *Washington Post* (July 12, 2001).

Page 298   "'Rove is Nixonian ...'" interview with anonymous political consultant.

Page 299   "'The thing is ... we used ...'" interview with anonymous Democratic consultant.

Page 299   "That means if you have to ..." *Washington Post* (May 14, 2002).

Chapter 16: The Baghdad Road

Page 301   "The three veteran Texas . . ." author Moore present.

Page 302   ". . . the same people who had advised . . ." *Washington Post* (September 24, 1999).

Page 302   ". . . significantly increase military . . ." *Washington Post* (September 24, 1999).

Page 303   "'Mr. Bush, when you . . .'" author Moore was debate panelist and asked question.

Page 303   "'All I know is . . .'" author present for Bush answer.

Page 303   "Actually, Bush's air wing . . ." *Washington Post* (July 28, 1999).

Page 304   ". . . missed a critical physical . . ." *Washington Post* (July 28, 1999).

Page 304   "'Exactly what kind of . . .'" Hughes asked question of author Moore at debate.

Page 305   ". . . outside of Houston . . ." *Washington Post* (July 28, 1999).

Page 305   "'I can't recall . . .'" interview with author Moore, notes (October 1994).

Page 306   "What Barnes did . . ." interview with author Moore, notes (October 1994).

Page 306   "'You need to understand . . .'" interview with author Moore, notes (October 1994).

Page 308   ". . . heap of problems . . ." *Los Angeles Times* (November 26, 2002).

Page 308   "Democrats were so optimistic . . ." *Roll Call* (July, 2002).

Page 308   "'It was just brilliant . . .'" interview with author Moore.

Page 309   "Even the Central . . ." Letter of CIA Director George Tenet delivered to Congress, quoted by the *Associated Press* (September 28, 2002).

Page 310   "'Well, that's a good . . .'" author Moore interview with Thurber.

Page 310   ". . . Wolfowitz and Vice President . . ." Defense Policy Guidance document, drafted for President George H. W. Bush, 1992, by Cheney.

Page 311   "'I will not stand by . . .'" Text of president's speech, at WhiteHouse.gov.

Page 311   "'All of a sudden . . .'" anonymous Democrat interview.

Page 311   "'I think this entire . . .'" anonymous Democrat interview, but different from note 20 source.

Page 312   "Rowley was the author . . ." *Washington Times* (June 6, 2002).

Page 312   "Jim Jordan, the director . . ." *The New Republic* (September 23, 2002).

Page 313   ". . . White House was resisting . . ." *New York Times* (September 7, 2002).

Page 314   "'The greater the threat . . .'" Text of president's speech, WhiteHouse.gov (September 20, 2002).

Page 315   ". . . the esteemed International Institute . . ." CNN.com (September 9, 2002).

Page 315   "'The American example . . .'" *American Conservative* (October 21, 2002).

Page 316   ". . . a U.S. Marine . . ." Foxnews.com (September 10, 2002); *NBC News* interview, undated.

Page 316   "Whisper wars had . . ." *Dallas Morning News* (December 2, 1999).

Page 316   ". . . holding up the Homeland . . ." *Arizona Republic* (September 26, 2002).

Page 317   "'So, I thought about . . .'" Author interview with Rove (Austin).

Page 318   "'Checking a box . . .'" Buchanan interview, University of Texas.

Page 318   "According to the . . ." *Washington Post* article quoted in *American Conservative* (November 18, 2002).

Page 319   "But the White House kept . . ." *American Conservative* (December 2, 2002).

Page 320   "Florida gubernatorial hopeful . . ." *Drudge Report* (November 4, 2002).

Page 320   "'It's almost eerie . . .'" anonymous political consultant interview.

Page 320   "'This,' he said . . ." *American Conservative* (November 18, 2002).

Page 321   "'It's a war without . . .'" anonymous political analyst interview.

Chapter 17: Yonder Goes Justice

Page 324   "'I went to prison . . .'" McRae interview with author Moore.

Page 324   "'I am a convicted . . .'" McRae interview with author Moore.

Page 325   "I realize there are . . ." McRae interview with author Moore at Fort Davis.

Page 325   "The state government funded . . ." *Country World News* (August 1, 2002).

Page 326   "In 1880, a young . . ." *National Archives and Records Administration*.

Page 327   "In the Fort Davis chapel . . ." *Fort Davis Historical Archives* (public display).

Page 328   "'I don't think he . . .'" McRae interview with author Moore at Fort Davis.

Page 329   "'No, this is not what . . .'" Moeller interview with author Moore at Fort McKavett.

Page 330   "'I was a public . . .'" Moeller interview with author Moore at Fort McKavett.

Page 330   "'A lot of it is . . .'" Moeller interview with author Moore at Fort McKavett.

Page 331   "'In terms of my . . .'" Moeller interview with author Moore at Fort McKavett.

Page 331   "'No, I read that . . .'" Moeller interview with author Moore at Fort McKavett.

Page 332   "'I don't think I . . .'" Moeller interview with author Moore at Fort McKavett.

Page 332   "'It certainly did not . . .'" Moeller interview with author Moore at Fort McKavett.

Page 333   "'Given where he is . . .'" Moeller interview with author Moore at Fort McKavett.

Page 334   "'I guess I have to say . . .'" Moeller interview with author Moore at Fort McKavett.

Page 336   "'If you look back . . .'" Author interview with Rove (Austin).

Page 337   "He doesn't make decisions . . ." Author interview with Rove (Austin).

Page 338   "Not many years . . ." author Moore interview with McRae in Austin.

Page 338   "'I guess one of the things . . .'" Author interview with Rove (Austin).

Page 338   "The campaign tour was . . ." Newsweek (September 2, 2002).

Page 339   "'It's a big state . . .'" Karl Rove transcript aboard Air Force One, provided to traveling press pool on California trip, WhiteHouse.gov.

Page 340   "When the president's plane . . ." Newsweek (September 2, 2002).

Page 340   "'I'm so proud to be . . .'" Associated Press (August 24, 2002).

Page 340   "'He's welcome to . . .'" Rove transcript aboard Air Force One, provided to traveling press pool on California trip, WhiteHouse.gov.

Page 341   "'I'm not aware . . .'" Rove transcript aboard Air Force One, provided to traveling press pool on California trip, WhiteHouse.gov.

Page 342   "'Well, we'd have to . . .'" Rove transcript aboard Air Force One, provided to traveling press pool on California trip, WhiteHouse.gov.

Page 342   "'We'd have to . . .'" Rove transcript aboard Air Force One, provided to traveling press pool on California trip, WhiteHouse.gov.

Page 342   "'This is a state . . .'" Rove transcript aboard Air Force One, provided to traveling press pool on California trip, White-House.gov.

Page 343   "In these settings . . ." President Clinton's remarks in Roosevelt Room, White House (February 19, 1999).

Page 344   "'I want to welcome . . .'" President Clinton's remarks in Roosevelt Room, White House (February 19, 1999).

Page 344   "'The army exonerated . . .'" President Clinton's remarks in Roosevelt Room, White House (February 19, 1999).

Page 346   "'Rove, with the assistance . . .'" Jesse Oliver's letter to President Clinton, October 31, 1996).

Page 346   "When he was leaving . . ." Jesse Oliver interview with author Moore in Dallas.

Page 347   "'You know, you get up . . .'" McRae interview with author Moore at Fort Davis.

Page 347   "We made mistakes . . ." McRae interview with author Moore at Fort Davis.

Index